book is printed
recycled paper

THE PASSING OF
THE MODERN AGE

John Lukacs

HARPER TORCHBOOKS
Harper & Row, Publishers
New York, Evanston, San Francisco, London

Chapters 9, 16, and 18 have previously been published in slightly different form in *Commentary*, *National Review* and *The American Scholar*, respectively, in 1970.

910.94
L96P
91355
Jan. 1975

First HARPER TORCHBOOK edition published 1972

STANDARD BOOK NUMBER: 06–131673–3

This book is dedicated
to Annemarie Gabrielle,
bourgeoise of the
twenty-first century.

Contents

I. ENDING

1. The passing of the Modern Age   3

   Why, as the twentieth century proceeded, more and more people felt that the end of the world was coming.

2. The Modern perspective   11

   Why the word modern *lost its attraction, and eventually its very meaning.*

3. The devolution   15

   How the decline of Europe proceeded together with the decay of civilization.

II. PASSING

4. The monstrosity of government   31

   How the rule of democracy has made people feel powerless and weak.

5. The impotence of Powers   44

How the greatest States, having accumulated unequaled powers, suddenly have found that they are becoming powerless.

6. The separation of races   55

How, after the abolition of slavery and the enforcement of equality, the races have discovered that their fraternity amounted to little.

7. The conformity of nations   63

How, notwithstanding the shrinking of the world, the nations of the white race have found that they must turn inward to face themselves.

8. The purposelessness of society   71

How, at the time when civilization has been most widespread, people have found that their aspirations are woefully empty.

9. The fiction of prosperity   84

How the impermanence of goods has rendered their possession unsatisfactory.

10. The dissolution of learning   99

How, at the time when education has become universal, people are discovering that their schools are teaching little or nothing.

11. The meaninglessness of letters   113

How literacy, having reached its peak, has fallen apart into a general state of decomposition.

12. The senselessness of the arts   125

How the highest refinements of artistic consciousness have degenerated into primitivism with astonishing speed.

13. The destruction of nature   134

How, in transforming nature, human civilization has discovered that it may be destroying itself.

14. The decay of science   145

How, at the time of their greatest triumphs, scientists have found that their basic principle of objectivity has proved to be an illusion.

15. The faithlessness of religion   155

How the updating of religion has led to a flight of faith from the churches.

16. The mutation of morality   168

How the emancipation of women has led to the pursuit of their degradation.

III. BEGINNING

17. The New Dark Ages   179

How, at the end of an age, some of its beginnings appear again.

18. The bourgeois interior   191

Why the most maligned characteristic of the Modern Age may yet be seen as its most precious asset.

19. The consciousness of the past   208

Why our future is our past, to a far greater extent than we are accustomed to think.

Index   219

I

ENDING

The passing of the Modern Age

Why, as the twentieth century proceeded, more and more people felt that the end of the world was coming.

During the twentieth century our world began to explode. Among other things, it hurled particles of itself first into the sky, then into the empty space of the universe. Early in this century two Americans flew for the first time in an engine above the sands of North Carolina. Sixty-six years later another two Americans were stepping cautiously on the moon. There was a great difference between these two events. In 1903 the flying mechanics rose into a light sky. In 1969 the astronauts were shot forth into darkness. In 1903 most people were optimistic; they greeted man's self-made liberation from the laws of gravity on earth. In 1969 many people looked at the moon with mixed emotions; the word that crept along the bottom of their minds was not liberation, it was escape. In 1903 most people of the white race, and virtually all of the American people, thought that their civilization was triumphant. In 1969 many people, including many Americans, felt that their civilization was collapsing. In 1903 people thought that the flight of the Wright brothers was the beginning of something. In 1969 they thought that

3

the moon flight of the American astronauts may have been the beginning of something but they also felt that it was the end of something. Between these two dates took place the evolution of the twentieth century, including a slow revolution of minds. We live now amidst the ruins of a civilization: but most of these ruins are in our minds.

Certain thinkers predicted some of this. In Europe, the realization that European civilization was mortal, that it was about to be endangered from the outside, occurred suddenly to Paul Valéry around the time of the Wright brothers' flight as he contemplated what the swift American victory over Spain and what the Japanese triumph over Russia meant for Europe. Ten years later a massive German cerebrator, Oswald Spengler, began the writing of his *Decline* or, more precisely translated, *Fall of the West,* the first volume of which was published during the dark summer of 1918. Another world war later a small volume, comprising a series of lectures by the German-Italian theologian Romano Guardini, entitled *The End of the Modern World,* in 1950 expressed, in a telling combination of philosophical reasoning and apocalyptic prophecies, what we may be coming to. But, then, the nineteenth century, too, had its share of seers and thinkers and poets who were the forerunners of these modern prophets of doom, who had seen that the civilization of their day was dangerously hollow. This made not much difference, at least not for some time. Most people had reacted to Nietzsche in much the same way in which they reacted to other professional pessimists: their reading of impending doom resulted in a bit of a shiver, a novel kind of intellectual recognition, after which they put this matter out of their minds.

At the beginning of the century the notion that Western civilization might collapse occurred but to a handful of people. By the time Spengler was published, many more people would entertain such notions, especially in the Germanies. By 1950 this notion had become a commonplace in the minds of many millions of Europeans and, for the first time in their history, even in the minds of some Americans. Most of us could still put this notion out of the conscious portion of our minds for long periods of time, relatively reasonably so. By the 1960's this became less and less possible. The notion that the breakdown in our civilization is actually occurring has been flooding the unconscious portions of our minds: it is now swimming up to the very surface of our consciousness.

❖

We live in a time when there is developing an increasing intrusion of mental processes into the structure of events. The dissolution of modern civilization is involved in this; indeed, it is to some extent the effect of this evolving "internalization." Now the crumbling of mental buildings rather clearly precedes the breakdown of material ones. Our civilization is in ruins because our beliefs about civilization are in ruins. We are far more beset by self-doubt than were our ancestors two or three hundred years ago. It is this self-doubt which has produced the end of empires. Few historians mustered the insight with which the philosopher Santayana, more than twenty years ago, wrote down his thoughts on the dissolution of empires, such as the British one:

> . . . England, for instance, in the eighteenth and early nineteenth centuries, acted the great power with conviction; she was independent, mistress of the sea, and sure of her right to dominion. Difficulties and even defeats, such as the loss of the American Colonies, did not in the least daunt her; her vitality at home and her liberty abroad remained untouched. But gradually, though she suffered no final military defeat, the heart seemed to fail her for so vast an enterprise. It was not the colonies she had lost that maimed her, but those she had retained or annexed. Ireland, South Africa, and India became thorns in her side. The bloated industries which helped her to dominate the world made her incapable of feeding herself; they committed her to forced expansion, in order to secure markets and to secure supplies. But she could no longer be warlike with a good conscience; the virtuous thing was to bow one's way out and say: My mistake. Her kings were half-ashamed to be kings, her liberals were half-ashamed to govern, her Church was half-ashamed to be Protestant. All became a medley of sweet reasonableness, stupidity, and confusion. Being a great power was now a great burden. It was urgent to reduce responsibility, to reduce armaments, to refer everything

to conferences, to support the League of Nations, to let everyone have his own way abroad, and to let everyone have his own way at home. Had not England always been a champion of liberty? But wasn't it time now for the champion to retire? And wouldn't liberty be much freer without a champion?

The other great powers, for abdicating more unwillingly, have not avoided the same fate; they are embarrassed by greater inertia or rebellion at home, and by the same tangle abroad. . . .*

Increasing self-doubt; increasing weakness. The growing self-doubt of our civilization has evolved together with our growing self-awareness: yet this self-awareness may perhaps become the shining side of the coin whose other, dark side is self-doubt.

❧

The expansion of the white race, of Europe; the promise of science, of literacy, of the New World, of an age of Reason after an age of Faith: many of these things began to unfold five hundred years ago. By now most of these things are no longer happening—or, if they are still going on, they are increasingly devoid of meaning and sense, because fewer and fewer people believe in them.

As late as one hundred years ago increasing numbers of our ancestors still believed in them, in all of them. They shared a conviction in common: a conviction that the progressive growth of life and of morality depended on the progressive applications of justice and of reason. It was because of the strength of this belief that the nineteenth century was, in many ways, a golden age of the Western world: the century of the greatest material progress, the rate of which was far greater than what we have experienced during the twentieth century.†

Some of our ancestors foresaw the material and technical circumstances of our lives not at all inaccurately, a century or even more ago. That by 1970 people might expect to live, on the average, seventy years or more, that their houses would be scientifically heated and cooled, that the thoroughfares of their towns would be

---

* *Dominations and Powers* (New York, 1950), pp. 278–279.
† See below, pp. 73–74.

bathed in electric light, that they would move along in self-pro-
pelled cars, that their doctors would be able to transplant human
organs, that giant airships would traverse oceans and continents in
hours, that men would land on the moon: these were accepted ideas
a century ago. People are amazed at the accuracy of Jules Verne's
"science-fiction" projections: in his book, *From the Earth to the
Moon*, published in 1865, the first astronauts were Americans, they
were fired out of a tremendous rocketing gun, situated in Florida; on
their return from the moon they splashed down into the sea: there
were more such details. "Men of letters," wrote the Scottish mystical
poet Alexander Smith, at that time (in *Dreamthorp*, 1863), "forerun
science like the morning star the dawn." Moreover, Jules Verne's
books were mostly read by boys. We live in a civilization whose
imaginative achievements are very much geared to the adolescent
mind. And the imaginative capacities of adolescents, no matter how
strong, are limited in their range: their ideas are their projections of
the things in their minds.

Most of the technical inventions of the twentieth century were
predictable; they were the applications of ideas that existed at least
one hundred years before. If one of our more intelligent ancestors
were to reappear suddenly among us, the very things that we would
expect him to be surprised at might surprise him the least: the
electric kitchen, the automobile, the telephone, television. He would
marvel at first, touching them, switching them on, seeing them
work. Still, to his mind, none of these things would be entirely new.
Do you want to see the earliest pictures of skyscrapers? Do not
merely hunt for early browned photographs: go to a large library
and look up certain European picture books of nearly a century
ago—those, for example, that were written and drawn by Robida;
they are all there, the pictures of skyscrapers, helicopters, elevated
and underground railways, masses of people crowding brilliantly lit
buildings and avenues at night.

Our ancestors expected most of this: indeed, they already saw
most of this—New York, for example, as the center of the civilization not only of *The*, but of *A* New World, the largest city of the

greatest Power. What they did not see was the state of the minds
and hearts of millions of well-fed and well-clothed men and women in
these air-heated and air-cooled rooms. They could not imagine how
in the greatest city of the Western world millions would be living
next to each other as entire strangers: that millions of the better off
would flee the city at night on crowded trains, abandoning entire
portions of it to hostile people of various races; that in the richest
and largest of buildings robberies would occur at any hour of the
day; that no one would dare to cross the city parks, and few would
dare to walk midtown streets at night; that an enormous body of
policemen, large enough for the armed forces of a Middle European
republic, would be distrusted and feared and yet be unable to
insure order and safety; that many of the schools of the city would
fulfill only a desperate and necessary function of daytime custodial
prisons, with police patrolling their corridors, where teachers and
overgrown boys and girls would confront one another with screaming hatred and concealed weapons; that hundreds of thousands of
people, including children, would be dependent on narcotics; that
thousands of well-to-do people would implore their psychiatric
doctors to place them in certain hospitals where, injected with
soporific drugs, they could be put into a state of cold sleep for
months.

Some of our ancestors foresaw mass poverty during a socialist
machine age and the horrors of some new kind of police state.
They did not foresee how widespread despair, hopelessness, loneliness, boredom would become in the midst of material abundance
and under the regime of increasingly meaningless freedoms. What
Lord Elgin wrote about Old China a century ago: "the rags and
rottenness of a waning civilization" have seeped into our very
midst. It may be seen around Forty-Second Street and Times Square
in New York, within the once throbbing and triumphant heart of
America's steely civilization, in the very place where twice during
this century millions of the masses of democracy poured out to cele-
brate the victorious end of a world war.

It is not an especially filthy place—physically, that is—although even at glistening noon hours the street is littered with the paper and metallic refuse of the new world, whirled about in a wind; even on the bluest of days the air has poisonous yellow and gray streaks in it, and there is the repulsive smell of hamburger grease wafting over these enormous cold Northern thoroughfares just as in the hot kitchen of a disreputable and sleazy household. What is filthy, beyond the imagination of the gloomiest visionaries of the past, is the imagery of the place: the lettering and the pictures, what their forms and combinations represent, and what they evoke: not so much the commerce with the human flesh but a sort of commerce with the Devil. It is not so much the material abundance of pornography as the cheap ugliness of its presentation that is pervasive: it is the spirit, not the matter, of the place that is horrid and depressing. It crawls onto the countenances of the loitering people, a frozen grin rather than a carnal leer. Contrary to the liberal belief, the dissolution of authority and censorship has not lifted burdens off minds. No one can close his mind to the imagery of Forty-Second Street, no matter how he wishes to pass through it; a low kind of diabolical interest burns and scratches on the bottom of his brain, like a pebble at the bottom of a shoe. It is this vile imagery that is unavoidable, it clings to the mind just as bad smell clings to clothes. It is no longer in the material slums of large cities that the depths of modern degradation are to be found; it is in this slum of slums of the Western spirit. This most crowded of streets of the greatest city of the greatest country of the greatest civilization: this is now the hell-hole of the world.

⁂

There is another condition that our ancestors could not foresee: that the end of our civilization is arriving with both a bang and a whimper. They thought in terms of the crashing fall of majestic empires, of barbarians battering down the gates, the horrendous extinction of light. We do not have walls or gates now, and we cannot speak of the waning twilight of our civilization. There is little that is twilit; there is, rather, a strange and perhaps unprecedented mixture of darkness and light, of the old and the new, perhaps even of good and bad. Already richness and poverty, elegance and sleaziness, sophistication and savagery live together more and more; they are next to each other not merely in the same streets but in the same minds. I believe that this condition will continue for a long time, this strange compound of light and darkness. As the coherence of a certain civilization dissolves, with it dissolves the coherence of our lives and our minds.

"To the world when it was half a thousand years younger," the great Netherlands historian Johan Huizinga wrote, fifty years ago, beginning his *The Waning of the Middle Ages,*

the outlines of all things seemed more clearly marked than to us. The contrast between suffering and joy, between adversity and happiness, appeared more striking. All experience had yet to the minds of men the directness and absoluteness of the pleasure and pain of child-life. . . . Calamities and indigence were more afflicting than at present; it was more difficult to guard against them, and to find solace. Illness and health presented a more striking contrast; the cold and darkness of winter were more real evils. Honours and riches were relished with greater avidity and contrasted more vividly with surrounding misery. We, at the present day, can hardly understand the keenness with which a fur coat, a good fire on the hearth, a soft bed, a glass of wine, were formerly enjoyed. . . .

It is different now. The outlines of things are blurred, and we have grown accustomed to this curious coexistence of winter and summer, of night with day. We experience little physical suffering and little spiritual joy. The contrast between illness and health, adversity and happiness is less striking. We have progressed from child-life to a state of the world in which we are all adolescents now. And this painful mental state of adolescence (a word whose literal origin, from Latin, contains the element of pain) marks our condition half a thousand years after the waning of the Middle Ages, at the time of the passing of the Modern Age.

The Modern perspective

Why the word modern *lost its attraction, and eventually its very meaning.*

We see the past from the present, and the present from the past. So did our ancestors. They regarded the Middle Ages as a dark trough in the middle between the shining ideal past of Antiquity and the beckoning sunlit uplands of the Modern Age of Reason. This, for example, was the view professed by Edward Gibbon, that most bourgeois of eighteenth-century Englishmen, in retrospect, at the peak of the Modern Age. When we read Gibbon on Antiquity, we learn as much, if not more, about the eighteenth century than about, say, the third century A.D.; we learn more about *his* mind than about Constantine's. This is a natural thing, and it does not reduce the merits of the author. Gibbon had a low opinion of the Middle Ages, which was typical of the eighteenth century, in Western Europe at least. Therefore he was rather optimistic of the future. He exemplified this in his chapter "General Observations on the Fall of the Roman Empire in the West," which is a summary of his view of history, of his deductions from the past for the sake of the then present.

11

We ought not be apprehensive, he wrote. "We cannot determine to what height the human species may aspire in their advances toward perfection; but it may be safely presumed that no people, unless the face of nature is changed, will relapse into their original barbarism. . . ."

We may therefore acquiesce in the pleasing conclusion that every age of the world has increased, and still increases, the real wealth, the happiness, the knowledge, and perhaps the virtue, of the human race.

This kind of optimism we no longer have: Gibbon's early modern belief in the modern notion of progress sounds very naive to us. We have fewer illusions: but, perhaps, we are also more critical, and introspective. But Gibbon was writing near the peak of the Modern Age.

This vision, or perhaps we should say perspective, lasted for a long time. Still, soon after Gibbon, it was beginning to change. Some of our ancestors, moved by the Romantic reaction against the increasingly hollow classicism of the eighteenth-century Enlightenment, about a century and a half ago discovered some of the virtues of the Middle Ages. The two adjectives of "dark" and "medieval" gradually ceased to be analogous in their minds. An increasing number of people accepted the argument that there was something to be said not only for the art but for some of the institutions of the Middle Ages. In certain minds, and among certain peoples, especially in the Germanies, this restoration of the repute of the Middle Ages eventually led to dangerous political and cultural excrescences. By about 1910 even cultivated Americans, who had no medieval past to look back upon, accepted the notion that the Dark Ages and the Middle Ages were different things, despite their overlapping.

There was another thing, another revision. Certain historians discovered that the break between the Middle Ages and the so-called Renaissance was not as sharp as people have been accustomed to presume, that in many matters the Modern Age had begun earlier, and the Middle Ages had ended later, than they had been accustomed to think, that the sixteenth and the seventeenth centuries could be more properly considered as the last great period of transition, of the coexistence of the Middle with the Modern Age.

And now there has come another change in our dispositions: the notion, gradually emerging, that the Modern Age itself had begun to pass. This has been a relatively recent phenomenon, almost entirely the product of the twentieth-century mind. But there is a difference. Centuries ago the Middle Ages were passing, without people noticing what was passing. The very term "Middle Ages" and the division of history into Classic–Middle–Modern Age did not become accepted notions until at least two hundred years after the waning of the Middle Ages had set in. To us, the passing of the Modern Age and the recognition of its passing are much closer indeed, at times so close as to be almost simultaneous. Is it possible that, like an increasing number of human illnesses, the decline of a civilization is psychosomatic? It is possible: to some extent the recognition may bring about the development itself—another illustration of the important condition that we are experiencing an increasing intrusion of mental processes into the structure of events.

Last and least, a small but significant symptom: the very word "modern" has lost some of its earlier shine. A little more than a generation ago "modern" meant something functional, fresh, youthful, airy, a welcome breakaway from the heavy and dusty categories of Victorian tastes (consider the appeal, and the novelty, of modern architecture, modern art, modern furniture in the 1920's). But, by 1970 "modern" has become far less attractive; its appeal has decayed, while its former antonym, "old-fashioned," has risen in our estimation.

The notion that we live in a time of transition is no longer a platitude; it is embedded in our minds:

The older perspective:	*Our perspective:*
Antiquity (till about A.D. 500)	Antiquity (till about 500)
	Transition: Dark Ages (till about 1100)
Middle Ages (about 500–1500)	Middle Ages (till about 1500)
	Transition (1500–1700)
Modern Age (from 1500 on)	"Modern" Age (1500–19–)
	Transition (19– –?)

Each transition, as each of the great ages, has been different. What will the third transition be? A second Dark Ages? A second Renaissance? A mixture of both? I cannot tell. But I can tell this: the term "Modern Age" no longer fits; it is no longer real.

The devolution

How the decline of Europe proceeded together with the decay of civilization.

There are at least three major instances in which Gibbon's contemporary prophecies have proved wrong because they were shallow. They concern Europe and Russia and America.

He saw Europe "as one great republic, whose various inhabitants have attained almost the same level of politeness and cultivation." This was not true. There were enormous differences between, say, Poland and England, or France and Spain in Gibbon's day, indeed far greater than now. In retrospect, the great diplomatic historian Albert Sorel could write, exactly a century after Gibbon: "this 'Christian Republic,' as some have been pleased to call it, was never more than an august abstraction. . . . In the eighteenth century such progress was only one of the beautiful theories of philosophers." Gibbon could not imagine that the dangers threatening Europe would come from within, and that the very unity he postulated was not much more than a chimera.

Russia, Gibbon wrote, "from the Gulf of Finland to the Eastern Ocean," now assumes the form of a powerful and civilized empire. The plough, the loom, and the forge, are introduced on the banks of the Volga, the Oby, and the Lena; and the fiercest of the Tartar hordes have been taught to tremble and obey. The reign of independent Barbarism is now contracted to a narrow span; and the remnant of Calmucks and Uzbecks, whose forces may be almost numbered, cannot seriously excite the apprehensions of the great republic of Europe. . . . Cannon and fortifications now form an impregnable barrier against the Tartar horse; and Europe is secure from any future irruption of Barbarians; since, before they can conquer, they must cease to be barbarous. Their gradual advances in the science of war would always be accompanied, as we may learn from the example of Russia, with a proportionable improvement in the arts of peace and civil policy; and they themselves must deserve a place among the polished nations whom they subdue. . . .

This Russia, during Gibbon's lifetime, was ruled by Tsars and Tsarinas who tortured their sons, poisoned their husbands, quartered people: many of Gibbon's contemporaries were aware of this, even in England. The present rulers of Russia no longer expose the bloody limbs of their drawn and quartered enemies in the public squares of Moscow where civilization reigns in the form of the automobile and the rocket gun: but not even an indulgent Marxist would now, two hundred years later, refer to Russia as a particularly civilized empire, a "polished nation."

About America Gibbon's optimism was unalloyed. The few sentences he wrote about it could have been penned by Benjamin Franklin. (Dr. Johnson, who distrusted Franklin, saw otherwise: "When the Whigs of America are thus multiplied," he wrote, "let the Princes of the earth tremble in their palaces. If they should continue to double and to double, their own hemisphere would not contain them. But let not our boldest oppugners of authority look forward with delight to this futurity of Whiggism.") Many Englishmen, however, saw a golden glow in America: they included the visionary Blake, whose archaic vision of the world was otherwise very different from the Gibbonian view of progress. He saw in America the earthbound Green Jerusalem that England may eventually become.

Tho' born on the cheating banks of Thames,
Th' his waters bathed my infant limbs,
The Ohio shall wash his stains from me:
I was born a slave, but I go to be free.

Ohio! The first American who flew up from the earth in an engine, the first American who stepped down on the moon, were born in Ohio.

❊

The zenith of the Modern Age was reached between 1750 and 1850, earlier for some nations, later for others. I write *nations,* because their formation was the most important event in modern times, the most important development of democracy. Gradually the ancient states became nations, something that was far more important than what happened to their social classes or even to their modes of production or to their forms of government. Nations were becoming the main instruments of historic change. Their relationships would eventually dominate everything else. This was true even of great events, such as the French Revolution. Had the French been beaten by the Austrians and Prussians in 1792, as they nearly were, their Revolution would have been snuffed out, at least for a while; it would have amounted to little in the long run. Because of the dissensions, the disorganizations, and the machiavellian stupidities of the monarchical states of Europe their alliances were incomplete, their armies were defeated. The French now spilled over into neighboring lands and eventually succumbed to the leadership of Bonaparte whose personal ambitions, too, were intensely national: having been born a Corsican, he wanted to become a famous Frenchman. He succeeded only too well, at least for a while. His French armies carried French flags to the four corners of Europe. The less national the opposing armies were, the easier his armies beat them. Eventually they were defeated by national hordes springing up in Russia, in Spain, in the end in the Germanies. The French were now outnumbered. Napoleon showed and scored some brilliant tricks on the fields of Europe, but once he was badly outnumbered he could do little or nothing. The era of nations meant the era of numbers. On St. Helena, where he had ample time to speculate, Napoleon realized that this boded trouble not only for the future of France but for that of Europe. The two World Powers of the future would be the United States and Russia. He was quite right. These were the only two Powers that could be defeated but never really conquered. Other statesmen knew this also. Russia was the biggest land Power at the Congress of Vienna where the monarchs and statesmen of Europe got together to redraw the map of the Continent after Napoleon. The shadow of the United States was present, too. The English could not have done much on the Continent had they not wound up their war with the United States beforehand.

The reactionary statesmen and monarchs of Europe now thought that they should make an effort to stick together. They, too, were entirely right. In the history of Europe the Holy Alliance was a step forward, not backward. For the first time in centuries there was an attempt to create something like a political system for the Continent. Eventually the Holy Alliance fell apart, but the benefits of a balance of power on the Continent continued. There was now no single Power that could dominate the Continent. These political conditions were the basis for the zenith of the Modern Age, of its high bourgeois period. The greatest progress in the history of nations usually occurs during periods of restoration, not of revolution. For some time after 1815 most conservatives were becoming liberal, and most liberals were becoming conservative. This made not only for a golden age of political philosophizing, it made for a period of prosperity and of real progress. Thus in the Lowlands, in the Germanies, in northern Italy, in the Austrian Empire the zenith of the Modern Age came during the first half of the nineteenth century, not before. Things were changing, sometimes rapidly; the first steam engines started puffing, the mass movement of people from the countryside to the city began. Still there was a long moment of rich stillness, a kind of interior equilibrium that lay on the bottom of the aspirations of the restoration years.

❈

This temporary equilibrium of change and stability in Europe was involved with the destinies of the Russian Empire and of the North American Republic, to a far larger extent than most people think and most historians teach. The Russian Empire was, after all, an element of European stability. Had it not been strong, the emerging nationalities of Eastern and Central Europe might have plunged that portion of the Continent into an unending battlefield during the nineteenth century. The stability of the Austrian and Prussian monarchies depended on the stability of Russian Tsardom, for an unconscionably long time. On the other hand the Russian state, conservative at home, would on occasion instigate revolutions abroad. In another sense, too, the Russians—their government and the people—were instruments of profound change. Their mistreatment of the Jews, most of whom lived in the western provinces of the Russian Empire in the early nineteenth century, led to the extraordinary migration of Jewish millions to Europe and eventually to America where they were among the vanguards of liberalism, progress, change.

The influence of the United States was different. The ideas coming from Russia had few effects on Russia's neighbors; rather the contrary. The very image of the North American Republic was an incitement to democracy. Had it not been for the existence of the United States, some of the radical and liberal ideas might have been unpopular, even in England. In another sense the United States was a great factor for European stability. Mass immigration from Britain, Ireland, Europe performed the functions of a safety valve. The lower classes of Europe lost their potentially most restive elements, potential agitators, revolutionists, criminals, most of whom soon became solid citizens, reputable pillars of church, society, state on the other side of the Atlantic. In 1848 the American conquest of California may have affected Europe more than all of her abortive revolutions during that noisy year: because of the former, the notion of an American El Dorado revived again before the eyes of millions of Europeans.

Within the continent of Europe there was one single event during the nineteenth century, more important than all of her revolutions. This was the unification of Germany. During the nineteenth century there was no single European nation that could unite itself and establish her independence without the help of a foreign Power. Led by Bismarck, the Germans were the only ones to do it alone. After that the French were no longer much of a match for them. Their very unification would upset the European balance of power: they were the biggest power on the Continent. The meaning of this dawned only slowly on some of the Great Powers, including England, in part because of the Germans' reputation for cleanliness and godliness. The knowledge of their cleanliness made them boastful, in an oddly self-conscious way. The knowledge of their godliness eventually led to their belief that they were now the Chosen People of God's Will, a faith from which no sane people ever recovered without having been badly mauled by God's will, sometimes twice in a row.

It is wrong to believe that the Great War of 1914 caused the decline of Europe. In many ways that war was a consequence, not a cause. Between Europe and Asia and Africa there lay the Ottoman Empire, with its rebelling provinces, sprawling rotten. Over these some of the Great Powers had been quarreling for a century or so. This, called the Eastern Question by our great-grandfathers, resulted in successive amputations until the Ottoman Empire was finally reduced to Turkey. This decline of the Ottoman Empire, stretching over at least three hundred years, hung over the edge of the Modern Age with fateful consequences, at least one of which—the creation and the perils of the state of Israel—are with us yet. The other, greater devolution was what should have been called the Western Question. Between Europe and the Americas there stretched the Spanish Empire, also sprawling rotten. Over its great decaying heritage, in successive stages, England and France fought their world wars during the eighteenth century. In the end the Spanish inheritance was to be collected by neither of them but by the United States. This was a great devolution whose meaning has not been grasped by Europeans even now. In the 1890's the United

States, fired by its own brand of imperial ambitions, attacked Spain in order to pick up the overseas remnants of this Western European empire. The Powers of Europe showed not the slightest inclination to get together or to assist Spain or even to protest against this kind of American aggression: on the contrary, each and every one of them sought the benevolence of the United States. This was especially true of the British, who had now concluded that the principal fundament of their statesmanship must be to insure the friendship of the Americans, at the expense of everything and of everyone else. Their alliance with France, with Russia, their going to war with Germany in 1914, and in 1939, is not really explicable except with this consideration in mind. It eventually cost them not only their Empire but their status as a Great Power, surely an event worth pondering.

❊

The civilization that we still know was a European civilization. The Modern Age belonged to European history. To speak of the Indian or Chinese Middle Ages is nonsense. There is only one thing wrong with this otherwise common-sense argument, as there is indeed with the even more common-sense argument about the fatal impact of the War of 1914 on Europe. In many ways there was no such thing as Europe before 1914. In one way Russia belonged to the European system of states; indeed her high culture was more than considerably European. On the other hand when a Russian was packing up in St. Petersburg for his annual cure or debauchery in France or Germany or Italy, he would say to his friends that he was going to "Europe." Educated Greeks, Rumanians, Bulgarians, or Montenegrins, situated nearer the middle of the Continent, would say the same thing. In one sense Europe began somewhere near Budapest, in another sense in the Urals, in yet another sense at Vladivostok. This was confusing enough, but there was even more to it. The people of the British Isles, for example, their alliance with France notwithstanding, felt closer to Australians and New Zealanders than to their European neighbors across the Channel. When the war broke out, no European Power had the slightest compunction in allying itself with Japanese, Chinese, Arabs, against some of its European neighbors. The utopians, the pacifists, the self-professed pioneers of a united Europe or of a united world were not much different. Their ideas of a more perfect union, of international law, of woman suffrage or progressive education or the secret ballot were stimulated by the American example, as indeed were the business practices of the more enterprising bourgeois. Like the bureaucratic advocates of a united Europe in the 1950's and 1960's, against whom de Gaulle used to rail, they were talking Europe but thinking America. European bourgeois civilization was coming apart at the seams. What remained of the old aristocracies regretted the coming of the war in 1914 which all of the other classes cheered on.

That war, the greatest of them all, was decided in the end by American intervention. That was a great milestone in the history of mankind, the sixth of April in 1917, the American declaration of war, compared to the importance of which the Russian Revolution amounted to little. What the Russian Revolution amounted to was Russia's dropping out of yet another European war and eventually the substitution of a half-European kind of tyranny by a half-Asiatic one. Indeed the Russian Revolution proved to be a boon for the other nations of Europe. It weakened the Russian Empire to such an extent that she hardly counted as a world power for the next twenty years. What the American intervention meant was the reversal of a political and migratory tradition that had rested on three centuries of American doctrine and political experience. The breakdown of Russia's alliances and of her government may have been predictable in 1914; the enthusiasm with which the American people and their government were to fling themselves into a European war in order to come out as the arbiters of the world was not. If we judge events by their consequences, the great world revolutionary was Wilson rather than Lenin. About Wilson his Postmaster General said that he was a man of high ideals and of no principles, a formula applicable indeed to some of the more successful Presidents of the Union. It was Wilson's espousal of the idea of national self-determination, not Lenin's much-vaunted international rising of the working classes, that vastly transformed Europe and much of the world after the First World War, setting the stage for the Second, and perhaps even for a Third. Lenin and Wilson died, by a curious coincidence, only a few days apart in 1924, around the time when a famous American progressive (Lincoln Steffens) returned from Russia to announce that there he saw the future and it worked. He had not seen the future at all, even though it was right under his long Puritan nose. The future was America, with its mass production and mass consumption, with its publicity and technology, an automobile civilization "thickening to empire," as an American poet (Robinson Jeffers) put it around that time.

During the preceding one hundred years of the Modern Age the evolution of statesmanship among the principal representatives of the white race from Washington and Pitt and Talleyrand and Metternich to a Wilson, a Lloyd George, a Clemenceau, a Czernin was enough to disprove all of the theories of Darwin. I am paraphrasing Henry Adams, but there was more to this devolution than statesmanship. The War of 1914 beat the stuffing out of the bourgeois. Not only revolutionary ideas but radical new forms of manners, of art, of fashion, of entertainment, of publicity became commonplace, especially in the great capitals of the Western world. The Americanization of Europe, indeed, of much of the world, was in full swing. Not only was the United States the richest country in the world, entire governments depending on its financial decisions: now there were millions of people in Europe who knew the names of Hollywood film stars while they knew not the name of their own prime minister. American music, American movies, American techniques of production and of publicity were emulated everywhere. The revolutionary enemies of the bourgeois order were not exempt from these inclinations. The only foreign models of industry and of production that the chiefs of the Soviet Union would admit were American ones. Among Hitler's more successful and enduring achievements were the promotion of a more-or-less classless society,

German versions of American picture magazines and the building of automobile superhighways. When the Second German War began in 1939 the United States, unlike in 1914, was a decisive factor in everyone's calculations from the beginning. Had they not known that the United States might eventually come in on their side the British would have made peace, or at least an armistice, with Hitler, especially after the fall of Paris. Probably the same was true of Stalin, after the fall of Kiev. Hitler, in turn, put up with every one of Roosevelt's planned provocations until his allies, the Japanese, chose to go to war with the United States on their own, a reckless kind of imbecility unparalleled in the entire history of the war.

By 1942 the prospective Americanization of the civilized world was a foregone conclusion. The exception was to be eastern Germany and a large portion of Eastern Europe, Roosevelt's gift to Stalin or, rather, his easy quittance for the fact that the victory over Germany cost the lives of twenty or thirty Soviet soldiers to every American one. Like Lenin and Wilson, Roosevelt and Hitler died merely a few days apart, in 1945. Now Russian and American infantry met in the middle of Europe and in the middle of Germany. An era of European history had come to an end, though the end of modern European civilization had not yet. The intervention of the United States saved much of this civilization from Hitler. The immediate interests of the United States had not been much involved in this. Whatever their other faults, Americans were not a selfish people. They still aren't.

※

There was another great event in 1945: the atom bomb. Its meaning was more portentous than its effects. Its use, during the Second World War, marked the end, not the beginning, of the mass bombing of cities: also, fewer Japanese died by the atom bomb than Germans died during the more "regular" bombing of Dresden. There was yet another thing that the making of the atom bomb should have suggested: the continued dependence of America on European ideas. The splitting of the atom and the putting together

of the bomb was the idea of European refugee scientists. It was
made possible by American wealth and American technology. This
pattern remained typical of many things, from lingerie to the moon
rocket. Their fashions and the designers came from Europe, their
producers and public relations men were Americans. There was one
fatal flaw in this division of labor. The ideas of Europeans were no
longer very good, or even very original. Still Americans dealt with
Europeans rather gingerly. For a while those nations of Europe that
found themselves on the western side of the iron curtain were relatively fortunate, partly because of the generosity of the United
States. They enjoyed a decade or more of pseudo-bourgeois restoration, the depth of which may have been shallow but which was also
extraordinarily widespread. On the eastern side of the iron curtain
entire peoples lived in misery, subjugated by local tyrants at the
beck and call of Moscow. These populations saw the Western world
as one of freedom and prosperity and sunlight. This was pathetic,
first because the West would offer them nothing beyond occasional
sympathy, second, because the Western peoples, with the exception
of Americans, were deeply affected by their own sense of weakness.
They took much comfort from their prosperity, sensing—unlike
Americans—that this must be temporary. They were, unanimously,
in favor of modernization which, in most instances, meant Americanization. Few people recognized this synonymity, least of all the
progressive intellectuals and the kind of youth who liked to indulge
in a rhetorical anti-Americanism almost completely devoid of substance. Most people knew that they lived on borrowed money; what
is more important, they felt that they were living on borrowed time.
They showed no desire to correct this. When someone like de
Gaulle came around to exhort them to think and act more independently, he was soon unpopular. On the other hand entire
generations of Europeans had learned during the twentieth century
how to live under the shadow of doom, that life was indeed
stronger than theory, a kind of existentialist attitude that may be
even more practical than pragmatism in the long run. We hope.
Gradually, after 1945, Americans discovered that they, too, were

not exempt from the decay of the modern world. Being still a youthful kind of people, they would propagate this discovery with great enthusiasm. Still, for a while—this was the greatest difference between Europeans and Americans—this discovery remained largely the jealous and profitable rhetorical property of American intellectuals. Gradually, however, the element of despair, always latent beneath the thick dynamic surface of American life, turned into a cult that began to smell of death. It is an interesting coincidence that this national mental condition began to emerge after 1960, at the same time when the election of John Kennedy meant a super-American revival of the cult of youth. This Kennedy phenomenon was of considerable significance. Here was an American President whose name, for the first time, was known to virtually everyone in the entire world. Had elections everywhere in the world followed the American practice of popularity polls, Kennedy could have been elected as the first President of the World, including President of Europe. To hundreds of millions everywhere Kennedy and his family represented *the* image of the successful New World: youthful, powerful, sun-tanned, and rich. This marked something that went beyond the nineteenth-century image of America: it marked the Californization of the dreams of the world. But this kind of aspiration, like much of the Californian way of life, was largely devoid of substance. It was not only that the Kennedys were marked by premature death, it was that they may have represented the last gasp of a cult of youth, that, in reality, smelled of death. John Kennedy, born in 1917, had in his inaugural address "served notice to the world," as he put it, that "the torch has now been passed to a new generation." Hordes of this generation would soon demonstrate their pyromaniacal inclinations, on both sides of the Atlantic.

By the middle of the 1960's most people of the Western world, even in America, felt the prevalence of despair. This was a new experience for civilized mankind, especially for Americans. In Europe there reigned cynicism and calculation, something that to many people of the Old World was at least not entirely unfamiliar.

Americans were beset by the fatal flaw of their mental habits, their tendency to state human problems wrongly. They were preoccupied with the persistence of violence whereas their problem was the re-emergence of savagery. It seemed that this once Indian land may have left a curse on its conquerors. In more and more places American civilization was succumbing to the temptations of a motorized and drugged witches' sabbath, at the edges of which reappeared the impassive savage ghost of the Indian.

In any event, the old things and beliefs were now beginning to go very fast. In many ways the end of the Modern Age, of the only civilization that some of us have known, began to set in. The foregoing pages were nothing but an outline of an outline of this devolution which was now visible in almost every field of life. The monstrosity of government, the impotence of Powers, the separation of races, the conformity of nations, the purposelessness of society, the fiction of prosperity, the dissolution of learning, the meaninglessness of letters, the senselessness of the arts, the destruction of nature, the decay of science, the faithlessness of religion, the mutation of morality were, all, at hand. I shall now attempt to sketch their devolution, in turn.

II

PASSING

The monstrosity of government

How the rule of democracy has made people feel power-less and weak.

Toward the end of an age more and more people lose their faith in their institutions: and finally they abandon their belief that these institutions might still be reformed from within.

At the beginning of the twentieth century among the civilized peoples of the world faith in political reform was still strong. Their political vocabularies—"Right," "Left," "conservative," "liberal," "radical," "nationalist," "socialist"—still made much sense. Only a few groups of extremists professed a cynical indifference to the potential benefits of constitutional government.

Except for two republics (France and Switzerland) as late as 1910 every European state was still a monarchy, but the actual political power of the monarchs was dwindling everywhere. Using the terms in their classical sense, it could be said that the peoples of the Western world before 1914 were governed by a mixed system of democracy and aristocracy. On the one hand the rise of democracy was being accepted almost everywhere, and universal suffrage existed in more and more countries. On the other hand governmental influence was still largely exercised by a relatively small class of people, a kind of functioning bourgeois aristocracy which was no longer a nobility whose distinctions had been based on birth. The distinction of this amorphous class rested largely, though not exclusively, on wealth or, rather, on the large and nearly limitless influences that wealth could procure around that time.

In retrospect we can see that the influence of this kind of transitional aristocracy was bound to disappear rather fast. Developments such as the passing of the House of Lords Bill in Britain or Theodore Roosevelt's measures in curbing the powers of plutocracies in America showed this even before the cataclysm of 1914.* All of this meant a gradual increase in governmental intervention in the lives of citizens. In certain states in Central and Eastern Europe a considerable portion of the population were employed by the state, in one way or another. Still, as A. J. P. Taylor put it: "Until August 1914 a sensible, law-abiding Englishman could pass through life and hardly notice the existence of the state, beyond the post office and the policeman."

He could live where he liked and as he liked. He had no official number or identity card. He could travel abroad or leave his country forever without a passport or any sort of official permission. He could exchange his money for any other currency without restriction or limit. He could buy goods from any country in the world on the same terms as he bought goods at home. For that matter, a foreigner could spend his life in this country without permit and without informing the police. . . . The Englishman paid taxes on a modest scale . . . rather less than 8 per cent of the national income. The state intervened to prevent the citizen from eating adulterated food or contracting certain infectious diseases. It imposed safety rules in factories, and prevented women, and adult males in some industries, from working excessive hours. The state saw to it that the children received education up to the age of 13. Since

---

* The shortsightedness of the Marxians was apparent even then. They were still agitated about the powers of a capitalist aristocracy whose authority was diluted each year. A few intelligent thinkers around 1900 saw further: they were aware that thoroughgoing reforms of society were to be stultified by an entirely new factor, by the emergence of managerial bureaucrats, including those within Socialist parties and trade unions.

January 1, 1909 it provided a meagre pension for the needy over the age of 70. Since 1911, it helped to insure certain classes of workers against sickness and unemployment. This tendency toward more state action was increasing. Expenditure on the social services had roughly doubled since the Liberals took office in 1905. Still, broadly speaking, the state acted only to help those who could not help themselves *

"All this was changed by the impact of the Great War." The Great War, as wars usually are, was a powerful motive force in the further development of democracy. It united peoples more than anything before it (or perhaps even after). The influence of the upper classes continued to wane. As usual, governments were slow in catching on. They were, generally, incapable or unwilling to realize the new necessities of the welfare state. Parliaments and parties began to look old and weak. This made certain people, mostly intellectuals, talk about radical political solutions. Some of them considered anew the virtues of Marxism, no matter how bankrupt these had proven in practice. The constitutional dishonesty of most of these intellectuals was such that they refused to see what was rather obvious: that the Communists won in Russia because Russia was still much of a barbarian country, the government of which became even more barbarian after the revolution than it had been before.

Between the two world wars the failure of democratic governments was not that they governed too much but that they governed too little. This is why most of them were no match for the new kind of government that arose in Central and Southern Europe, where the democratic evolution of the masses was, on occasion, exploited by national and centralized dictatorships. In the classic Aristotelian terminology, therefore, the new mixture was that of democracy with monarchy—or, in modern terms, it was dictatorship with mass consent. It provided potent and sometimes efficient governments of a kind that other people envied, not altogether without reason. In the United States the democratic reforms toward a long overdue governmental administration of welfare were presided over by Franklin Roosevelt, for all practical purposes an

* *English History 1914–45* (Oxford, 1965), p. i.

elective monarch. In Europe the rise of Germany under Hitler was so spectacular that she could have dominated much of the Continent by the reputation of her governmental efficiency alone. For some reason, however, Hitler was not sufficiently confident of this; he wanted to make this kind of German domination unquestionable. The result was the Second World War, at the end of which his monstrous government was destroyed. In most of Western Europe, freed mainly by American and British armies, a partial restoration of liberal democracy took place after the war. In most of Eastern Europe another monster, Russia, imposed her form of government, with or without the consent of the Atlantic democracies. The United States had become, not only economically but militarily, the greatest power of the world, with the result that the originally, and constitutionally, limited powers of the executive arm of the American government grew to enormous proportions.

At the time of this writing the United States and the Soviet Union are still the two supergovernments of the world. The governmental bureaucracies of the smaller Western nations have been growing, too, though generally at a lesser rate. Unlike before the last war, however, fewer and fewer people feel that their governments are not powerful enough: rather the contrary. During the last few decades not only the different forms of governments but the different words designating political ideas have become empty of meaning. A "conservative" in Russia designates a Stalinist. In the United States "conservatives" distinguish themselves by their espousal not of the Constitution but of the FBI. "Liberals" in the United States and earlier in Britain long ago turned advocates of the socialist state. In many European countries the Socialists have turned middle-class par excellence. Elsewhere, the Communists have become antirevolutionaries. During the last war "nationalists" in many countries distinguished themselves by advocating that their country surrender to Germany. Like the ancient designations "Right" and "Left," less and less of this makes sense any longer.

Today disillusionment with politics and with government is widespread to an extent which was not foreseeable even a decade ago. It is not only found among people who are ruled by dictatorships or authoritarian governments, such as exist in Eastern or Southern Europe or in South America, or among people whose politics have been palpably corrupt or inefficient, like those of the French in the 1930's. It has begun to spread among the peoples of the oldest and most stable democracies of the world. It is no longer only the attitude of an oversensitive and largely irresponsible intellectual class: it has begun to penetrate the minds and the hearts of large numbers of people.

To some extent this development was predictable. When were peoples ever satisfied with their government? Not very often: certainly not in modern times, when it seemed as if they appreciated the relative virtues of their governments only in retrospect (*"comme la République était belle sous l'Empire,"* said the French). But here is the difference: in the past, disillusionment with politics was one thing, the dislike of government another. When politics were rotten, people looked forward to a new kind of government; when government was tyrannical, people looked forward to a new political system. Now, however, disillusionment with politics and with government go hand in hand.

In the Western democracies the respect for politics depreciated before the respect for government. This is registered by our languages. The word *politic* three or four hundred years ago meant something akin to "wise," "temperate," "civic-minded," in England. In France the *politiques,* at the end of the sixteenth century, were the moderate Catholic party, a party of reason, of Henry IV and of Montaigne: the noun had a largely approbatory meaning, since it contrasted them with the *fanatiques,* the Holy League men during the religious civil wars that racked and grieved the French. But by the twentieth century "he is a politician"; "politicking"; "playing politics"; "politiquant"; "espèce de député" are, all, condemnatory. Significantly, the older the democratic practice of politics, the more condemnatory they are.

At the end of the Middle Ages, having literally become sick and tired of the violent and unpredictable rule of aristocracies, people had welcomed the strong rule of the first national monarchs. The middle classes, nearly everywhere, profited from the rise of the centralized state. Four hundred years later the modern state and its centralized form of government have become so enormous that large numbers of people fear, distrust, dislike and disrespect it.

To point out the evils of centralization does not belong here: most of the conservatives and a few thoughtful radicals of the nineteenth century wrote about these things well enough. But I must say that the argument for decentralization which has recently become somewhat fashionable, will not go very far in our times, when people have begun to question not only the distribution of power, but its very exercise; not only the structure of government, but its very nature.

Of course it is very often true that officials of a central government, sitting in their capital, gravely and injudiciously interfere with the lives and properties of citizens in distant provinces or towns, without having consulted them at all, and without either considering or understanding their particular problems. But there is no longer any guarantee (if there ever was) that people elected or appointed locally will be more capable or even more considerate. In the United States, for example, federal authorities have often acted more considerately than have local authorities in matters involving the civil rights of certain groups. Of course there have been many instances when the reverse has been true. But the newfangled advocates of decentralization have not asked themselves this question: Why is the election of supervisors of townships, or mayors of small towns, an even less inspiring exercise of one's civic duties than the election of a governor or a president? Is it because people feel that in these times of centralized government these locally elected men have little power? Not necessarily: the budgets that local governments and school boards handle nowadays are enormous, their powers of regulating properties are very large indeed. The answer, I submit, is to be found elsewhere. People have become distrustful of the kind of men and women who are interested in holding this kind of power at all.

In the long run the rule of aristocracy has been succeeded not by the rule of democracy but by the rule of bureaucracy. Let us examine this pallid aphorism a little more closely. If one does not like aristocracy one is, most probably, a democrat by preference; or the other way around. But one's exasperation with bureaucracy is a different matter: it is at the same time more superficial and more profound than our dislike of either form of government. The democratic exercise of periodic elections does not compensate people sufficiently against their deep-seated knowledge that they are being ruled by hundreds of thousands of bureaucrats, in every level of government, in every institution, on every level of life.

These bureaucrats are not the trainees of a rigid state apparatus, or of capitalist institutions, as their caricatures during the nineteenth century showed them. They are the interchangeable, suburban men and women of the forever present, willing employees of the monster Progress. They, without exception, are employed in the external administration of life, at a time when people are becoming aware of the frightening condition that the internal freedom of their lives is shrinking. Hence the monstrosity of government even in the most democratic of nations.

❖

During the second quarter of the twentieth century it seemed that a very new kind of monstrous government had arisen in the form of the totalitarian state, exemplified by those of Hitler, Stalin, and of their numerous imitators and satellites. Monstrous as they surely were, the word "totalitarian" (a stammering sort of word, at that) does not really fit them. Total government is an impossibility, even under Hitler, even under Stalin. In retrospect, it is surprising how many fields of everyday life were—sometimes deliberately— actually untouched by these cruel regimes. (This does not mean that fanatical ideologues would not rather see the entirety of the lives of peoples governed by regimes that incarnate their own ideology: but there is little that is new in that.)

Relatively new, however, were three or four features of these modern dictatorships. First, they were democratic, at least in the sense that they ruled with the consent, sometimes active, sometimes passive, of the large majority of their people. (This was especially true of Hitler's Germany.) Second, they were capable of vast misdeeds because of the instruments of modern science. (No gas chambers: no Auschwitz. The SS may have killed one million Jews at random, but not four million.) Third, the execution of such crimes, together with all of the huge operations of the regime, were made possible not so much because of the existence of a minority of radical fanatics and perhaps not even because of the existence of large insensitive majorities as because of the existence of a considerable number of sufficiently efficient and sufficiently indifferent bureaucrats (indifferent, that is, not to their own lives and careers but to moral standards and considerations that lay outside their authority). Fourth, for more or less sensitive people the most horrible trait of these regimes was not so much their practice of injustice as it was their propagation of untruth.

Now, the monstrous matter with modern government is this: every one of these features exists within our mass democracies, too. The consent, sometimes active, sometimes passive, of the majority for governmental misdeeds in the name of efficiency; the criminal applications of modern technology; the eagerness of professional specialists to be employed by the government; the prevalence of untruth (practiced, to be sure, not by hardheaded government censors but by eager or stupid journalists). Thus it sometimes seems that the differences between a modern dictatorship and a modern democracy are merely differences of degree, not differences of kind.

Let us not underestimate differences of degree! They are very important, except for those who believe in the possibility of something like perfect government on earth—utopian idealists who are often potential fanatics, whether they know this or not. The actual extent of these differences of degree is manifested by the movement

of the people who flee, whenever they can, from Communist Eastern Europe to democratic Western Europe, or from Castro's Cuba
to Nixon's United States; there were very great differences of
degree, too, distinguishing, say, a dictatorship of the Franco kind
from Hitler's. Nevertheless, at the end of an age, the elements of
governmental evil are probably alike, no matter how tempered they
are by separate traditions and, what is more important, by different
national characteristics. As Bernanos wrote after the Second World
War: "The democracies have been decomposing, too, but some
decompose more quickly than others. They have been decomposing
into bureaucracies, suffering from it as a diabetic does from sugar,
at the expense of his own substance. In the most advanced states,
this bureaucracy itself decomposes into its most degraded form,
police bureaucracy. At the end of this evolution, all that is left of the
state is the police. . . ."

꠲

More than one hundred and thirty years ago Tocqueville, in a
famous passage, attempted to describe the "sort of despotism
democratic nations have to fear." It would not be like the tyranny of
the Roman Caesars. Modern democratic despotism "would be more
extensive and more mild; it would degrade men without tormenting
them. . . . [The] same principle of equality which facilitates despotism tempers its rigors." But this was scant consolation; he went
on. "I seek in vain for an expression that will accurately convey the
idea . . . the old words *despotism* and *tyranny* are inappropriate:
the thing itself is new, and since I cannot name, I must attempt to
[describe] it."

I seek to trace the novel features under which despotism may appear
in the world. The first thing that strikes the observation is an innumerable multitude of men, all equal and alike, incessantly endeavoring to
procure the petty and paltry pleasures with which they glut their lives.
Above this race of men stands an immense and tutelary power, which
takes upon itself alone to secure their gratifications and to watch over
their fate. That power is absolute, minute, regular, provident, and
mild. . . . It covers the surface of society with a network of small complicated rules, minute and uniform, through which the most original

minds and most energetic characters cannot penetrate, to rise above the crowd. The will of man is not shattered, but softened, bent, and guided; men are seldom forced by it to act, but they are constantly restrained from acting. . . .

I have always thought that servitude of regular, quiet, and gentle kinds which I have just described might be combined more easily than is commonly believed with some of the outward forms of freedom, and that it might establish itself under the wing of the sovereignty of the people.

In 1945, when a new edition of Tocqueville's *Democracy in America* was published, American critics declared that Tocqueville had been unduly pessimistic, that he put too much emphasis on the tyranny of the majority. Twenty-five years later this kind of reaction is nowhere to be found. Not only disgruntled conservatives or con-venticles of intellectuals but millions of people now experience a sense of impersonality and of powerlessness: impersonality, because of the hugeness of democratic organizations and the myriads of interchangeable human beings who make up most of their person-nel; powerlessness, because of the knowledge that votes, appeals, petitions amount to so very little at a time when people have become accustomed to accept the decisions of planners, experts and power-ful governmental agencies. The result is the sickening inward feeling that the essence of self-government is becoming more and more meaningless, even though the outward and legal forms of democracy remain. In spite of recent advances of civil rights, in spite of recent juridical extensions of constitutional freedoms (sometimes permitting the propagation of all kinds of licentious-ness), people sense that they are facing a growing erosion of privacy, of property and, yes, even of liberty.*

---

* Another element in the growing disillusionment with democracy (the very word itself has become bland and meaningless, and not only because practically every government in the world now claims to be "democratic," very much including the Communist "people's democracies") is the growing realiza-tion of its abstract character. For who are "the people"? Rule by "the people" is not only difficult, it is abstract. While it is possible to find out (and later relatively easy to reconstruct) what a certain ruler or even a certain ruling group wanted, who can say what "the people" want? When do "the people" really speak? A statement by Napoleon is a statement by Napoleon: a state-ment by the people is, almost always, a statement made *in the name* of the people—a profound difference.

Yet at the very time when this soulless kind of democratic despotism has arisen, fulfilling to the jot and tittle the prophecies of Tocqueville, symptoms have begun to appear of a development that he could not foresee. As I wrote earlier, the growing disinterest in politics has developed into disillusionment with government in general. The recent rebelliousness of young radicals whose ideas otherwise are rather unoriginal (since they are seldom anything but extreme projections of radical and anarchistic ideas that had been articulated many decades earlier) would be unimportant and ineffectual in the long run, were it not for another, emerging factor: at the very time when modern governments have accumulated enormous powers and fantastic weapons, their very powerlessness is beginning to appear. The monstrous growth of modern democratic government seems to carry within itself the fast-sprouting corpuscles of decay.

Tocqueville saw that in the age of democracy great revolutions would become rare (let us not forget that Hitler or Mussolini assumed power through largely nonrevolutionary means). His foresight proved extraordinarily accurate for one hundred and fifty years, which may be the undisputable world record for political thinkers. What he could not foresee was that for many people existence in a technological and standardized society might become so meaningless as to be intolerable—either because of their appetite for individual freedom, including many of its excrescences, or because little in their education had prepared them to live on their inner resources in the midst of a standardized and depersonalized external world.

❊

There are only three basic forms of government, Aristotle said: monarchy, aristocracy, democracy. Others, as for example Montesquieu, added that in essence every government is a mixture of these forms in one way or another. For a long time it seemed that liberal democracy would eventually degenerate into a new kind of elective monarchy, that increasing centralization and the degeneration of elections to the levels of vast popularity contests would lead to this. This danger is by no means past. But another possibility has now arisen: a new compound of democracy and aristocracy—the latter, however, not a spiritual or hereditary or financial or intellectual aristocracy, but a novel kind of aristocracy of brute power.

I find it not at all impossible that the disintegration of regular civic authority might eventually lead to the establishment of a new kind of relative safety and order desired by people in neighborhoods and small towns—which, however, would no longer be imposed by the traditional and lawful authorities alone. It would depend upon the cooperation of criminal gangs who had grasped and maintained portions of power and authority in their neighborhood during the time when traditional authority was disintegrating. The gangs that already control certain very clearly delimited portions of streets and blocks that their members call "turfs"; the successful criminal who is a hero among the young people of a neighborhood or perhaps of an entire social or racial group; the tightly knit group of adult criminals who, indirectly or directly, secure contracts from this or that arm of the government and consequently guarantee safety and profit for those who do not object to cooperating with them—all of this, including the actual cooperation of certain elements of the police with certain groups of criminals, reminds one of the beginnings of feudalism in the Dark Ages, of the end of one thing and the beginning of something else from which a new kind of law and a new kind of order would eventually grow. At least in the United States we have suddenly traveled very far from Tocqueville's centralized democratic government whose power is "absolute, minute, regular, provident, and mild."

The idealist (or, more properly, the sentimentalist) radicals among our young people are therefore quite mistaken in thinking that because of the bankruptcy of the established political and institutional ideas they, and their ilk, are bound to inherit authority and power, whereafter the building of a new Jerusalem may begin. To the contrary, power will be quickly grasped by those who want it for themselves, who would sneer or laugh at the notion that after the old order comes down, the first item of business would be the discussion of the new philosophical ideas that should govern new institutions. Something like this happened in the autumn and winter of 1917 in Russia, or during the ridiculous play at revolution by the students in Paris in May 1968, toward the end of which juvenile criminals from outlying districts began to appear in the university buildings, terrorizing and blackmailing students and their girls who already after two weeks were exhausted from debating and playing at revolution. Their compatriot Proudhon, a much deeper seer than Marx, was, after all, entirely right in saying that people react less to ideas about social contracts than to the realities of power.

Does the history of government alternate between periods in which authority prevails, degenerating eventually into tyranny, and other (usually much shorter) periods in which liberty prevails, degenerating eventually into anarchy? It seems so: and the best times in the history of modern civilization were those decades when there existed a tolerable compound of authority and liberty. In these matters, however, the compounds are marked not by the proportions of their quantities but by their qualities. In our times, then, when the principle of popular democracy is supreme, when elections are popularity contests at the same time when the common citizen before government is powerless; when he is the potential victim of atomic accidents, of atmospheric booms, of exploding gases or chemicals, at the same time when he is at liberty among pictures, advertisements, books, theater and moving-picture scenes representing the mutual degradations of naked men, women and children, to talk of a balance of authority and liberty is nearly nonsense: it is tyranny and anarchy that are beginning to hold each other in sway.

The impotence of Powers

5

How the greatest States, having accumulated unequaled powers, suddenly have found that they are becoming powerless.

Toward the end of the Modern Age we may observe two contradictory developments: the increasing concentration of power on the one hand, and the beginning of its disintegration on the other.

This may be traced, relatively clearly, in the relations of the Great Powers that, after all, have remained until now the most important relations in the historical development of modern mankind.

The unprecedented progress and prosperity of the white race during the nineteenth century may have depended on the existence of a continuous balance of power among the Great Powers of Europe. The functions of this balance of power were often far from salutary: still there were no world wars and no all-European wars during the century before 1914. There were five Great Powers in Europe. Politically speaking, our world did not become round until the end of the last century. At that time two new and dynamic states, the United States and Japan, became World Powers; and the European balance was profoundly affected by their influences. Thus at the outbreak of the First World War seven Great Powers existed (or six, if we exclude Austria-Hungary, which was growing feeble, and the only one among the seven that possessed no colonies). Twenty-five years later, at the beginning of the Second World War, five states remained that could still be properly called Great Powers: the United States, Britain, Germany, Russia and Japan. At the end of that war two were defeated and the third, nominally a victor, was weakened to such an extent that the United States and the Soviet Union were the only two Great Powers left.

To most people it seemed that thereafter these two Superpowers were engaged in a global struggle involving, in essence, the domination of the world. The Soviet Union was now the only Great Power on the European continent; she had incorporated entire states within her system; she professed to incarnate an expansive and revolutionary world ideology. The United States, financially and industrially the most powerful state on earth, accepted the dependence of Western Europe on its presence and support; thereafter, rapidly and perhaps thoughtlessly, it extended its system of overseas bases and alliances to dozens of states on five continents.

After a decade of so-called "cold war," however, it began to appear that the two Superpowers were not seeking to destroy each other, even though for the first time in history they were capable of doing so with their rockets and atomic bombs. In certain places of the world they were actually beginning to retrench and to withdraw. Their maneuverings showed that the world was still too large to be dominated by a single Power, no matter how much nonsense was being prattled about "One World."

During the last decade, then, the two Superpowers proved on occasion incapable or unwilling to prevent a partial disintegration of their own spheres of influence. Communist China shook off all Russian influences and became an outspoken enemy of the Soviet Union; the President of France could terminate the presence of American troops and military installations within his country; the United States had to tolerate the existence of a self-proclaimed Communist dictatorship in Cuba, on her southeastern doorstep; the Soviet Union tolerated the existence of a more-or-less independent

Rumania, on her southwestern doorstep; after several years of frustrating fighting in Vietnam the United States started to pull out; there appeared other symptoms of this kind of retrenchment and withdrawal in other parts of the world.

It is still too early to say whether this partial disintegration of the *de facto* empires of the two Superpowers would develop further, whether they might proceed beyond a certain point (the Russian crackdown on the independent-minded Czechs in 1968, and perhaps the continued American presence in Guantánamo suggested that, for the time being, there are certain limits beyond which this military retrenchment will not go). But it is not too early to point out the existence of a monstrous paradox: at the very time when the Superpowers have accumulated arms of fantastic and incredible power, when they have shown themselves capable of hurling rockets to Mars and men in capsules onto the surface of the moon, their influence over their neighboring peoples has become gradually weaker.

※

Why this incipient weakness? We can detect at least four elements bringing it about. They are:

the impotence of technology,
    the democratization of warfare,
        the deterioration of sovereignty,
            the "internalization" of human personality.

During the last twenty-five years the dreadful arms produced by the Superpowers have often rendered them impotent. For about four years after 1945 the American government had an absolute monopoly in the possession of atomic bombs: but the thought that this awesome monopoly ought to be exploited in bringing pressure on the Soviet Union to make her retreat from the forward bastions of her bloated empire was banished from the deliberations of the American government at the time. Britain had her first atomic bomb in 1952, her first hydrogen bomb in 1957: her decline from the status of a Great Power has been precipitous since that time. Sixty years ago the submission of Cuba or, at that, of any Latin American country could be secured by the presence of a few American warships; all of the hydrogen rockets and all of the nerve gas stored in American arsenals do not seem to have given Castro a single sleepless night. Deeply influenced by his early political memories under Franklin Roosevelt during the New Deal era's illusions of benevolent omnipotence, President Johnson believed in 1965 that the technological superiority of the United States, together with massive aerial bombing, would be sufficient to insure the defeat of the guerrillas of Vietnam; he was tragically mistaken, and hundreds of thousands of American soldiers had to be sent there to wage that interminable war.

There are two sides to this impotence of technology, one external, the other internal. The external side is obvious, to the point of a platitude. You cannot kill a fly with an elephant gun. What is perhaps more significant, you cannot even threaten it, which is the other side of the coin. Technology has become cumbrous and useless in far more instances than people have been accustomed to think. But there is more to this: the reluctance to use a horrible instrument (because of its unforeseen consequences) reduces its fearful reputation. This does not mean that accident or miscalculation could not, in an instant, let loose enormities upon the world. But, as I wrote earlier in this book, the end of the so-called Modern Age is arriving with the cacophony of bangs *and* whimpers.

❧

After the first atom bomb had been cast on Japan, after the end of the last war there was widespread agreement among intellectuals and statesmen. From now on there were to be only two alternatives: world peace or an atomic world war; world government or world destruction. They were wrong (perhaps because at the end of an age intellectual consensus is almost always wrong). We have entered into a period not of large wars but of protracted small wars.

There is little reason to rejoice in this. These small wars are, in many ways, more savage and barbarian than were many of the great armed conflicts of the still recent past. The democratization of violence has now begun; it is one of the elements in the impotence of the Great Powers.

Perhaps one of the high marks of civilization was not the absence of wars but its capacity to keep wars within certain limits. Before 1914, wars were fought among the Powers within tacitly accepted ground rules. There was a definite distinction of soldiers from civilians, of combatants from noncombatants, of conditions of peace from conditions of war. Wars were practiced by the armies of states rather than by entire peoples. (At the same time small municipal forces of police or of a watch were sufficient to insure tranquillity and safety in the cities of the Western world.) There were exceptions to this, here and there, during the nineteenth century. On the edges of civilized Europe, the Spanish and Russian peoples practiced *guerrilla*, "little war," against their French invaders as early as one hundred and sixty years ago; during Sherman's march through Georgia, as during the Prussian siege of Paris, there gleamed something new and barbaric, the determination to punish an entire people. The democratization of war went on: it made the carnage of the First World War patriotic and popular. Still the traditional distinction between soldiers and civilians was observed; Clausewitz's grave little platitude, a typical summary of the history of the Powers during the Modern Age, was still valid; war was the continuation of politics by other means.

All of this was changing during the Second World War. Hitler, for example, chose to regard the extermination of millions of people as one of Germany's principal war aims; the Germans as well as the Allies regarded the methodical bombing and killing of enemy populations from the air as regular methods of warfare. The Germans found that while they could conquer states, they had still to face the armed hostility of entire peoples, bursting forth in the guerrilla warfare of the so-called resistance movements. This was to happen to them in Poland, Yugoslavia, Greece, Russia and, after a while, in France, Italy and a host of other countries. This, not the bomber or the rocket or the snorkel submarine, was the most revolutionary change in warfare during the Second World War. It was fraught with the greatest significance even when we recognize its limited military importance at the time. (Had the Great Powers, Britain, Russia, America not continued fighting Germany with the prospect of ultimate victory, these patriotic guerrilla movements would have dwindled to nothing or, in many cases, they would not have come into existence at all.)

During the last quarter century, then, the dissolution of the once traditional boundaries between peace and war has proceeded very fast. During the so-called cold war many of the practices of the Superpowers demonstrated the reverse of Clausewitz's famous dictum: politics served now as the continuation of war. In the Middle East we could see the existence of a new kind of war, erupting in violent movement every ten years or so, never subsiding into real peace in between. In sum, the original and literal meaning of *guerrilla*, that is, "little war," small-scale war, seems to mark the violent conflicts of our times. In Vietnam, for example, the war goes on between armies and peoples; trafficking civilians of the day turn into savage warriors at night, or the reverse. The occupying soldier does not know who among the natives is his ally, who is his enemy; neither do some of the natives themselves. With the democratization of war, and of violence, the symptoms of a new kind of savage life have appeared, not only on the frontiers of the Great Powers but in the hearts of their cities themselves. They amount to the possibility that with the disintegration of traditional distinctions we may be facing the coexistence of perpetual war with perpetual peace, a nomadic guerrilla existence symptomatic of the new Dark Ages, against which all of the fantastic rockets and bombs in the secret arsenals of the Superpowers will amount to nothing.

❋

The democratization of warfare means simply this: from wars between states we have passed through the massive phase of wars between nations to the newest phase of wars between peoples. We have, thus, arrived at a stage of civilization where *international* relationships have only begun. Let me explain this. The word "international" has been a misnomer. We have been using it for one hundred and fifty years or so in the wrong sense, since when we speak of "international law," "international organizations," "international treaties," "international relations," we almost always mean something *supranational,* something that involves the relations of states, not the relations of nations. On the other hand phenomena such as the seasonal migration or the tourism of millions of people from one country to another; the image that one people has of another through books, magazines, translations, movies, television; the attraction or the dislike that one nationality has for another, are truly *inter*national relations, democratic phenomena which the governments of traditional states often cannot determine: they can only attempt to influence them.

We have, thus, come to the end of hundreds of years when the history of civilized mankind consisted principally (though never exclusively) of the relations of states, since states were the only sovereign powers on this earth. Again it is technology which has eroded the earlier exercise of nearly unlimited sovereignty. How curious this is! The state in the second half of the twentieth century is less potent than it was a hundred years ago, even as its bureaucratic intervention in the daily lives of its peoples is greater than ever before. How ridiculous were (and are) the attempts of those international lawyers who still assert that the frontiers of states extend vertically, too, into air and space—into the stratosphere? to the moon? beyond it? The Soviet Union, which guards the frontiers separating her even from her own satellites by minefields, wire fences and watchtowers, had to tolerate for years the rapid flight of American spy planes above its vast territories. While it is true that long-range aerial bombing and long-range aerial observation have proven far less effective weapons than what had been believed for a long time, it is also true that our modern states cannot stop intrusions into the air over their lands. I submit, further, that the time is coming when they will not be able to stop foreign incursions on land. I am not only thinking of guerrilla or commando raids, I am thinking of the sudden migratory pressure of large populations, sloshing across frontiers. Except in still largely uninhabited territories, against them not even atomic bombs would do.

In Southeast Asia, in the Middle East, and perhaps elsewhere in the world, too, wars are now being fought without ever having been declared by the states that fight them. But, then, these are wars involving peoples, and not only the armies sent out by states: in such conditions state sovereignty amounts to very little indeed. In other portions of the world the once civilized relations of governments that are not at war with each other have eroded fast. During the 1950's, at the height of the cold war between the United States and the Soviet Union, and during the 1960's between the United States and Cuba, not only agents and spies but criminals and delinquents fleeing from one state would find asylum in the other. The power of transmitted images and words, too, erodes the independence of the once sovereign state. There exist situations now in which revolutions could be provoked in neighboring countries without sending a single agent across the frontiers. The riots in East Berlin in 1953, and perhaps even the Hungarian Rising in 1956, could have been fanned into general uprisings in East Germany and Eastern Europe merely through radio and television appeals across the border, had the American and West German governments so decided at that time. (Because of the American unwillingness to risk a general war with Russia, they did not choose to do so.)

How ironic it is, then, that during this phase of history millions of people were told to put their faith in assemblies of bureaucrats such as the League of Nations or the United Nations, falsely believing them to be the first "international" organizations in history, when, in reality, they represented nothing but the governments of states—at a time when the sovereignty of states that has marked the history of the last four hundred years, counted less and less.

In one important way the world is *not* becoming smaller, rather the contrary. Politically speaking, we have reached a contradictory phase: integration contradicted by disintegration. We used to be told, not so long ago, that small states were obsolete: but look at the number of new states that have come into being in Asia and Africa, some of which are breaking up further into tribal components. Nor is this entirely attributable to savagery. During the last few years independence movements have sprung up in old regions of Europe itself, in Scotland, Wales, Brittany, the French-Swiss Jura, the South Tyrol, struggles have erupted between Flemings and Walloons in Belgium, Protestant and Catholic Irishmen of the North, not to speak of the tribal nationalism aflame among black Americans, Mexican-Americans, French- and English-speaking Canadians. In one way these movements have been the results of the increasing consciousness of nationality: in another, of the decreasing authority of the traditional state. Of course the power of the state is often still strong, and the stake of many ordinary people in the existing order of things is too large (especially in Europe) to seek a desperate showdown with the state. Yet there are few reasons to doubt that the power of the state will sooner or later become affected by the erosion of its authority. Instead of being archaic remnants of a patriotic past, these tribal or regional revolutionaries may herald the future.

❈

Power brings authority; authority includes power; we live at a time when both the power and the authority of the modern state are diminishing. The authority of monarchs, dictators, presidents, governments generally evoke less and less of the traditional loyalty of the citizen. The decline of both power and authority is now involved with the decline of credibility. Thus even in these times of mass production and mass communication, in spite of massive bureaucracies, the influence of the state on the citizen may be weaker than it was before, for the simple reason (the reason may be simple but its consequences are complex) that the government can exercise but a limited influence over the individual person's mind —not so much because individual minds have become more independent as because people themselves have become more and more aware of this condition.

❈

Should we rejoice over these developments? It would seem, at first sight, that the developing feebleness of enormously powerful states is something to which free men and women ought to look forward with confidence. To some extent this is so; but we ought to consider the great and looming danger, that of revolutionary anarchy loosened upon the world. The impotence of the world Powers among themselves is eventually inseparable from their incipient weakness within themselves, the latter being both cause and consequence of the former. In the largest cities of the greatest power of the world today entire sections exist where police cannot guarantee order. Elsewhere a few thousand students are capable of defying governments possessing atom bombs for the simple reason that the government would not dare to kill them.

When Tocqueville wrote that in the coming democratic age great revolutions may become rare, he did not exclude their possibility altogether. He warned that such revolutions, if successful, would have terrible consequences—they would for a while destroy the basis of civilized life. Still he thought in terms of big revolutions, not of small ones. He did not consider what the waning authority of government could mean for an increasing number of people. We are beginning to learn what this might mean: not the appearance of a democratic Caesar, "the man on the white horse" liberals fear (reading history wrong, as usual), but a new and brutal kind of order where the police bureaucracy and a criminal elite work hand in hand. We have seen examples of this in the Nazi concentration camps where the right hand of the Nazi guards were a camp aristocracy of criminals, wherefrom the so-called Kapos were recruited. We know that in Soviet camps and prisons too, a criminal elite rises to the top in collaboration with the armed guards.* In the United

* In 1943 the intelligence agencies of the United States employed the services of the Mafia of former Sicilian immigrants to aid the crusade of the democracies during the invasion of Sicily and southern Italy, with propitious results, in the short run at least. Of all the rulers of Italy Mussolini was the only one who, to some extent, succeeded in breaking the rule of the Mafia in Sicily. This is a fragmentary example: but is it too extreme to think that, all of democratic indoctrination and sincere revulsion from dictatorship notwithstanding,

States organized criminality is not always the enemy of political authority: the cooperation of the criminal, of the political, of the labor, of the industrial bureaucracy is widespread, and not only on the local level.

In sum, the growing powerlessness of the modern state reflects the abdication, first of the convictions, then of the courage, of its erstwhile governing classes; and it is at least probable that in its wake there will follow not the blessings of increased liberty but a long transitory brutal period of insecurity and terror.

---

the time may come when a generation may seek something admirable in people such as Mussolini and Hitler as if they had been the potential last-ditch defenders of Western civilization?

The separation of races

How, after the abolition of slavery and the enforcement of equality, the races have discovered that their fraternity amounted to little.

One of the strangest elements of human nature, certainly one of the most mysterious components of the unity of mankind, is the existence of various races.

During the present phase of our mental evolution the realization of what this diversity means has not yet emerged from the depths of our minds to the surfaces of our consciousness. On the one hand the reactions of large masses of people to their confrontation with problems of race are still primitive and fearful. On the other hand it was hardly more than one hundred years ago that the first attempts were made to confront the problem of the diversity of races on the higher basis of detached intellectual study: but none of these attempts, whether by racialists or anti-racialists, have left us with anything but a sense of shameful and confused inadequacy.

At the end of the Modern Age the coexistence of peoples of different races within certain regions of the earth, often within the same country, has suddenly become problematic; and the pattern of world settlement that was characteristic of the last five hundred years seems either halted or reversed.

People sometimes think that race (as distinct from heredity) played no part in the savage animosities of the Christian Middle Ages: but this is not so. No matter how truly revolutionary the doctrines of Christianity were by virtue of its proclamation of a faith that was potentially open to slaves as well as to masters, to our remote ancestors race and physical heredity meant much of the same thing. Even a superficial acquaintance with the history of the Spanish Inquisition tells us, for example, how the popular hatred for Jews and Moors in Spain involved more than the profession of religion, that a narrow and fanatical preoccupation with the potential evils of alien blood pursued the troubled descendants of the sincerest of *conversos* for centuries.

Still, nowhere outside of Europe were whites to be found five hundred years ago. The white race then discovered other continents, inhabited, sometimes sparsely, by other races. The racial geography of the world was transformed. In the course of four centuries one hundred million white people migrated across the oceans. They conquered four continents; they settled North America, Siberia, Australia, which were harboring a few million people of primitive races; in Central and South America they mixed with large numbers of the natives; in Africa and Asia in their capacity of a superior and governing minority they ruled vast lands and large peoples. This expansion of the empires of white nations reached its peak as late as seventy years ago when, for example, all of Africa, save for two weak native states, was a colony of one or another European nation. Doubts were beginning to rise about the benefits of colonialism and about the validity of imperialism among the peoples of the white nations themselves. But their prestige was still high. All of the peoples of the world, possibly even those Chinese and Japanese who pretended the contrary, envied and emulated them.

A little more than fifty years ago this was beginning to change. The Japanese proved, for instance, that they could defeat Russians, Frenchmen, Englishmen, to the point of humiliation, even though they were to be defeated by the Americans in turn. The abject surrender to the Japanese of the rabbit-toothed British commander in Singapore in 1942 was a significant event, though it made probably a deeper impression upon the consciousness of a generation of Englishmen than upon East Asians. For more important than the ups and downs in the contests of states were the mutations of beliefs. After the Second World War few Europeans still thought that the nations of the white race ought to rule over other races of the world. The two new Superpowers, burdened though as they were by the presence of various races in their midst, were propagandists of anti-imperialism, each in its own way. Then the diminished European Powers discovered, belatedly, that their possessions of overseas colonies cost them more than what they were worth. Thus they rapidly liquidated their empires within a few years: and, save for Siberia, South Africa, and a few small exceptions here and there, the political supremacy of the white race in Africa and Asia came to an end.

This meant the end of a great period in the history of the world: of the vast movement of the European race to the vast lands across the seas that had begun five hundred years before. But it was the beginning, too, of something else: of an increasing consciousness of what the coexistence of different races might really portend.

❉

The coexistence of races in the United States is an example of this. Hatred among people of different races, and the subjugation of one race by another exist, of course, in many other places of the world: indeed, its worst instances are often practiced by one colored race against another. But I must write about the United States, because I am concerned with what is happening within Western civilization, among the components of which the continent of Europe is relatively fortunate, inhabited as it is by different nations which are, however, all, whites.

More than a century ago the peoples and the governments of the Old World had chosen to put an end to slavery in their colonies and dominions even before the peoples of the New World were to do so.

During the obscure evolution of the history of South and Central America the aspirations and conflicts of different races and their mixtures were the profoundest of elements. In North America, too, the key to the Civil War in the nineteenth century was race and not politics or economics: had the slaves in the Southern states not been black, they would have been freed long before; indeed, they would not have been slaves at all. Nevertheless, freed they were, at the cost of a murderous war between their white masters. During the following one hundred years it became more and more evident that the legal emancipation of the black race was not enough. It had put an end to one great evil, while the evolution of society was creating others, because of the same principal elements in the revolution of its consciousness that we have encountered earlier, and that we shall encounter again. I am speaking of the shortcomings of egalitarian democracy, and of the increasing "internalization" of the human condition.

During the century that passed since the abolition of slavery in the United States the animosity between the two races of the American people has not decreased: alas, in many places probably the contrary is true. Not only were Negroes subject again to all kinds of legal restrictions, principally in the Southern states: even when these, too, were abolished, the Negroes found that the hostility of many of their white neighbors was as strong, if not stronger, than before. When they migrated to the Northern states, they were confronted by an insensitive and callous quality of industrial life that to them was new. They exchanged a condition of inequality that had been tempered by the reality of human contacts in the South for a legal condition of equality in the North where the personal relations of the races were often abstract and inhuman.

The main shortcoming of democracy facing the Negro race in the United States is not illiberality, it is abstraction. When we consider the Negroes' lives, the traditional conservative warnings to the effect that an undue extension of equality results in a diminution of liberty means little. Their sufferings have existed, rather, because equality is often but a legal category, so narrow as to leave the essence of personal relationships unaffected, entirely different from those feelings of fraternity which, as Péguy wrote, "have animated great men and great nations . . . whereas the desire for equality had only inspired very dubious revolutions."

The intellectual consensus of our times still believes—or, rather, it pretends to believe—that through their economic improvement the dissatisfactions of the Negroes will diminish and perhaps even disappear: and that with the growth of democratic education and legislation the two races will eventually mingle and mix to such an extent that they will no longer remain separate entities. Both of these liberal projections have already proven woefully wrong. The legal prohibition of segregation—declared, alas, on the basis of a woozy sociological argumentation by the philistine Justices of the Supreme Court of the United States—probably overdue by 1954, was proclaimed at the very time when the *de facto* segregation of the two races was crystallizing across the country. Since that time actual segregation may have proceeded faster than desegregation. There are virtually no whites who still live in Harlem or in other Negro sections of American cities. Public schools with Negro majorities are close to becoming all-Negro schools. Democratic education, at any rate, has meant nothing, since the egalitarian conformity of democracy actually impedes the free commingling of races: it is the lower class among the whites who hate and fear the Negroes the most. The nervous mingling and the self-conscious inclusion of Negro men and women in public institutions and public entertainment means little. More important, there is some evidence to the effect that, except on the fringes of bohemia, the number of marriages between Negroes and whites may not be increasing, all of the public preaching and propaganda of sexual freedom notwithstanding. Of course the distinction of the races would diminish if the number of children from mixed marriages increased; but the number of mulattoes in the United States is hardly increasing at all (in certain states of the South it was not inconsiderable one hundred years ago).

In sum, the two races live apart as before, and in certain important ways even more apart than before. That this is mostly due to the barbaric prejudices of white Americans is largely (though, alas, not always) nonsense; and those Europeans who claim that they cannot understand the stubborn persistence of racial apartness in the United States ought to keep quiet and thank their good fortune for their own lack of experience. It is easy for a Frenchman to point at the racial liberalism in evidence in the cafés of the Left Bank: were there one million blacks living in Paris the liberalism of the Parisians would yet have to be demonstrated.

During the last ten years, however, an important change occurred in the mental dispositions of American Negroes, the meaning of which goes beyond their discontent with the erratic and sometimes overdue legal enforcement of some of their civic rights. For the first time millions of them claim that the white majority, with all of its rights, ways, culture and civilization, is no longer to be emulated. For centuries the Negroes dreamed of becoming like the whites, to the point of imitating not only the clothes but the physical appearance of the whites. Now many of them are trying to convince themselves that this aspiration is not merely impossible but that it is also undesirable. "My blackness goes deeper than the color of my skin"—this, in brief, is the condition that certain thinking Negroes have discovered within themselves, having looked deeper into themselves than had their ancestors earlier. Thus Negroes, too, have been influenced by the evolving "internalization" of the human condition in the Western world: and the tragic, the sometimes horrible, and sometimes ludicrous excrescences of this assertion of their identity, bursting forth in the civil disorders of the last few years, ought not to obscure the significance of this condition.

The tragedy of American Negroes (and also of whites), then, is that this, far from ignoble, aspiration is practically unachievable: for, in spite of their fanciful exaltation of Muslimhood or of Africa, the American Negroes have no Zion whereto they may return. Their language is English, their entertainments (and, consequently, much of their everyday imagination) are American, they are condemned —if that is the word—to live in the United States. There they dwell, crowding into their narrow interstices between the white American population. Because of the decaying urbanity in American aspirations, they may come to occupy, here and there, more and more sections of American cities that are abandoned by whites: but a truly meaningful secession into a Negro community, a state within the United States, is impossible. Still, this self-assertion of their separate identity is an important event. Marked as it is, on the one hand, by the occasional reappearance of savagery in the midst of civilization, on the other hand it marks the end of an epoch of intellectual illusions. It suggests—temporarily or not—the waning prestige of the white race; and it exemplifies a development that is now crystallizing everywhere in the world.

※

Here, again, we encounter the dual development of integration and disintegration. On the one hand the world has become compact; every race has some contact with another; in many places of the world the members of different races are mingling freely; it seems as if the world were becoming one world, after all.* On the other hand the world is breaking up into vast racial regions; the various races are beginning to be sovereign within their own regions, somewhat like the nationalities of Europe that began to form themselves into national states toward the end of the Middle Ages. Except for the Americas and Australia, the white race has returned to Europe; Africa belongs to Africans, Asia more and more to Asians. There remains the huge question of Russia's empire in Northern Asia: at the end of the last century Bismarck was supposed to have said that the most important fact in the twentieth century would be that Americans speak English; it is not impossible

* The recent interest of white people in the cultures and artifacts of Africans and Asians would be an admirable thing in itself, a symptom of the broadening of minds and of perceptions, were it not that many among the professional practitioners of "non-Western studies" seem to be little more than intellectual opportunists, whose interest in alien cultures is hardly genuine: it is rather, the outcome of their ignorant disinterest in the history of the culture that should have been their own.

that the most important condition of the next hundred years might be that the Russians are, after all, white.

The civilization that has spread out from Europe and America now rules the world; but the prestige of the white race has become afflicted while its proportion of the populations of the globe is diminishing, too (at a slower rate than most people believe, principally because of high birth rates in Latin America). The coexistence of different races in the world is now a fact, but the question remains: what kind of coexistence? Alas, it is possible that before the racial geography of the globe crystallizes anew—like five hundred years ago, when the political geography of Europe was crystallizing—large popular wars might erupt, with entire peoples of different races rushing at each other. (In the chronic conflicts of our decades, between Arabs and Israelis, in Vietnam, between Russia and China, it is foolish to slur over the element of racial struggle beneath the ideological or political or economic claims, more than often pretexts.) On the other hand it is not impossible that such a murderous worldwide struggle among races might not take place, precisely because of their separate consolidation in different regions of the globe. In that event our descendants will smile at the modern illusion: the belief that masses of different races will coexist peacefully within the same nation, under the same government, elected by themselves; and that with their increasing consciousness their distinctness will disappear.

The conformity of nations

How, notwithstanding the shrinking of the world, the nations of the white race have found that they must turn inward to face themselves.

One of the main delusions of modern liberal political thinking is the belief that nationalism is a survival from a reactionary past, and that with the development of democracy it is bound to weaken and eventually disappear. To the contrary: nationalism, nationality, freedom of speech and equality in society have developed together. During the last golden age of political thought, during the last decades before 1848, most political philosophers could still overlook this condition. They wrote, with few exceptions, about what should be the proper compounds of liberty and equality, of liberalism and conservatism, ineluctable matters that may still engage our attention on occasion. Yet by about 1870, one hundred years ago, the liberal-conservative antithesis had largely lost its meaning. After the general acceptance of the democratic principle in the Western world, there were no real conservatives left. Now a few Socialists appeared, proclaiming that their ideology was a most important innovation in the history of mankind, that socialism was to be the successor of the liberalism that had been characteristic of the pass-

ing bourgeois phase. This was a half-truth, at best. The greatest
world developments during the last phase of bourgeois capitalism,
the dissolution of the Spanish and Turkish empires, the constitutional weakness of the Austrian empire, the rise of the German and
of the American empires, finally the First World War, had little
to do with conservatism or liberalism or socialism: they were caused
and promoted by nationalism.

That was a new phenomenon, the greatest consequence of democracy, the meaning and sometimes even the presence of which
was ignored by the Marxists. In 1914 there were millions of workers
in Germany, France, Britain, who, for the first time in history, knew
how to read and write; they were voters, they were Socialists. Many
intellectuals therefore believed that national wars could not happen
again, the dawn of socialist internationalism having risen. In 1914
the effect of the latter was that of a cold square pat of margarine in
a hot skillet. The peoples went to war with the greatest of enthusi-
asms, entire nations rushed at each other; not only did the bishops
of each nation bless their flags and guns, but the socialist workers of
each nation stoked the furnaces and cannons. No matter how much
still separated their lives at home or even in the trenches, officers
and soldiers, the sons of gentry and of workers were fused into one
cohesive national mass. The class struggle made no difference, it
hardly existed at all. The different currents of socialism were swallowed up by nationalism as rivers are swallowed up by the sea.
Much of the same thing was true of the Second World War, all of
the statesmen of which were national leaders, very much including
Stalin. The same thing remains true of the chieftains and dictators
of the last twenty-five years, about everywhere in the world: a
Castro or a Ho Chi Minh may be a Socialist or Communist by
choice while he is a nationalist by nature. Meanwhile not only the
brutal nationalism of the Russians themselves but the presence of all
kinds of nationalisms on both the western and eastern borders of
their empire reveals, again and again, the idiocy (though it is often
a profitable idiocy) cultivated by those propagandists and intellectuals who either praise or fear (some of them do this alternately)

the Soviet Union as if it were the incarnation of Communist revolutionary internationalism.

❉

A century ago in Eastern Europe there were still millions of people who did not know what their own nationality was. This has changed in the twentieth century. The democratic development of mankind homogenizes peoples; they become alike, they conform in habits, opinions, thoughts, they wish to identify themselves with the "cause" of their national state, they are suspicious of outsiders within their state even more than they are of foreigners, a form of nationalism becomes their tradition, their only ideology. This is different from patriotism, a more ancient phenomenon that means love for a certain land, for a certain town, for a certain people, something that is basically defensive and not expansive, anchored as it is in a living past. When Hitler wrote *Mein Kampf*, he understood this very well; he wrote that he was "a nationalist, not a patriot," since early in life he dedicated himself to the glory of the German nation but not to the preservation of the ancient Habsburg monarchical state. He had millions of followers, bursting with dynamism: for when people found that many of their earlier bonds and of their previous loyalties were dissolving or becoming meaningless, they discovered a new meaning within their own allegiance, the one to their nation.

This has been essentially a mental and psychic process experienced by millions during the democratization of nations. Thus, for example, the children and sometimes the grandchildren of immigrants in the United States became (often through the agency of the democratic school) the most potent instruments of "Americanism." This was especially so during the period from Presidents McKinley to Kennedy, when the expansion of the United States in the world took place. From the ranks of second generations of immigrants came some of the most vocal of America's nationalists. But this, too, may be passing now.

❉

At the very time when the practices and ideas of nationalism, coming from Europe, infected large parts of the world, the peoples of Europe were beginning to be cured of them. After the Second World War, among most of them a general revulsion against the excesses of nationalism set in. In spite of their humiliations (or perhaps, to some extent, because of them) the French, for example, no longer hated the Germans (and the Germans not the French). Save for certain exceptions, this tendency became the general mental experience for a new generation on both sides of the iron curtain dividing Europe. For one thing, wars among nations *within Europe* seemed insane, things of the past. For another thing, the states of Europe were now more nationally homogeneous than ever before: the presence of alien minorities within the traditional boundaries of the national state was an acute problem only in a few instances. This homogenization of the nations of Europe was very important: it made the first blossoming of truly international relations among the masses possible. For here we arrive at a paradox (or, rather, at two successive phases of the same evolution): democracy nationalizes; but, then, it internationalizes, too.

This is largely (though not exclusively) the result of modern mass communications. There is the development of mass tourism: tens of millions of people, virtually of every class and age, now visit other countries, other nations. There is international trade: millions in one country become acquainted with, they develop a taste for, the characteristic products of other nations. There is the massive presence of international information: through newspapers, magazines, radio, television, millions see and know something of certain people in other countries, a coronation in England or a presidential election in America becoming, thus, a vicarious experience shared by hundreds of millions abroad. There is mass entertainment: the images and the sounds of international film stars or popular performers of music are part and parcel not only of the mental equipment but of the household of millions across continents.

But we ought not exaggerate the effects of these massive international developments: no matter how widespread, they are often superficial. During the nineteenth century the movement of a few political exiles across the Pyrenees, the clandestine importation of a few pamphlets were sufficient to provoke revolutions in Spain; for more than a decade now fifteen million people are crossing from France to Spain each summer, without much effect on the stability of the Franco regime, or at that, on the political consciousness of the Spanish people at large. In many ways the internationalism of the cosmopolitan aristocracy of the eighteenth century, due to which Voltaire and Gibbon could write of Europe as a great republic of cultivated spirits, was something more substantial than the screaming cosmopolitan pervasiveness of the Beatles. Jay, Franklin, Jefferson were more at home in the France of the ancient regime than are Dean Rusk or Richard Nixon in the modern France of today. The now fashionable concern with the widespread presence of American industrial corporations in Europe, these fears of Europe's "Americanization" through the dollar, are exaggerated, too: for, while the adoption of certain American techniques of production is practically useful, the presence of American salesmen in Europe is practically useless: very soon the American corporation in France or Italy becomes staffed entirely by native administrators and clerks, whereby for all practical purposes the American-owned institution or corporation is re-nationalized.

The re-nationalization is an important point. After everything is said, democracy still nationalizes more than it internationalizes. One hundred years ago, even fifty years ago, a French banker had more in common with a Spanish banker than either of them had with their clerks. This is no longer so. Those intellectuals who prattle about nations being remnants of the past cannot see the forest for the trees. The contrary is true: we live in an age where the relations of nations have become even more important than the relations of classes.

But these relations of nations are something else than the older, more rigid and restricted, relations of states: for we must not confuse nations with states, and nationalism with nationality. The existence of nations preceded the existence of modern nationalism, and the former show every sign of surviving the latter. Indeed, there are some reasons to believe that the older the nation the less nationalistic it is: or, in other words, the older the nation, the less aggressive its nationalism which becomes, instead, a patriotism of another, deeper kind. The awareness of nationality, in successive generations, may become less pronounced on the surface, while it becomes an interior reality. The inherited and the acquired, the permanent and the vested interests that people have of their own nation accumulate, they become more genuine, part and parcel of the character of the person. Besides being merely political, nationality becomes a cultural phenomenon.

⁂

The history of the United States should furnish good examples of this. For a century the crystallization of American nationality was disrupted by mass immigration: and, as we have seen, among many groups of immigrants the second generation chose to be the representatives of a virulent, and particularly American, form of democratic nationalism. A generation or two later many of their children and grandchildren no longer felt the need for this kind of self-assertion. Thus, for example, the "Americanism" of John Kennedy eventually became less nationalistic and more internationalist than that of his father's generation. During the closing decades of the twentieth century one of the propitious developments within America may be precisely this novel crystallization of nationality in these very times of superficial internationalism: for, once the overwhelming majority of Americans are of the fourth or fifth generation, their sense of belonging to America may (note that I am not saying *will*) be secure enough so that they could afford to discard the aggressive and unsure suspiciousness of nationalist attitudes.

Thus democracy, having nationalized one or two generations, internationalizes the next; after which it re-nationalizes them, on a deeper level. In our days a Tocqueville would not, and could not, write *Democracy in America*, the accuracy of the title of which reflected the singular honesty of its author, since it was a work dealing principally not with America but with democracy. But now, unlike one hundred and forty years ago, the United States is no longer unique in respect to democracy. There exists an English democracy, a French democracy, a Scandinavian, a West German, a Dutch, a Swiss democracy; and a new book that is needed ought to bear the title *American Democracy*, emphasizing precisely those of its national and cultural characteristics that distinguish it from the democratic societies of other nations. In the democratic world these characteristics have not disappeared; they merely manifest themselves in new forms. A French car is different from an American car, and a traffic jam in Paris is different from a traffic jam in Chicago—not so much because of different physical conditions but because of the different people who are involved in them: when Frenchmen drive their cars differently from Americans (usually worse), this happens also because their cars mean something different in their lives.

Throughout this book I have emphasized the development, in the Western world, of "internalization," of the deepening—often painful and confusing—of human consciousness, through which people become more introspective, trying to come to terms with their personal characteristics, among which their national origin is a most important one. The recently fashionable phrases of "search for identity" or "identity crisis" are but superficial reflections of this condition. They are by no means extinct; they are existential. The first thing that we note in a person is that he is an Englishman, a Swede or a Portuguese; the condition that he is a liberal or a conservative, a socialist or a communist, an authoritarian or a permissive personality, are secondary to that. One of the reasons for this is not so much hereditary nationality as it is language. A deepening sense of consciousness involves an uneasy awareness that, on the one hand, perfect communication between two human beings is impossible while, on the other hand, the very imperfections and the traditions of different languages are full of unexpected meanings. This is what the greatest number of writers and poets of the last hundred years or so have sensed and experienced, sometimes to the point of their obsession with language. The older liberal ideas of an eventual international language—Esperanto or Volapük or even Basic English—have not taken root at all. It is true that among us now abounds a new kind of international art and lingo, exemplified by the movies or by certain facile writers whose language is so superficial that they are easily translatable and digestible by an international public. There exists even a kind of international American-English that is read and understood by a growing international clientele of scientific specialists. But this kind of supranational communication—for, again, this is supranational rather than truly international—satisfies people only on superficial levels of their minds. It accords with the conditions of mass technology but not with the other development of "internalization" which is becoming characteristic of the human condition, in the Western world at least.

There is every reason to believe that, unless a very great catastrophe rearranges the most elemental priorities of life, the nations of the Western world are far from becoming extinct. They are, rather, starting to turn inward, some of them having already done so, beginning uneasily to confront themselves, just as millions of human beings within them are compelled to do so. There are many signs indicating that the nations of the Western world may become what the smaller fatherlands, the *patriae,* were five hundred years ago. With the passing of nationalism in the West (and perhaps only in the West) both internationalism and a newer kind of patriotism may be rising, both in ways very different from which we are still accustomed to think.

The purposelessness of society

How, at the time when civilization has been most wide-spread, people have found that their aspirations are woefully empty.

The restless movement that is so characteristic of our times had begun almost two hundred years ago. Before that time the settlement of Europe, certainly of Western Europe, had been marked by a considerable permanence of residence. Vast numbers of peasants in the lands of Western Europe in 1800 lived not more than twenty miles from the places where their unknown ancestors had first settled one thousand years before, some of them even earlier, at the end of the large migrations of the Dark Ages. Many of the bourgeois stayed in their towns for centuries. But now this was beginning to change. The last great phase of the expansion of Europeans overseas was opening. In the century before the First World War perhaps as many as seventy million people left the old continent for new worlds. A far greater number of people were beginning to move within their own countries, leaving the countryside for the cities. After the First World War the first of these movements, the overseas one, slowed down to a trickle; the second is still going on. By the early twentieth century, therefore, a condition existed in the

Western world that had no precedent since the mass migrations of the Dark Ages. The number of people who lived in the same place where their ancestors lived even a few decades before was dwindling fast. This fact alone may explain the demise of the older kind of patriotism and the rise, instead, of modern conformist nationalism. In any event, this gradual mass movement of millions entailed such enormous transformations in the very landscape and in the structure of societies that, contemplating these enormous events in retrospect, one is tempted to speak of a dissolution that had set in at least a century or a century and a half ago.

Such a statement would be premature, for at least two reasons. In the first place there was a great exception: even as hundreds of millions moved from one place to another within the same state, few people moved from one nation to another on the same continent. (The only major exception to this exception was the Jews, an extraordinary minority.)* Thus this restlessness and the displacement of most of our ancestors coincided with the great event of their national consolidation, a development whose full meaning is therefore much more recent than what we have been accustomed to think, and whose full consequences are not yet.

In the second place the last two hundred years have been marked not only with a horizontal but with an ever increasing vertical mobility of society. The barriers of class were weakening, they were dissolving, with all kinds of results, some of which, surprisingly enough, made for more stability, not less. More and more people, for example, were discovering their ancestors. At first, as they abandoned their rural homes, they tore themselves away from an ancestral past: but, then, that was a past of the meaning of which they were hardly conscious. Having settled in their cities, their ambitions were no longer circumscribed by a seemingly endless atavistic routine. Their ambitions now encompassed their children. During the nineteenth century and after, this originally bourgeois aspiration diffused itself through society, including the working classes. Thus a paradox: that century of individualism and of the so-

* See below, pp. 161–163.

called atomization of society was also a century of the greatest family cohesion. Consequently the kind of people who had hardly given this a thought before began to remember their grandparents, and in some instances their great-grandparents who, in turn, were looking forward to their grandchildren with anticipation.

All of this had something to do, too, with the extension of life's span and also with that growth of past-consciousness which had begun to penetrate the minds of men and women after the beginning of the nineteenth century, though few of them recognized its meaning. Certain conservatives and anti-individualists asserted that in a stable society most people ought to remember the names of at least three of their great-grandparents. This was, paradoxically enough, becoming a reality in Western Europe around 1900, at the time of unbridled liberalism and individualism. This, again, involved "internalization": families were closer together mentally than before, even when some of their members were geographically more separated than before. Even those single men and women who tore themselves away from their families to escape or to seek their fortune on other continents craved this kind of respectability. They entered into family bonds overseas as soon as they could do so. (Few successful immigrants made a career in the United States as bachelors.)

These developments were unforeseen, unexpected and, even in retrospect, surprising. They vastly contributed to the relative stability of national societies, counteracting the massive movements of populations that otherwise may have led to the collapse of orderly society as early as a century ago. By 1970, however, we cannot say that they would be sufficient counterweights in the future: the social problems of the late twentieth century are not those of the nineteenth.

꙼

Fifty years ago our fathers and grandfathers were beginning to live substantially the way we live now. Between 1870 and 1920 the daily lives of peoples in the cities of the Western world had changed more than they changed ever before or after. Central

heating, cold and hot water indoors, electric lights were now at their
fingertips. In certain countries their life expectancy had moved up
to at least sixty years on the average while infant mortality
dwindled. The standards and practices of medicine, surgery, and
anesthesia current in 1920 bore no resemblance at all to the still
largely barbaric standards of 1860. (In some places these standards
of 1920 were also better than those of 1970.) To our fathers and
grandfathers the railroad, the steamship, the automobile, the telephone, the phonograph were old hat. The functioning of these
things was improving every day. Airplanes, airships, radios had
been invented. Much of this had to do with industrialization, and
with the mass production that followed. Most of this was also far
more in evidence in the cities than in the countryside. For the first
time in the history of the world in certain countries the production
of food was no longer the task of the majority of people. England
passed this point of no return first, during the ten years before 1880,
the United States next, during the ten years before 1920. The rest of
Europe and North America followed during the next fifty years, the
Soviet Union only in the 1960's. With the change of occupation
came the change of residence: in the United States, for example, the
1920 census showed that when for the first time the majority of the
people were engaged in industrial, not agricultural, production the
proportion of the people living in towns and cities became a majority too. It seemed, therefore, that Industrialization meant Urbanization, simply and squarely. It still seems so to most people.

In reality, this impression is deceiving. First, this mass abandon-
ment of agriculture and of the countryside was often the result of
depression, not of progress (as Ensor wrote of the agricultural
depression in England after 1870: "For twenty years the only
chance for any young or enterprising person in the countryside was
to get out of it.")* Second—and this was a more universal phenomenon—the majority may have ceased to be rural but the city
population also ceased to grow. Between 1800 and 1920 the population of Paris had multiplied five times, of Vienna, more than seven

* R. C. K. Ensor, *England 1870–1914* (Oxford, 1936), p. 118.

times; of London, nine times; of Berlin, twenty-five times; of Philadelphia, thirty times; of New York, one hundred times. During only the thirty years before 1920 they doubled, on the average. During the thirty years after 1920 none of them doubled in size; on the average their populations increased by one-seventh. During the last twenty years the population of some of these great metropolitan cities (Vienna, Berlin, Philadelphia) hardly grew at all.* But, then, after 1950 many of these statistics became meaningless: for it is no longer possible to draw a reasonable definition separating cities from the suburbs. The old municipal divisions count hardly at all.

What have grown enormously during the last half-century are not cities but suburbs. The decay of cities has begun, fastest in the United States, where their growth, too, had been the fastest. By ceasing to be rural, the majority of people have become neither urban nor urbane. Instead of their *embourgeoisement,* instead of having become bourgeois, the influx of masses—especially after their incomes had risen to the levels where they bought automobiles—went on to destroy many of the standards of urban bourgeois life† whose zenith had been reached before the First World War in the cities of the Western world.‡ The suburb,

---

* During the last twenty years the cities that grew the fastest in Europe were Madrid and Moscow. This, among other things, indicates that the fastest growth in the population of cities usually occurs during the last phase of what is still largely an agricultural society. Thereafter it slows down.

† Before 1920 the heights of urbanity, of urban civilization and comforts, were to be found in the very cities whose populations were expanding very fast. After 1950 the attractions and comforts—now increasingly old-fashioned —of urbane life continued to exist precisely in those cities whose expansion has slowed down, sometimes dwindling to a minimum: in Vienna rather than in Paris, for example.

‡ There is, of course, another factor that we must frankly admit. Many of those standards depended on the existence of domestic servants. They had come from the countryside. The diminution of this reservoir of an agricultural population, even more than the rise of wages, gradually put an end to their availability. This was a great change. For a long time the great social divide was between people who could afford domestic servants and those who couldn't. After the 1920's in the United States and after the Second World War in Western Europe this division faded away. People kept telling themselves that machines would make up for servants in their homes. Of course they didn't. With the disappearance of servants traditional standards of bourgeois urbanity were bound to disappear—consider, for example, the seated dinner party or the care and training of children in their own rooms. Yet, because of the

especially in the United States, originally meant to become a bridge
between city and country, became a sprawling monster, devouring
both. In sum, deruralization did not and does not mean urbanization. Rather the contrary: we have been witnessing the gradual
destruction of the countryside and of the city alike.

These massive shifts of residence again corresponded to a massive, though for long unrecognized, shift in occupations—a change
whose effects on society may yet be the profoundest of all. By 1956,
for the first time in history, most people at work in the United States
were engaged neither in agricultural nor in industrial production
but in administration. Thus, at least in one sense, the urban period
and the period of industrial production, involving the majority of
populations in the Western world, had been much shorter than we
are accustomed to think—perhaps one hundred years, at the most.
In the United States this period was even shorter, the great urban
phase lasting perhaps fifty years at the most, and the phase of
predominantly industrial employment, forty at the most. Theorists
came now forth to call this phase the Second Industrial Revolution.
This was largely nonsense: it was an administrational, not an
industrial one. The view of the future that had been shared by the
believers in progress a century ago, and that still forms the mental
categories within which most social savants and urban planners are
hopelessly captive, has been wrong. They saw the future of societies
as increasingly urban, industrial, proletarian or bourgeois. None of
these terms fit the lives and the ambitions of the new interchangeable middle class in the interchangeable suburbs. Indeed, even the
term "middle class" makes less and less sense: for are they still in
the "middle," between the upper and lower classes? In the United
States at least it may be argued that this, too, is no longer so.

※

One of the greatest motive forces of the bourgeois epoch was the
connection between social respectability and personal aspirations.

---

prestige and attraction of these bourgeois standards, hundreds of thousands
of women are still struggling, with valiant determination, to keep them up on
occasion. We should bow before these heroines.

During the nineteenth century this had affected all of the classes. At that time social aspirations became dominant in the minds of many millions of men and women. They were woefully misread by both Marx and Freud, who ascribed them to the category of secondary phenomena, to excrescences or superstructures of the social order or of the sexual psyche. Marx was unwilling to recognize that the striving for wealth is only rarely an end in itself. Freud was unable to recognize the tremendous social element in sexual aspirations, especially in those of women. Some of the great novelists of the nineteenth century recognized this better, though most of them did not know that this, too, was a passing condition, typical of the flourishing phase of the bourgeois epoch. For this obsession with social aspirations was so widespread because the classes of society were now within hailing distance from each other. It was possible for people to move from one social group to another. This had an enormous influence on the bringing up of children. The bourgeois began to limit the number of their children, a practice which then filtered down to the lower classes. They did this because of their love for children, not because of their abhorrence of sexual profligacy; and they did this long before contraceptives became well known. The worst catastrophe that could befall people now was to have their children slip below them on the social scale. The common insurance against this was education. All of this had manifold consequences. There were now generations of spoiled children, stretching way down on the social scale of classes. What is more important, the period of adolescence, that originally narrow and merely transitional phase of a year or so between the worlds of childhood and those of adulthood, became extended, so that, like the suburb into city and country, adolescence began to bite far and deep into both.

Then in the United States during the 1920's—an adolescent decade par excellence—something new was beginning to happen. Until that time the shape of virtually every society resembled an irregular pyramid or, rather, a Christmas tree of sorts. But now the middle portion of the pyramid or tree had become so enormous that it was bulging out, in every direction. It began to resemble a balloon, an onion, a square glass jar. There would be a small, and eventually ineradicable, section of poor people on the bottom and a flat little onionlike peak of the very rich on top. In the vast and increasingly square-shaped middle the differences of class were losing their meanings, including even the invisible line that for a while was perhaps the most meaningful of all, the one separating the lower middle class from the upper middle class.

This dissolution of what remained of an earlier class structure has had very thoroughgoing psychic consequences. It deprived millions of people of their earlier aspirations. Let me explain this. The flourishing of social aspirations during the late bourgeois period developed together with the burgeoning of "internalization," with that increasing intrusion of mental factors into the structure of events. What happens to people is always to some extent inseparable from what people think happens to them, but with the development of "internalization" the second becomes ever more important. The wife of a roustabout wants to pass as a woman of gentle birth: well, as long as people think that she is of gentle birth—or, rather, as long as she thinks that people think that she is of gentle birth—she is content. Now, during the late nineteenth century something like this was becoming possible for more and more people. But during the recent decades, especially in the United States, these things were losing their meaning. (I am not speaking of feverish snobberies since snobs, like the poor, will always remain with us: I am including the gentlest and most honorable aspirations, those of the working-class mother wishing for respectability for her children, or of a workingman developing a certain appetite for learning.) Life is becoming, life is the wish for more life, life is worth living when we have something to look forward to, life involves aspirations; and people's aspirations, more than often, involve their relationships with other people. When the sense of some of these aspirations disappears, they are alone and bewildered.

The dissolution of classes, in any event, has advanced further in the United States than in certain European nations. But in the

United States the consequent weakening of social aspirations was compensated for a while by a related movement, typical of the conformities of a democratic society. While few people wanted to rise above their social groups, most people still wished to rise within them, and with them. Eventually, by the 1960's, this kind of aspiration also lost most (though not yet all) of its significance. This happened at the time when, as we have seen, the majority of the people were employed in administration, no longer in production. This kind of employment involved less and less individual enterprise and more and more standardization within huge corporations. Thus the lives of many people, instead of becoming enlightened, became burdened by the meaninglessness of their social aspirations as well as by the growing meaninglessness of their work.

This has had many consequences, one of them being that now people felt that they had to prove that they knew what to do with their leisure time. To a younger generation the entire pragmatic and middle-class ethos of work was collapsing. In 1924 Huizinga could still write: "Modern man is a worker. To work is his ideal. The modern male costume since the end of the eighteenth century is essentially a workman's dress."* A generation later this was still true. During the 1960's this began to change. Fashions are always matters of some significance: at the present time their tendency toward opposite extremes—miniskirts and floor-sweeping robes for women, Viking hair and Regency garments for men, the confused gropings for extremes of ugliness on the one hand and the extreme aestheticism of vivid colors, soft fabrics, ornaments on the other, radically breaking away from the recent past and at the same time showing a surprising amount of nostalgia for the habits of past ages—reflects the extraordinary confusion of the interregnum in which we live. On the one hand the forms of a new age have not yet begun to crystallize. On the other hand they suggest the rejection of middle-class, even more than bourgeois, concepts of life.

So it is now, and only now, that the purposelessness of traditional

* Huizinga, *The Waning of the Middle Ages*, p. 39.

social aspirations has come to mean the dissolution of society in its traditional sense. During the last world war Hitler and Goebbels used to say that, whatever its outcome, the bourgeois were finished once and for all. Because of the fact that Britain and the United States shared with the Soviet Union in the victory over Germany, because they liberated at least one-half (and the more-or-less bourgeois half) of Europe, this statement was premature then. Also, the prevalent mood in Europe after the war, all superficial impressions to the contrary notwithstanding, was essentially conservative; the traditional liberties and comforts of the bourgeois past still had much to offer to people, especially when they had been deprived of them during the war. Since then, another generation has arisen; and for the first time in many centuries the cohesion of national societies themselves has been weakening. There developed, too—again especially in the United States—a new kind of nomadism, a large floating portion of society in which the average citizen changes his employment and, more often, his residence every few years. Not all of the occasional nomads were employees: there arose a considerable number of new nomads, unwilling and unable to settle down even after they had sown their wild oats, people whose modes of life reflect a return of savagery in the midst of civilization. The cohesion of families has been weakening, too, with the rise in the number of divorces and with the separation of generations. Degrees and certifications have become more and more necessary to secure a certain level of administrative employment and income. Thus formal education has become more and more important. For an ever increasing number of young people the school years would last longer and longer: the period of adolescence extended more and more.

The practices of permissive education meant that not only the end but also the beginning of adolescence was pushed back further and further. The worldwide cult of youth also contributed to this. But now young people suddenly discovered that they were not looking forward to adulthood. Childhood, and even adolescence, in the past meant not only protection but preparation for adulthood.

Because of its urges and restrictions, adolescence was painful; therefore boys and girls looked forward with anticipation to their day of liberation, when they would graduate into adults and finally become free. This day has now been postponed more and more; indeed, it ceased to be a recognizable day, or time, at all. With the fatal weakening of adult self-confidence it has also become meaningless: for, having acquired most of the pleasures and privileges of Young Adulthood in their teens, adolescents were fearful of the future. They wished to stay in the present, *their* present.* This is the very obverse of the aspirations of the Bourgeois Age. They are not a futuristic generation; far from it: their occasional (and usually verbal) wish to destroy existing institutions is accompanied by their unwillingness to look forward into the future. The grim idiocy of their intellectual categories, and their humorless indulgences in promiscuity, anarchy, drugs, suggest those primitive fears. Of course these are deeply disturbing phenomena; and many people think that with the dissolution of the traditional bonds of society the fundamental cell of civilization, the family, too, will either disappear or become transformed beyond recognition.

I do not think so. Not that I believe that the recent sexual and social revolution of manners (it is more the latter than the former) has run its course: far from it. Nor do I believe that the traditional ideas of conservatism are still widespread enough to produce a massive reaction. The present emergence of a meritocracy on the top of society, the condition that now distinctions of formal education and of public celebrity mean more than distinctions of wealth or distinctions of birth, is transitory, too, and nearly entirely without promise: for the weakness and the arrogance of such a meritocracy are such that it cannot inspire confidence for long, and thus it cannot

* In this respect it may be said that the situation of adolescents *in time* resembles the situation of what the lower middle class used to be *in society*. What distinguished the lower sections of the middle class from the rest was the fact that their snobberies were merely negative: they had few aspirations beyond proving that they had left their earlier proletarian status behind. So the modern adolescent has few aspirations beyond that of having left childhood behind.

be even remotely expected to restore or to rebuild a more stable society. We are approaching a social situation when the most envied, and admired, people will be those who can afford privacy, not merely financially but culturally speaking, by which I mean people who have inherited or acquired a largely private way of life, who are able to live by themselves with their families, who are not entirely dependent upon the standardized and mechanical features of mass society and of mass culture, of mass entertainments and of mass leisure.

In the age of feudal aristocracies the most enviable people were those whose birth had rendered them self-sufficient; in the Bourgeois Age the most enviable people were those whose wealth made them self-sufficient; and in our times they are those whose education and culture make them self-sufficient. About sixty years ago Charles Péguy wrote that the true revolutionaries of the twentieth century will be the fathers of Christian families. There have been, alas, only too few of them in sight. It is not impossible that the true revolutionaries of the twenty-first century will be the fathers of decent and civilized children.* Their families will not be exclusive, like those of the nineteenth century: but they will be culturally self-sufficient.

Meanwhile the number of families whose children can still expect to rise above the cultural and social level of their parents may be decreasing. For most Americans this is not bad but good news, surprising as this might seem. One hundred years ago (in 1869) a successful American, Charles O'Conor, "an ornament of the New York Bar,"† proclaimed that in America "a man is accounted a failure, *and certainly ought to be,* [my italics] who has not risen above his father's station in life." This ornament of the New York bar could not see how this suggested the refusal of one's parents—as indeed the rejection of the Old World whence many of them had

---

* This involves more than manners, even though the present decay of manners is a sign of profound moral chaos: as Goethe said, "there is not an outward sign of politeness which has not a profound moral foundation."

† Carl N. Degler, *Out of Our Past* (New York, 1962), p. 269.

come—something that was one of the weakest sides of the American psyche, for to be ashamed of one's parents is the deepest of psychic wounds. But soon, for the first time in history, vast numbers, probably the overwhelming majority of the children in the American aquarium, certainly of the former middle and upper classes, can no longer expect to rise above their "father's station in life." Does this not mean that, after having grown up, these children, unlike untold children of untold immigrants, will come to respect their parents? Together with the crystallization of American nationality the slowing down of vertical mobility within America may yet be a great blessing for the United States in the next few decades.

This, of course, can develop only if much of civilized life, say fifty years from now, remains substantially intact, if no enormous civil or biological catastrophe occurs. Otherwise the decimated populations of the once civilized portions of the world will be reduced to leading nomadic and at least partially savage existences. This would probably last for a long time, until around the more intelligent and powerful tribal leaders new cells of permanent order develop, through the emulation of which a new society slowly begins to form.

The fiction of prosperity　　　⑨

How the impermanence of goods has rendered their possession unsatisfactory.

At the time of this writing the peoples of the Western world have come to experience a strange admixture of prosperity and disillusionment. This would have surprised our ancestors. There exists, of course, an old and simple explanation for this strange state of spirits. Human nature is such that prosperity does not necessarily bring contentment: when people have it too good they become spoiled. This, vulgarly put, certainly explains something of our present condition. But this explanation is no longer sufficient. The current disillusionment with the availability of the goods of this world has not been merely the psychic consequence of the oceanic wave of popular prosperity that is now engulfing large portions of the world. The two conditions have not been successive: they have developed together. Our unprecedented affluence has been accompanied (and in some ways it has been furthered) by a sense of impermanence and of uncertainty.

All of this was very different at the beginning of the twentieth century. Money, at that time, was much more powerful than ever before or after. It could buy practically everything, including power and prestige. Conversely, people without money, including those who were only temporarily deprived of it, experienced personal humiliations and miseries that may have been unknown to their ancestors, and are largely unknown to us. On the one hand wealth, more than ever before, was a most powerful and rapid solvent of class and caste barriers: it made social mobility possible to an extraordinary degree; it was, thus, a very important factor in the democratization of peoples. On the other hand this hard reign of wealth to many people seemed to be more unjust and immoral than the injustices of earlier societies that rested, rather, on distinctions of birth. In any event, few people remembered the latter while they contemplated the former. Few people also realized that the capitalistic order (if that is the right word) was about to come apart by its very success, and in the very opposite pattern from the one with which Marx had knit his hoary theoretical rug together: the rich, instead of becoming fewer and fewer, were becoming more and more numerous, and in the most capitalistic of countries quite a lot of money was filtering down to the lower classes. The circulation of money increased apace with the circulation of people: sociologically, the decades before 1914 were decades of democratization, that is, of the inflation of society.

Surprisingly enough, monetary inflation did not follow as yet. This is one of the most extraordinary phenomena of the one hundred years before 1914 to which social savants, not to speak of economists, devoted no attention at all. The social order, especially on the top and bottom, was becoming faster and looser: yet money continued to be as good as gold, and as solid as the rock of Gibraltar. In 1900 the pound, the dollar, the franc, the florin, the crown, the mark, the lira—all of these national currencies with their names that reach back to the Middle Ages—were worth, in each other's terms, the same everywhere. Their value had not changed in decades, for some of them not in one hundred years. They were available in the form of gold pieces,* silver coins, and bills, freely exchangeable at one's convenience. Silver coins were heavy, gold

---

* Except in the United States during the Civil War.

dreams of avarice. The last were most important, because a respect-able portion of the population was involved in them, not without a periodically nagging feeling of insecurity, or perhaps even of guilt. In late 1929 the stock-exchange boom caved in. Such stock-exchange panics had occurred periodically in the European and the American capital markets before 1914 with few important effects in the long run. The panic of 1929, too, would have been no great loss for the United States and the world, had it not been for two new elements without precedent: the speculation now included millions of people, not merely a few thousand financiers and fast-money men; also, the international economy of the civilized world was connected with the finances of the United States, otherwise a self-proclaimed isola-tionist Power. The result of the American people's sudden collapse of confidence in their own speculations was the international de-pression that engulfed the entire Western world for five or six years. Eventually it was corrected by such men as Hitler, Mussolini, Roosevelt, who, to their own good fortune, knew nothing of the laws of economics.

This depression—no matter how widespread and temporarily tragic were its effects (in the United States the depression, not the two world wars, was the traumatic experience of an entire genera-tion)—was an anomaly, a flat footnote in the history of the twenti-eth century, hardly qualifying even for the proverbial exception that proves the rule. The rule of the twentieth century was inflation, not depression. 1929 was a nineteenth-century event in the midst of a twentieth-century society. The next government of the United States discovered that its prime duty was to provide some-thing like full employment, not only at the cost of balanced budgets, national debts and other fictitious bookkeeping figures but eventu-ally at the cost of productive efficiency and of solid money. After 1934 Americans were no longer allowed to exchange their money for gold. Most other governments did the same thing. Money was now simply worth what the government said that it was. When the government was powerful and prosperous, as for example in Hitler's Germany, this proved to be no trouble at all. When the government was not prosperous but very powerful, as for example in the Soviet Union, this proved to be not much trouble either. Money and production followed power, not the other way around. During and after the Second World War the confidence of the peoples of Europe in their governments would collapse first, the deterioration of the value of their money would follow. Surprisingly enough, economic life and even the volume of production would go on, and even rise on occasion. Journalists would write of this or that state "on the verge of bankruptcy": no state ever became bankrupt, not even Egypt. Still after the end of the Second World War only a few currencies remained solid: the dollar, the Swiss franc, and old coins of gold. The first had become the predominant international currency, because of the power of the United States and because of the prestige of her productivity.

This is still largely true at the time of this writing: but meanwhile the solidity of the dollar itself had begun to crack. After 1966, for the first time in history, American money was no longer exchangeable into silver equivalents. Silver disappeared from American coinage that was struck, or in some cases pasted together, of cheaper and baser materials. The American people were told that all of this meant nothing, which they no doubt believed, though they did not act accordingly. The relatively moderate inflation of prices and costs that has marked their economies for thirty years now began to accelerate. The dollar bills themselves, for the first time in history, became dirty, soiled, and torn, since they were passing from hand to hand with increasing rapidity. They were no longer folded and handled and kept with a kind of anxious respect; they began to resemble the soiled and ragged and inflated money of Europe after the war. (When the finances of a state are sound her money is crisp and clean.)

This, in all probability, is not a superficial phenomenon. It is no longer explicable—reasonably, that is—let alone controllable, by professional economists. The raggedness of money reflects, as a matter of course, the raggedness of government. The debasement of coinage has always reflected the debasement of governmental authority: but now there is more to this: the purposelessness of money is beginning to catch up with the purposelessness of society.

*

At the beginning of the century not only the value of monies seemed permanent: so did the possession of goods. Private property and public property were two different things, both of them protected by the strictest of laws. The state did not and could not interfere with private ownership. There were a few exceptions. Taxation was slowly increasing because the role of government was growing: the movement toward the welfare state had begun. With the development of industry and of urbanization the primacy of the public domain had to be asserted, here and there, especially over real estate. None of these exceptions counted, as yet, very much. The sense of their encroachment on private wealth was counterbalanced by the permanence of things that the latter could buy. The more one paid for some things, the more lasting they were. The solidest of bourgeois built the solidest of houses, with foundations twenty feet deep and walls two feet thick. The most expensive motor car or overcoat was the longest lasting, all of the whirligig of fashion notwithstanding.

Much of this was true of the United States as well as of Europe, but there was an important difference. This was due to the deep-seated restlessness of the American character. Americans, who are possibly the least materialistic of peoples in the Western world, all of the imbecilic clichés to the contrary notwithstanding, were moving from one place to another, and they were buying and selling and exchanging their properties at a rate which to most Europeans would have seemed incredibly fast. People who are exchanging their material possessions that fast (while their ideas change at a very much slower rate) are not materialists—far from it. At the very peak of the Money Age, around 1900, Americans were not individualists, either: the primacy of their social considerations dominated their individual desires. In the western part of the United States, superficially the openest and freest portion of American society, legal limitations of private property existed (for example, the right of the public domain governing the use of bodies of water) that a Western European bourgeois would have regarded intolerable, whereas to Americans these were matters of course. Unlike Europeans, jealous of their possessions and of their privacy, Americans did not build walls around their houses. They still don't.

These are profound matters that seldom figure in the statistics and practically never in the limited imagery of economists. They meant that even a century ago the sense of ownership, and of possession, among the American people was different from that, say, of the French. The consciousness of this most modern of peoples was different because their ambitions were different. The enormous wealth of the United States, too, was not simply attributable to its prodigious production. That production was the consequence of the first mass market in history, not the cause of it. Until the Second World War more than 90 percent of the goods produced in the United States were acquired or consumed by the American people themselves. This was nearly a fantastic fact of success, from the consequences of which American businessmen have not yet recovered.* It was made possible, among other things, by giving credit (in more sense than one) to the masses. "On ne prête qu'aux riches"—one has to be rich to be able to borrow—was a common European witticism of the world before 1914, indeed, before 1945. This had no meaning in America at all, certainly not after 1920 when the shape of American society was beginning to bulge out.

The depression changed the development of this tendency toward mass ownership not at all. True, stocks and bonds could no longer be bought on the basis of tiny down payments (not many people wanted to buy them in the Thirties anyway). More important was the change in the ownership of industries. During the Thirties the

* By this I mean: Americans were, and still largely are, producing for Americans. The conditions of their production (high wages), of their prices (dependent upon the expense accounts of an enormous bureaucracy of merchandising) and of their salesmanship (talking in American accents, to American men, women and children) are not advantages, they are handicaps on the world market.

line separating public from private properties was beginning to be washed away. Factories and corporations were no longer owned by capitalists and their families, they were governed by managers. Huge amounts of stocks and bonds, too, were no longer owned by individual investors and speculators: they were managed by financial bureaucrats for impersonal institutions and pension funds. During the Second World War the government became the single largest purchaser of American production. This practice continued after the war. Whether General Electric under Eisenhower was nationalized or not made as little difference as whether Krupp under Hitler was nationalized or not. Both depended on government orders, on government regulations, their employers had to be screened and supervised by the government. By 1960 perhaps as much as 30 percent of American industry was dependent upon government orders, certain industries more than 90 percent. Their leaders would make speeches on occasion, extolling the virtues of the American private enterprise system—a tribute to the national habit of self-deception, no doubt. Others would call this "people's capitalism" instead of recognizing what this was, and still is: a peculiarly American form of socialism, corresponding to American democracy.

At any rate, this American kind of national socialism, unlike the Soviet one, made for an unprecedented kind of affluent prosperity. The most important development in the lives of people after the Second World War was the mass consumption of new goods. Standardized mass production and standardized mass credit, helped along by the inflation of wages, made it possible for hundreds of millions to acquire and to consume things that they themselves had not thought of but a few years before. Around the turn of the century, the millionaire J. P. Morgan, with a somewhat wooden witticism, said something to the effect that the kind of person who had to think what a yacht would cost him couldn't afford it. By 1955 the reverse was true: the kind of person who was thinking of having one would go ahead and afford it. In this new and increasingly classless society thousands of truckdrivers had power boats if not yachts, the wives and daughters of plumbers would go on winter cruises in the Caribbean. Millionaires now counted much less than before, not only because of inflation and taxation but because in the new credit economy earning capacity—which for the overwhelming majority meant regular employability—counted far more than the possession of wealth. More important, this became a worldwide phenomenon. After 1950 mass production, mass credit, the welfare state made it possible for the societies of Western Europe to move in that direction. A few years later it became evident that even the miserable Communist states of Eastern Europe would not exempt themselves from this kind of development.

By the 1960's a new kind of disillusionment was beginning to set in. People sensed that their newly found prosperity was somehow insecure, even though few of them knew why. Inflation was a tangible—or, rather, an intangible but nonetheless visible—villain, especially in the United States. The economists and the financiers who had now converted themselves to preach the virtues of controlled inflation found that the controls no longer worked (if they ever had). Their mental constructions were upside down, as usual: inflation was a consequence, much more than a cause, of this widespread feeling of instability and mistrust. For there was more to inflation than the sinking value of money. The inflation of society led to the inflation of goods, not only of their quantity but of their quality too—they have become impermanent. Unlike even a few decades ago, the high cost of a certain item was now due to its relative rarity rather than to its durability. This was true not only of clothes but of machines and houses. It had something to do with the decline, and in some places with the virtual disappearance, of individual craftsmanship. It had much more to do with another subtle transmutation of the sense of ownership. On paper more Americans owned houses and cars by the 1960's than ever before. In reality they were renting and discarding them. Long before they paid off the last installments of their mortgages they would move away. Millions of people still found it more satisfactory to buy houses than to rent them: but, since they were moving every few years, their sense of ownership was less than that of people who have been living in the same rented house or apartment for a long time. In Europe, too—indeed, on both sides of the iron curtain—the use of a company automobile for a businessman was quite a satisfactory substitute for its ownership.

In short, the consumption of things has become far more widespread and important than their possession: and the previously clear distinction between the ownership and the rental of properties has begun to blur. The American social thinker Thorstein Veblen who had castigated the materialism of the wealthier class of Americans for their "conspicuous consumption" sixty years ago was not too far wide of the mark, though he was a little premature. The principal instrument of keeping up with the Joneses—or, rather, of thinking of how to keep up with the Joneses—at the time was the conspicuous possession of things: their conspicuous consumption came only later. By the sixties the meaning of the adjective "conspicuous" paled. Consumption remained the overwhelming reality: but this was different from materialism: for the very act of consumption involves the disappearance of matter. (Eventually it would also mean the narrowing of choice: but that is another problem.)*

You may expel nature with a pitchfork but it comes back to you, Horace wrote: no longer a very telling metaphor but a true one nevertheless. The transformation of society meant the transformation of goods and the transformation of money:† a credit-card

* Deeply impressed with the privations of the Thirties and with the bureaucratic cruelties of the modern police state, George Orwell in 1947 prophesied that in 1984 people would be reduced to mass poverty, they would be ill-fed, run-down. The opposite happened. Halfway to 1984 prosperity has risen: and the danger is not, as Orwell saw it, that entire generations of once prosperous countries would no longer know such things as wine, oranges, lemons, chocolate: it is, rather, that traditional tastes and table habits are about to be washed away by a flood of frozen and synthetic foods, available to us every hour of the day. It is true, on the other hand, that fresh vegetables, unfrozen meat, unprocessed and unchemicalized foods may become an expensive rarity. The mass distribution, even more than the standardized production, of goods is beginning to reduce their variety. Therefore increasing affluence may no longer mean increasing choice.

† In a society where most people were engaged in administration, not in production, costs of administration were not only passed on to consumers but this was now openly admitted. Thus, in the early 1950's, this writer was

economy in which most transactions were handled on paper. Even people who were habitually taking advantage of this felt unsure about it, on occasion. No matter what governments said about it, and no matter how they tried to keep its price down, for a minority of hardheaded skeptics gold remained attractive because it was secure. Already during the Second World War the price of gold outran even that of the dollar on the black markets of the world. After the restoration of their battered currencies most Western European governments, in the late 1950's, thought it best to insure confidence by allowing their people to exchange them for gold; the United States government did not do so, but it is very questionable whether it could for long maintain confidence in its money at a time of increasing inflation.

At any rate, from the late 1950's onward the most spectacular rise in prices included things that were not new but old: old paintings, old houses, old furniture, old artifacts: things that were irreplaceable and, therefore, permanent.*

*

This reflected something that was more than mere snobbery; it had, also, little to do with nostalgia or with the veneration of the past. As I wrote earlier, inflation means that when there is more and more of everything it is worth less and less. "It is as simple as that." Yes—but this simple reaction takes place in the most complex organ of the most complex organism in the entire universe, in the minds of human beings. The condition that what happens is inseparable from what people think happens is even truer in the "factual" and "quan-

---

amazed to read how the president of a large American cigarette manufacturing company would explain to a congressional committee that the rise in the price of cigarettes was due to "increasing production *and advertising costs*" (my italics). No one questioned this argument which would have made our grandfathers turn purple with rage.

* Irreplaceable, but not only because of their historical uniqueness. By 1960 the price of a good 1900 reproduction of, say, a Louis XVI table had risen, sometimes to fantastic heights—probably because people knew that with the disappearance of craftsmanship even such reproductions were no longer reproducible.

titative" science of economics than anywhere else, since the value of any thing is not only inseparable, it is determined by what people think its value is. This has always been true. But the effects—including all kinds of side effects—of this truth are gaining momentum as people recognize its existence. That ways of thinking may not only modify but transform hard material economic facts would have seemed nonsense to people sixty years ago, to Americans even later. By the late 1960's a book entitled *The Money Game*, attempting to prove the common-sense truth that people are buying and selling stocks not only because of economic reasons of security and gain but also because of psychic motives to play and to win, was a national best seller. We may yet witness a most momentous transformation of economic life in perhaps a thousand years, involving a transformation of the meaning and of the function of money as well as of the welfare of peoples, eventually knocking the bottom out of the still prevalent dogmas of economists with their hopeless materialism. I write "eventually," because probably decades will pass before these new doctrines and the new theories appear, having crawled up through the labyrinths of the meritocracy, following events at a hopeless distance, expostulating and explaining them when it is already too late. They almost always do. *

* The original meaning of economics was "knowledge of the household," *oikos* meaning "house" in Greek, a word that still lives on in the German *Wirtschaft*, which means both "economics" and "housekeeping." During the last two hundred years a change in this meaning took place. Because of the availability of statistical information and because of the invention of modern accounting, modern economic information became more accurate—but only up to a point. In the first place, after a while it became evident (or, rather, it should have become evident) that the increasing accuracy of economic information did not at all mean a corresponding increase in our economic knowledge. In the second place (and this is more important), during the twentieth century the accuracy of economic information itself began to decay because of its inflated categories. An example of this is a figure such as the "national debt" which in the twentieth century has become not much more than an abstract item within intranational accounting. Certain international financial transactions have become abstract, too, in the sense that the movement of monies that they register are often transfers on the level of bookkeeping, not physical transfers from one country to another. This does not mean that they are meaningless: but it means that what happens in such transactions is something quite different from what we are told happens and that, consequently, some of their consequences may be different, too, from what

We have already begun to experience some of the consequences of this mutation in our economic consciousness. Consider, for example, the extraordinary meaning of mass tourism in the relation of peoples. In this age of so-called "industrialization" there exist now kingdoms and republics in Europe, and states in the Union, whose principal source of income is tourism. This has become true of industrialized republics such as Austria or of the cradles of American industry, the New England states. Entertainment, vacation, recreation have become more and more important in the economies of people and of the welfare state. The production of consumption becomes more important than the consumption of production. There is every reason to believe that this tendency will continue.

But in a world where consumption has become most important, all kinds of new problems arise. On the one hand the sense of the pervasive impermanence of most things may destroy the prospects of all civilized life. On the other hand it is most unlikely that the mutation in economic habits would amount to a mutation in human nature, that consumption would ever become a satisfactory substitute for possession. In this sense the recently fashionable terms of an "Acquisitive" or "Affluent Society" are off the mark. "Acquisitive" means an eagerness to possess and to keep. "Affluent" means a kind of prosperous ease that flows from the possession of considerable personal reserves. None of these adjectives fit the new millions of buyers and renters and consumers who discard things almost as fast as they buy them. In the past, when money was scarce, people who earned or acquired some of it may not have been well educated: but they certainly knew what to do with it. A principal problem of our modern welfare programs, again especially in the United States, is

---

people would expect. Or consider the famed figures of Gross National Product —what do they mean, especially for societies where most people are no longer employed in production? The two martinis that an advertising executive buys for a winsome secretary for lunch, the junket of a kolkhoz secretary for a carouse in Moscow—they, all, figure in the computations of Gross National Products. As in the vocabulary of politics, these gross corrupt terms no longer fit realities: to paraphrase Tocqueville, a new kind of science of economics is needed for a new kind of world.

not only their bloated bureaucracy; it is that an increasing number of people do not know what to do with their money. This, in many ways, is not merely the result of insufficient education. Nor is it only the problem of the poor on the bottom of the economic jar. This waning interest in durable possessions, together with their—less conscious—frustration with the pleasures of consumption, is characteristic of the "new poor": men and women and children whose poverty is not material but social, psychic, spiritual.

In one sense their crisis may be part and parcel of the increasing spiritualization of matter which marks the evolution of our consciousness. But this evolution has not yet become sufficient to counteract the sense of impermanence that bedevils their lives. While large regions of the "old" poverty still exist, everything indicates that the "new poor" are becoming more prevalent. Increasingly, their poverty has less and less to do with their material conditions. Thus, at the end of the Modern Age, this paradoxical condition: now, when people are prosperous as never before, immense numbers of them are unhappy and confused. Millions of people are now aware, often painfully, that they do not live by bread alone. And yet this is happening at a time when the mechanical interpretation of life and materialist interpretations of human nature are most widespread. This is no longer a paradox. It is a ridiculous condition of the modern intellect. Centuries ago there was often a real connection of cause and effect between the rise of a few pennies in the price of flour and the peasant riots that ensued. Such a relationship between economic "causes" and "effects" in the recent history of the Western world does not exist; none of its revolutions in the twentieth century are attributable to economic "causes." And yet it is now that not only econometricians but political scientists and certain opportunist historians believe—or, rather, pretend to believe—that to all social wisdom the mathematical computability of economic "facts" is the key. It is high time that people recognize the antiquated character of this intellectual absurdity: that the categories of materialism and of its offspring, modern economics, are not "facts" but mental constructions, as indeed are most things in this world, our world.

The dissolution of learning

10

How, at the time when education has become universal, people are discovering that their schools are teaching little or nothing.

At the time when this is written serious troubles have broken out in the higher schools of the Western world. Certain people of an optimistic (and others of an opportunistic) bent of mind see nothing very wrong in this: they welcome the restless dynamism of the young, and seek solace in the fact that in the past, too, student riots punctuated, occasionally, the long venerable history of universities in the West. Other people who are more pessimistic (including defenders of their own vested interests) go so far as to say that higher education is now being wrecked, for the foreseeable future at least. The latter may be right: but not for the reasons which they commonly advance.

They believe that the recent riots reflect the indiscipline and the arrogance of a generation that no longer wants to obey or learn anything. I believe, on the contrary, that the young are engaged in a desperate search—not very intelligently, or even consciously, to be sure—for some kind of authority; and that their indiscipline and arrogance are but the reverse sides of their insecurity and fear.

The pessimists are correct, however, as they recognize that this

rash of rebelliousness has been different from the student rebelliousness of the past, including the recent past. Students, especially
in Europe, often enjoyed being in the vanguard of political radicalism. Their, usually immature, idealism made them more recep-
tive to new ideas, or, rather, to what they thought were new ideas.
The universities, then, were the central places for this. Consequently on occasion students would march out, shoulder to shoulder
with some of their professors, to the streets, sometimes as far as the
first few barricades. This was not true of 1789 (the university of
France had little or nothing to do with the great revolution) but it
was true of much of the nineteenth century in Europe, and of a
good part of the twentieth. (It included a generation of Fascist and
Nazi students who had their own favorite professors and teachers.)
This intellectual and spiritual comradeship between students and
teachers still exists on exceptional occasions, and it will probably
exist until the end of time. But it is no longer as prevalent as in the
past: for the young are now actively dissatisfied not only with the
institutions but with the content of education itself. With all of their
inarticulate respect in front of intellectuality, they have suddenly
come face to face with the dissolution of learning.

❖

At the same time it is unduly optimistic to believe that this kind
of unrest is principally intellectual, and that is the particular problem of institutions of higher learning. Here and there it has begun to
seep down to the level of the middle schools, where it may yet lead
to literally incalculable consequences. In the United States it has
been evident for a long time now that the high schools are the
weakest links in the entire educational chain.

We must understand that the school, as we know it today, came
into being only during the Modern Age. True, we are still the heirs
of the Graeco-Latin tradition of learning, in some ways more than
we think. But these traditions were preserved consciously only in
the universities. They had little to do with the modern idea of the
school—more precisely, with the modern idea of the function of the

school. During the Middle Ages and the Renaissance the prestige and the size of the universities of Western Europe waxed and waned but there were few schools worth mentioning. Whatever education there was, it was mostly private, within the family—though not necessarily within one's own family. The school that we know had arisen in Europe only during the seventeenth century.* It was originally a bourgeois idea, for their own children, at first exclusively for boys. "The great families of the nobility and the artisan class," as Philippe Ariès put it, "remained faithful to the old system of apprenticeship, providing pages for grandees and apprentices for artisans. In the working class, the apprenticeship system would continue down to our times"†—let us add, on the Continent.

At first there was much hostility to the idea of school; even men such as St. John Baptist de la Salle had to surmount what to us seem incredible prejudices, not the least among the clergy. Yet the rise of the "middle range of the hierarchy of classes," and of their ideology, would make the repute of systematic education unassailable. The eighteenth-century idea of perfectibility (or even of the improvability) of man: what else was this but trust in his educability? A century later, education—compulsory education—became universal in the Western world. In many places its institution preceded even the institutionalization of democracy. (It is not commonly known that in the Tsarist Russian Empire in 1917 the portion of illiterates was *less* than in Italy, or that one of the most extensive and successful systems of elementary education was introduced in the Austrian Empire *before* 1848.)

At any rate, by the middle of the last century most people in the United States, and by the end of the century the majority of the people of the white race, had at least a few years of formal schooling, and they knew how to read and write. (They *really* knew how to write: compare the handwriting of a twelve-year-old boy in 1900 to that of a twelve-year-old boy today, I care not whether in

* The *Oxford English Dictionary* records the first usage of the systematic, as distinct from the household, meaning of *education* in 1661.
† *Centuries of Childhood* (London, 1961), pp. 370–371.

America or in Europe.) This elementary schooling was a great success: no matter how crude its circumstances in some places may have been, people have been unable to improve upon its basic methods for a century.

At the same time we may ask ourselves: did universal education mean a great change, in the long run? At first sight it seems that the acquisition of literacy opened up a new dimension in the consciousness of people. But this has been true only of a minority. The majority of people during the last one hundred years who learned how to read and write made little use of it. I want to make it clear that I am not falling back on the reactionary (though not always unreasonable) argument that many people would have been happier without their compulsory education, for consider only the abuses of literacy that followed: the penny newspapers of the *Daily Mirror* type, the brutal primitiveness of certain mass magazines. My argument is the opposite: in the long run the literacy of the masses made surprisingly little difference. The newspapers of the European nations that had a very large responsibility in whipping up sentiment for a war in 1914 were written by and for the middle classes. Nothing like the *Daily Mirror* existed in Germany in 1933. Most of the consumers of pornography, too, come from those classes. The imaginative capacities of the lower classes were, and are, of a different order: less literary and, therefore, more feeble. In the end, with the advent of television (and with other methods of mass communication) it is becoming evident that the written and printed word plays a lesser role in their lives than before. The extension of universal education is still going on: but we must accustom ourselves to recognize that that is one thing, and that the extension of universal literacy (especially in depth) is quite another. The greatest achievements of the latter, too, may be already behind us.

In the long run the function of the middle schools may have been more important than those of the elementary ones. For already before 1914 it was beginning to appear that they, especially in Europe, marked the existence of the most important division within society, between the "working classes"—meaning manual workers—

and the rest. The diploma, attesting to the completion of the middle school, was the crucial document. Without it a young man could hardly be anything but a manual worker, a peasant, a municipal or civil servant of the lowest janitorial ranks, at best engaged in commerce on a low level. Thus it may be said that already before 1914 the present trend toward a meritocracy (or perhaps one should call it an examinocracy) was there: the privileges based on formal education were replacing privileges based on wealth, or on birth. True, wealth could still buy education,* whereas education could not buy wealth. But without their credentials of having completed their secondary education, the children of the middle classes could not expect to secure a certain level of income and status.

There is not much to be said for the universities of Europe during the early Modern Age. As late as during the eighteenth century most of them smelled of camphor; they were relics of the Middle Ages, they were not at all in the vanguard of progress. During the nineteenth century they began to flourish anew. An increasing number of young people frequented them, the minority in order to gain degrees that would qualify them for certain professions, the majority because with the increasing inflation of society the span of formal education was increasing, too, and their university degrees (in law, for example) would qualify them for higher positions in the bureaucratic order. With the applications of the modern scientific method the national universities of Europe became the prime repositories of organized knowledge and the places for research, in more and more fields of learning. Most of the research took place in the laboratories, libraries, seminars of the universities. Their golden age, too, were the decades before 1914. Some of the greatest teachers were also the greatest researchers. By 1900 the status of a university

---

* That, too, was true only in a limited sense. The tuition fees for secondary schools on the Continent were low. The middle classes could afford to send their children there because they, unlike many of the poorer classes, were not dependent upon the earning capacity of their children. On the other hand, because of their own limited aspirations the workers would not send their children to the academic secondary schools, even when this earning capacity was becoming less important.

professor had risen far above that of a century before, when they had been treated (often with reason) as mere antiquarians or bookworms. During the nineteenth century the Ducs de Broglie were very learned men, historians of antiquity, who had nothing to do with universities. When in the twentieth century the grandson of one of them became a university professor he was no longer regarded as having come down in the world.

This relatively new—and transitory—golden age of the universities nonetheless depended upon a cultural situation outside of them. They—on the continent of Europe at least—had no monopoly on culture, not in the least; before 1914 they did not even have a monopoly on higher learning, except for some research in the natural sciences. Before 1914 one could meet many cultivated men in the cities of the Western world who had had no university training at all. It is seldom recognized how much of the study requirements of the universities, and also of the higher secondary schools, depended on this condition. It was taken for granted that most of the cultural equipment of a young man would be collected, gathered, provided for him (and later by him) outside of his formal learning, in his private and family life. (In the universities of Europe it is still sometimes taken for granted that a student will do his basic reading on his own, with little, if any, guidance from his professors.) Among other things, this condition made it possible for the university to concentrate on the training of specialists, not all of whom turned out to be cultivated men in the broad and deep sense of the word, since they, at best, "knew more and more about less and less," as their enemies were wont to say. More important, the character and the moral courage of many of these scholars turned out to have been stunted. This would not have surprised our ancestors before the nineteenth century or, at that, during the Middle Ages. It surprised many people in the twentieth century, since they had been taught that the pursuit of knowledge was the noblest thing in the world, that the objectivity of the scholar was the only way to the truth, that an intellectual elite was the truest elite of all. In his *Pasquier Chronicles* Georges Duhamel described the shock and disillusionment of a young intelligent Frenchman, *anno* 1908, as he discovered that some of the greatest scientists were moral dwarfs. Certain Germans discovered this in 1933, a few Americans in the 1960's. Still this kind of disillusionment involved far more than the universities within whose walls congeries of honest and dedicated men continued to exist; it involved an entire new class of intellectuals, a topic to which I shall return.*

More important, at this point, is the condition that a mere few decades after their golden age the universities became antiquated vessels, not so much because of the heavy seas outside as because of their structure which was creaking and breaking, overloaded. The inflation of society was filling these aging structures with hordes of students until they, in the 1960's, were literally beginning to burst. In old and dirty lecture-halls hundreds of students were crammed together, pretending to listen to the lectures of a single erudite; more often than not, the kind of specialized information that he was imparting was hardly in accord with their interests or needs. Whereas in the past the university could provide, on occasion, for personal contact with the world of scholarship, now the universities became even more impersonal than the world outside. Paradoxically enough, it was now, at a time of the cult of youth and of democracy, that contact between teachers and students was becoming impossible. But this was not merely a practical problem of how to accommodate ever more students. The latter were beginning to sense, too, the cultural crisis of our times, though they have not recognized its paradoxical nature: that, apace with its dissemination, the dissolution of learning began.

❧

To all of this the United States—and, perhaps until recently, the British Isles—were, again, the exception. The greatest of American dogmas was—at least until recently—the belief in the perfectibility of man; or, if we look a little closer beneath the surface of the

* See below, chapter 11.

rhetoric, in the perfectibility of society (which is why the European Enlightenment of the eighteenth century was something different from American modes of thought). Nowhere, with the possible exception of Soviet Russia, did people have such a naive trust in the powers of education as in the United States. Schools sprang up like little mushrooms, everywhere in the colonies, even in the slow, slavery-ridden South. During the nineteenth century compulsory education, starting from New York and New England, spread across the vast country. There was not much difference between American and European primary schools, but toward the end of the nineteenth century the secondary schools on the two continents became rather different. In America more and more children were compelled to attend school longer and longer, eventually well into their teens. A large bureaucracy of educationalists developed, combining peculiar programs of extraordinary extravagance with extraordinary narrowmindedness. The American people tolerated this because of their self-conscious respect for Experts. They were also greatly relieved to find that their schools were taking over those cultural responsibilities that were said to be the necessary accompaniments of one's rise in society. The schools took care of the transportation, of the lunchtime feeding, and of the cultural spoon-feeding of boys and girls, increasingly together. They also taught manners, morals, dancing, driving, sports, and, most important, Americanism and Good Citizenship. The more expensive American private schools and colleges were slightly different, emulating English models: fortunately for their inmates, with little success. In England most boys and girls hated their schools, pining for the day when they'd be free of it. In America they rather liked their schools, knowing that their teachers were causing them as little trouble as possible. Still the American and the English systems had one vague thing in common: the purpose of school was social rather than intellectual.

The development of the American university, around the time of the Second World War, was beginning to change this. Universities which were comparable to those of Europe evolved from their colleges in America only around 1890, less than a century ago, when it became evident that without a systematic establishment of higher standards American professional training, in medicine for example, could be dangerously deficient. Thereafter American universities and colleges were to dispose of very large sums of money; they accumulated the most splendid of laboratories and libraries, and began to attract scientists and scholars from Europe. During the first years of the Second World War this intellectual migration from the Old World to the New developed into a veritable flood, the fear of Hitler bringing to these shores an untold number of scientists and humanists, including the proponents and producers of the atom bomb. By 1945 most universities of the United States had grown up, their programs resembling those of their European counterparts during the golden age of the latter. Much of the scientific research, and also some of the scholarship, in the United States, now surpassed the standards and, even more, the possibilities of Europe. Indeed, unlike in Europe, the universities became the monopolies of learning and of culture. Aspiring young novelists dreamed of becoming professors of literature, rather than the reverse. By 1960, presidents and politicians found that in engaging professors and scientists among their principal advisers, they would no longer incur public criticism, to the contrary, they might even be praised for that kind of thing. Americans were congratulating themselves on this. They did not see that the very success of the American university was destroying the American middle school. For with this inflation of education the value of a high school degree, indeed, even of a college degree, had dwindled. The public schools, especially in the cities, became vast custodial institutions (it was deemed safer and cheaper to lock hordes of adolescents in their schools than let them roam the streets), while the better private secondary schools were turned into first-class college preparatories. The hugeness of the universities, something that was quite new in the United States where even the most famous of higher institutions had been relatively small in size at the turn of the century, dominated not only the educational but the cultural scene of the United States in the 1960's. They became cultural and social centers, eventually at the expense of much of the learning that was (or, rather, that was supposed to be) going on within their walls. Despite (and to some extent, because) of the absence of certain archaic traditions the crises of the American university system by the 1960's began to resemble that of the European universities. In that respect at least the world has become smaller: the explosions that rocked the universities in recent years were nearly simultaneous on both sides of the Atlantic.

❧

We have seen that throughout the Western world the span of adolescence was increasing, in some ways unexpectedly, during the last few decades. The school years of the younger people now extended backward to the nursery school and forward to some kind of graduate university degree which became more and more necessary—a span of sometimes as much as twenty-five years. This extension of schooling led to an unnatural situation: to the postponement of intellectual maturity at the same time when the privileges and pleasures of young adulthood were made available to young people earlier than ever before. In other words, the stretching out of schooling has led to its increasing thinness: many of us have now met university graduates whose cultural equipment is full of astonishing lacunae (who, for instance, cannot spell).

But more was involved here than the consequences of social and educational inflation. Something else has happened within the mental processes of our children. The dissolution of learning has been developing together with the dissolution of attention. The latter is a deep-going psychic mutation of great importance. Its cause is the complexity and the superficiality of modern life. The bane and woe of teachers in the past, the dumb clod of a child, who was unable to entertain anything save for a single idea or a single matter, has given way to the nervous children of today who are unable to sit still and unable to concentrate on anything. These are not merely matters of the discipline of perception: they involve, among other things, diseases of the human imagination. In the past the ability to entertain various images or divergent modes of thought, the capacity of thinking and doing two things at the same time usually came with the growth of age and maturity. It seems that now the very opposite is happening: it is the ability to concentrate that is developing later in life.

If this is to go on much further our descendants may have to face the task of an entire revolution of our, still largely traditional, procedures of teaching, since these still depend largely on training children to appreciate the printed word *in the beginning*. And yet it is obvious that watching television (irrespective of the quality of the programs) involves a lower level of intellectual activity than that engagement of the imagination which comes with the kind of mental construction that is involved in reading a book. On the one hand we live in societies where the great majority are watching television, which can be watched both by young children who do not yet know how to read and by old people who no longer want to read. Thus the practice of reading is often restricted to only the educational portion of the life-span of democratic man, just as the Age of Literacy may have been but a passing phase in the development of the democratic society. On the other hand a minority of people generally advance from liking television to liking books. This, then, involves an advance in intellectual maturity; and since television represents the present, whereas the world of books represents the past, we encounter again a perhaps significant indication to the effect that increasing maturity means a growth of interest in the past—that, indeed, the future *is* the past, strange and paradoxical as this might seem.*

There exists, in any event, a recent tendency—developing fast in the United States—whereby older people, especially women, return for courses in schools in their late thirties or forties, not always for the utilitarian purpose of earning a new degree or qualifying diploma for a new occupation but to "broaden" their minds through new intellectual experiences. This development of "continuing edu-

* See below, pp. 212–217.

cation" means a further extension of the functions of schools. Is it farfetched, therefore, to foresee a situation when the two principal classes of society will be those who teach and those who are being taught?

※

Beyond the relationships of teachers and students there looms the monstrous problem of the dissolution of learning among teachers and potential teachers, among the purveyors of learning itself. This problem has become monstrous because of its dimensions. The inflation of society includes the inflation of the world of teachers and of scholars. Their professional advancement habitually depends upon publications. These are now so numerous that sometimes more than one-half of the books and journals in respectable libraries may consist of publications of the last fifteen or twenty years. There exist harebrained men and women who hail this kind of thing as the Knowledge Explosion, whereas it is nothing less than the cancerous dissolution of learning. Until very recently scholars had been plagued by a scarcity of printed materials relevant to their discipline. Suddenly the very opposite has happened. The best of them struggle as they are snowed under by printed matter, while the weaker ones let their span of attention contract to the point of intellectual corruption.

One would think, at first sight, that all of this results in a dangerous fragmentation of learning, in an ever increasing trend toward specialization, then toward the specialization of specialization, at the expense of understanding, unity, synthesis. This is no doubt true, but the main dangers are already those from the opposite direction. For the first time in centuries it has become possible for first-rate specialists not to be aware of the work of other specialists in their own field, sometimes within the same country. Moreover, in a society which pays so much respect to intellectual ability, the most successful intellectuals, teachers, scholars are idea-mongers, people whose principal ability consists in their public exemplification of those general ideas that are becoming respectable and popular among intellectuals. Instead of the older specialist who may have learned more and more about less and less (which could be an honorable and honest admission, worthy of a scholar), these newer intellectuals know less and less about more and more (without, of course, admitting this). It is no longer the unworldliness but the worldliness of the scholar that corrupts: especially now when, perhaps for the first time in the entire history of the Western world, teaching and research have become not only secure but considerably lucrative occupations.

The dissolution of learning is an essential part of a general breakdown of communications. I think it was Matthew Arnold who said that the end of the Middle Ages came with the development of communications. The end of the Modern Age comes with their breakdown, which means, too, the increasing loneliness of people, very much including young people, surrounded though they are by more people than ever before. Our external communications are marvels, we can see pictures flashed from the moon, at the same time when our interior communications are breaking down, when parents and children, teachers and students, husbands and wives, colleagues, neighbors, lovers cannot, because they will not, listen to each other.

This is a great paradox: this enormous development of external communications at the same time with the breaking down of interior ones. And there is another great paradox: the superficially revolutionary character of our times, beneath which we may detect extraordinary extents of intellectual stagnation. Probably the latter, too, has much to do with the contracting attention-span and with the breakdown of interior communications: superficially we can receive, and dismiss, a fantastic amount of flickering images and messages while we are, more than often unconsciously, bored with their essential sameness. After all, the governing ideas of the twentieth century have been seldom more than projections and applications of nineteenth-century ones. In these times, when, superficially speaking, "anything goes"—we are in a traffic jam. To those few original minds who seek an escape the public roads are closed. Because of this deadening dependence on publicity, ideas move slower than they have for a long time. But this was foreseen by Tocqueville, who warned his contemporaries: they ought not mistake appearance for reality. "We have witnessed," he wrote, "very rapid changes of opinions in the minds of men; nevertheless it may be that the leading opinions of society will before long be more settled than they have been for several centuries in our history. . . ."

It is believed by some that modern society will always be changing. I fear that it will ultimately be too invariably fixed in the same institutions, the same prejudices . . . so that mankind will be stopped and circumscribed; that the mind will swing backwards and forwards forever without begetting fresh ideas; that man will waste his strength in senile and purposeless trifling; that, though in continual movement, humanity will no longer advance.

The sometimes hopeless slowness in the movement of ideas makes life difficult for the young who, even more than adults, are very much dependent upon the ideas of others. This is why the dissolution of learning will not at all eliminate their dependence on teachers, rather the contrary: and the great teachers of the future will be those who, through a kind of private wisdom, will direct their attention to all kinds of public untruths, very much including those propagated by the established public intellectuals.

In any event, the teaching profession will probably continue to attract all kinds of people, bad and good, if only because it will be one of the few fields of endeavor where it will still be possible for men and women to exercise their authority. Sooner or later, however, people will be fed up with the division of society into teachers and students: and when they recognize that nearly everybody can teach *something*, the day of a populist revolution against a meritocracy of intellectuals will be at hand.

The meaninglessness of letters

----

*How literacy, having reached its peak, has fallen apart
into a general state of decomposition.*

One of the most extraordinary consequences of the inflation of
modern society has been the appearance of a class of intellectuals,
of an intelligentsia. This phenomenon is less than a century old. No
historian has attempted to survey, as yet, the confusing phenomenon of its overall emergence.

A century ago the noun "intellectual" did not exist. There was, as
yet, no social or even cultural class of people it would signify. The
minority of people who knew how to read and write were not at all
like the clerics of the Middle Ages. They had no special qualifying
characteristics of their own. Those among them who could write
and speak well enough to attract attention would rise in society:
that kind of intellectual ability was translatable into social esteem
while only rarely into money. They sought the company of certain
people, cultivated hosts and hostesses who, however, did not belong
to a particular group; they did not form a class as such, they were
scattered among the upper and middle classes.

Compulsory education, and the beginnings of universal literacy, would change this. Certain men and women discovered that they were different from other people not merely through the fact of their literacy but by the quality of the latter. They were beginning to be bothered less by the prevalence of ignorance than by the prevalence of insensitivity. Oddly—or perhaps not so oddly—this new kind of social crystallization appeared first in Russia, then in America and in England. In the semibarbaric empire of the Tsars atop a majority of ignorant serfs there existed a class of barely (or, rather, narrowly) literate civil servants, a mean and low bureaucracy upon the functioning of which the brute absolute rule of the Russian government depended. This same government, having set up large schools and universities on the German model, produced hordes of graduates (and also some would-be graduates) many of whom were itching to prove that they were different from the pen-scratching bureaucracy of ridiculous governmental clerks. The latter were *clerks*, nothing more; but they were sensitive and cultured people, *intellectuals*. Thus an ancient and venerable Latin adjective was turned into a noun describing a particular kind of person. This word, "an intellectual," at first sounded odd to discriminating English ears, but soon it would become adopted among the conventicles of the English and American "intelligentsia"— another Russian word-import, designating a sort of community among intellectual men and women, a word which was not even transformed, merely transliterated for Anglo-American usage.* Few people are aware of the curious origins of these words, perhaps regrettably so.

It is significant, and melancholy, to observe how relatively early the very success of literacy led to disillusionment with its results. In the United States Emerson, around 1860, may have used the word "masses" for the first time in its pejorative sense. By the end of the century the first American groups of intellectuals, of an intelligentsia, were becoming visible. The more-or-less genteel literati of New York and New England, a somewhat special breed of men and women, still existed: but while their manners were quite different

---

* The "ts" in "intelligentsia" is a mere transliteration of the Russian diphthong *ts* (as in Tsar).

from the newer kind of an American intelligentsia, their ideas about the function of an intellectual aristocracy within a democracy were not. For the intelligentsia depends on snobbery, sometimes of the worst sort. No matter how "Leftist," radical, socialist, pro-Communist, demophile the political opinions espoused (more than often irresponsibly) by the intelligentsia, there is this sorry side of their dishonesty: their distrust, and dislike, and their sometimes neurotic fear and hatred of the common people, perhaps especially in the United States.

A famous essay by Van Wyck Brooks, written in 1914, established the term "highbrow," distinct not only from the barely literate "lowbrow" but from the literate but largely tasteless "middlebrow" portion of the population. In England this tendency was there, too—the Americanism "highbrow" stuck—but with a difference. There the alienation of artists from public opinion ("the bald man in the back of the omnibus," Bagehot wrote) grew with the philistinism of the late Victorian period; it was artists rather than intellectuals who were appalled by the insensitivity of people in the age of literacy. Unlike in the United States, the beginnings of a self-conscious British intelligentsia were marked by their aspiration to set themselves apart as men and women of superior taste rather than of superior judgment. Still we can glean from the tragic pages of Gissing the intensity of a pathetic longing for intellectual comradeship in the midst of a materialist and callous society, which was perhaps more depressing in the London of the 1880's than anywhere else in Europe.

In most European countries at that time the usage of "intellectual" as a noun did not yet exist. A century ago "ein Intellektueller," "un intellectuel" (as distinct from "un homme intellectuel"), "un intellettuale" would have sounded odd. In the great cities of Europe, too, a growing number of men and women existed who professed contempt less for ignorance than for insensitivity. Most of them, however, had something to do with art rather than with thought. The rhetorical contempt of artists for bourgeois standards and for bourgeois behavior was cultivated by some of them in Paris already before 1848. But now an important difference: by 1900 this bohemianism, and this kind of avant-garde radicalism, were no longer the particularity of artists and writers. An increasing number of men and women were hanging around them. The world of artists and the world of the intelligentsia overlapped more and more. They came to depend on each other, especially in countries such as the United States where both felt that they were a small, indeed a misunderstood, minority among the large mass of their countrymen. Soon this mutual dependence became more and more lopsided, as the artists turned to depend on the intellectuals for their sustenance. Eventually the intelligentsia world would devour and absorb them, the world of art having become but one portion of the world of intellectual reputation.

But that is another story, this contemporary catastrophe of art, to which I must turn in the next chapter. Something else, perhaps something more important, was happening. The race of independent cultivated men and women, on whose active patronage, sustenance, interest not only the world of art but the world of ideas used to depend, was beginning to disappear after the First World War, certainly after the Second. The reason for this was education rather than taxation; it was intellectual rather than financial incapacity. In a world of increasing intellectualization there were fewer and fewer people who were self-confident enough to form their opinions and tastes independently, without much consideration for an intelligentsia that was becoming more and more numerous and the opinions and the ideas of which were publicized more and more.* These people of formerly independent means either wished to be accepted as fellow travelers of the intelligentsia or dropped out of

---

* Already in 1927 Ortega y Gasset wrote: "I have the disturbing conviction that, at least in our time, there are no intelligent men other than intellectuals." He added: "And since the majority of intellectuals are not intelligent either, it turns out that intelligence is an exceedingly rare event on this planet. This conviction, the pronouncement of which will probably, and justly so, irritate the reader, is also extremely painful and upsetting for the one who holds it. . . . There are periods . . . the end of Roman history, in which bravery becomes so rare that finally no one is brave other than military men. So there are other periods in which intelligence becomes restricted to intellectuals and hence a profession. . . ." "Olmedo's Solution," in his collection of essays On Love (New York, 1956), pp. 162–163.

it, abandoning the burden of their cultural interests in their advancing years.

In any event, the influence of intellectuals of all sorts in the mass societies of the twentieth century was rising, not falling, contrary to their frequent assertions of self-pity. We have seen that the intelligentsia absorbed the world of artists after 1900. We have also seen that it made such inroads in the formerly elevated and elegant landscape of cultivation on the top of society that the latter was leveled into a kind of upper middle class suburban development. Finally, after the First World War, the attractions of the intelligentsia were beginning to intrude into the life of scholarship, something with which they had had little or nothing to do before. The distinctions between professional and amateur intellectuals were beginning to disappear. One of the causes of this was relatively simple: with the swelling of bureaucratic societies, of publicity and of propaganda and of education and of administration, all kinds of jobs for all kinds of intellectuals were increasing. This had been foreseen by few people, least of all by their beneficiaries.

Looking back at the last fifty years of rapid intellectualization of modern life, we encounter this inflation of intellectuals which is so formless that it is difficult even to sketch its outlines. Who is an intellectual, who is not an intellectual? Who belongs to the intelligentsia, who doesn't? It is extremely difficult to tell, with any degree of accuracy. Nevertheless we may observe one very significant condition: the presence of intellectuals in a state represented something new, a state within a state, no matter how amorphous—not a social class, not even a social function, but *a state of opinion*. This prospect may have pleased our conservative or liberal ancestors a century ago, since they had feared that the advent of mass democracy might lead to soulless materialism, with fewer and fewer people paying heed to the world of ideas. This has not happened; our ancestors, however, are fortunate in not having to witness its consequences: the catastrophe in art, the decay of intellectual honesty, the dissolution of learning, the meaninglessness of letters.

The performance of the intelligentsia during the last fifty years has been generally marked by cowardice, opportunism, dishonesty, and irresponsibility, far more than by intellectual courage, self-dedication, rectitude and responsibility: honorable exceptions have been few. Of course intellectual occupation is seldom conducive to exceptional bravery: the clerks and the theologians of the Middle Ages, too, were wanting in the latter. The difference in the twentieth century was that now people had been taught to expect much from intellectuals who then deceived them. In Stalin's Russia, Hitler's Germany, Mussolini's Italy, in France at the time of her defeat, etc., etc., the intelligentsia were both unable and unwilling to provide an example of moral resistance, let alone moral leadership, for the people. There were some exceptions, not all of them honorable. When their own existence was threatened by tyranny, certain intellectuals would proclaim their opposition to it, usually from a safe spot outside the reach of the tyrant. At home, once they discovered that resistance to a crumbling tyranny was becoming both safe and popular, intellectuals would appear in the vanguard of the opposition, at times with commendable bravery: but we must not overlook the element of opportunism even in such temporarily inspiring performances as those of the Hungarian intelligentsia in 1956, or of the Czech and Slovak one in 1968.

For more than thirty years most intellectuals in the more-or-less free democracies in the West nurtured illusions about the Soviet Union that were not only fanciful and exaggerated but that told a story that was the very opposite of what was happening in that backward country, with its Byzantine rulers. The medieval theologian writing about celestial battles of angels and devils was merely indulging in a little lyrical nonsense when we compare that, say, with the performance of the Webbs, of these most respectable exemplars of the English liberal and socialist intelligentsia who, returning from Russia in the early Thirties, composed a work of encyclopedic nature in which every chapter was false, the very contrary of every one of their arguments being true. This was not only an example of the shortcomings of the modern methods of social scientific objectivity; nor was it merely an example of the frequent inability of certain intellectuals to see what stands before them. It reflected their deeper, moral failure, their unwillingness (rather than their mere incapacity) to see, and their willingness (together with their all-too-human capacity) to deceive themselves. Again there would be nothing new in this, were it not for the influence of the intelligentsia in the world of ideas. Having first deceived themselves, the Webbs were on the way to deceiving countless other people. Eventually most Western intellectuals would turn against the Soviet Union: but only after, not before, they discovered that their confreres living there were also getting the ax.

Preoccupied with justice (which was seldom more than a reflection of their fear of experiencing injustice), few intellectuals had a comparable preoccupation with the elusive, and yet far from unreal, character of truth. During the Thirties C. M. Bowra, the Oxford scholar and classicist, visited his sister in San Francisco. He found the party conversations of rich Californians extremely boring: "The only ideas which interested them were those which they had in common and repeated like incantations to one another in the hope that this would make them feel good." Soon this would be as typical of the intelligentsia as of the bankers at the Golden Gate, perhaps even more so. For this single sentence, in Bowra's *Memories,* sums up, admirably, the shortcomings of the modern democratic ethic of rhetoric. It also suggests the main reason for the intellectual stagnation and for the deadening slowness of the movement of ideas which I mentioned in the former chapter. The modern professional intellectual was becoming less and less of a specialist, more and more of an idea-monger. Hence the extraordinary conformism of the intelligentsia in our times which is merely masked by their superficial radicalism and by their recondite vocabulary. Eventually this kind of moral corruption would corrode the very functions of their minds. There are innumerable instances suggesting that modern intellectuals do not believe themselves, that they don't really believe what they say, that they say certain things only in order to assure themselves that they possess opinions and ideas that are different from those entertained by the common herd of men.

Opinions! Again, contrary to what all the experts have been

telling us, the development of communications in the twentieth century has led to a dissemination of opinions rather than of information. For one thing, during the twentieth century, with their cooking of news, the older practice of the newspapers with which they had attempted to separate their presentation of information from their presentation of opinion was disappearing. This was especially true of the newsmagazines, movies, television. The modern reader was getting opinion, usually disguised as information. This led, then, to a most curious condition of intellectual life. People, especially the young, were actually looking for opinions, not for information. They were buying unorthodox opinions in much of the same way in which they were buying unorthodox clothes. The parallel is telling, for in both cases they were wearing them, not swallowing them. In the past it was believed that information must precede opinion. Now it became apparent that opinion was preceding information. The nineteenth century erroneously believed that they could be separated. During the twentieth century the intelligentsia were still paying lip service to their separateness. Yet anyone could see that they were interested, first *and* last, in opinions, for even scholarship was becoming impressive usually to the extent in which it related to the exemplification of opinions that were current and respectable among the intelligentsia.

All of this was involved with the lessening of the attention-span, with the dreary superficialization of mental habits which was current among intellectuals no less than among others. The principal vehicles of intellectual commerce, too, were no longer books but magazines. Because of the tyranny of opinions, people were more and more afraid of having the wrong opinions than of having insufficient knowledge. They could always plead insufficient information, whereas to show one's wrong opinions was worse than to show one's dirty linen. For the first time in centuries to have the wrong opinions was worse than to have bad taste. The most successful magazines of the intelligentsia were publishing less and less prose or poetry or excerpts from books, they were publishing reviews of books, and, in the end, reviews of reviews. By that time

(the early Sixties) most successful and reputable books were themselves nothing but reviews—of other books, of other interpretations,
they were interpretations of interpretations.* In the United States
most reviewers, editors, publishers gave up reading altogether.† And
now, when even the intelligentsia were no longer reading, not even
each other's books, Professor McLuhan came on, prophesying the
coming meaninglessness of letters, probably too late.

∷

There were a few pessimistic seers who during the nineteenth
century forecast that universal literacy would lead to the meaninglessness of letters and to the end of literature. These gloomy predictions were premature. Looking back at the nineteenth century we
see a rich literary landscape, full of the greatest individualities, its
highlands as well as its lowlands fertilized by the kind of economic
gain that was offered by the presence of a mass audience. For the

---

* Jacques Ellul: ". . . le livre cessait d'être élément d'un ensemble per-
sonnalisé . . . l'oeuvre d'art est devenue spectacle et . . . le livre est devenu
opinion." The book has become opinion. *Métamorphose du bourgeois* (Paris,
1967), p. 136.
† In 1963 a disastrous little experience taught me how intellectual corruption could lead to the almost total meaninglessness of letters. The instrument
was an unreadable book by a very highly respected American social thinker,
of Central European origin. "Unreadable" is a metaphor, meaning usually
something that is difficult to read. But large chunks of this book were not
merely difficult, they were virtually impossible to read, as if it had been written in a foreign language that one did not know. (A better simile would be a
kind of dish, say, of porridge, whose ingredients and whose taste one knows
but which is undercooked to a degree where it is not merely distasteful or
indigestible but literally unswallowable because of the size of its lumps.)
Having worked my way through it I came to the conclusion that no one had
read this book through: not the editors, not the author, not the reviewers, not
the readers, not the scholars, many of whom subsequently found it propitious
to include its title in their bibliographies, probably because of the intellectual
reputation of the author. One of the more eminent reviewers whom I asked
about this (he had published a mildly favorable and respectful review) admitted to me as much: he couldn't read the book, not really, he said. This first
encounter with a wholly unreadable—and not merely indigestible—book in my
private life was a great event, it drove me on to the condition *ubi saeva in-
dignatio ulterius cor lacerare nequit,* where rage and resentment can no longer
eat into the heart.

first time in all history certain men and women would earn enough money simply because other men and women were buying their books. We ought not underestimate the importance of this stimulus. Scott, Byron, Dickens, Balzac, Tolstoy, Dostoevsky, Conrad, Mann were best sellers. The novel was particularly suitable for mass consumption, partly because of its prose form, partly because of its description of certain scenes and of certain men and women with whom readers could identify themselves. As the century proceeded the literary marketplace became more complicated. For one thing, the businesses of printing and publishing were now separate. The distribution and the marketing of books became more important (and eventually more costly) than their printing. The writer now became dependent on his publishers, more than ever before (or even after). Publishers, in turn, needed writers—all kinds of writers. There arose now a large gap between successful writers and unsuccessful ones, often not at all related to their respective literary merits.

After 1900 the gap seemed to widen, to the point when sensitive writers would earn less and less money when compared to the earnings of more-or-less-talented literary hacks. But now the inflation of intellectuality within the inflating societies of the twentieth century came to the rescue of the former. Even the least talented among them could take solace in contemplating himself as a member of the avant-garde, one of a band of *poètes maudits*, of an intellectual aristocracy in an age of swinish democracy. During the Thirties the situation improved further: they were invited to write scripts for movies or propaganda for governments, it hardly mattered which. Finally, after the Second World War, the respectability of art rose high enough so that no sensitive poet or avant-garde writer would starve any longer, since all he needed was to go through the motions of being a member of the intelligentsia. Once he was so recognized, his income could be assured from public funds or foundations; there would be a well-paying place for him in colleges and universities. As a matter of fact, his books would be actually bought (bought rather than read) by libraries and students to whom they would be assigned, but this now mattered little. Still in the long run this development of writers writing only for other writers led to a cultural chaos, and eventually to the dissolution of literature together with the dissolution of language.

But, again, these developments involved something more than the reactions of people to the material conditions, including those of the literary marketplace. They involved the evolution of consciousness within the better writers themselves. Beginning, perhaps, with Flaubert's early insistence on the *mot juste* more than one hundred years ago, writers became more and more interested, sometimes to the point of obsession, not only in their writing but in the conditions of their writing, including the conditions of language. The consciousness of writers about the limitations of their craft was deepening. The Impressionists and Symbolists among the poets of France were early examples of this, producing poetry of a comprehensible irrational kind of beauty (though interlaced, at times, with incomprehensibility) that had no precedents. Other writers were plumbing the depths of their native languages, occasionally reaching heights of subjective beauty that was poetic in intent and hence largely lost even in the best and most scrupulous of translations. All of this meant that high literature was turning inward not outward. T. S. Eliot was less translatable than Tennyson, Proust than Balzac, Evelyn Waugh than Mark Twain. Others, obsessed with the recognition that words and phrases, not sentences, were the deep substances of thought, experimented with what was to be called "interior monologue" or "stream of consciousness." Again others, usually lone heroes, went even further, or rather deeper, recognizing that there was more to this: not only were words the results of thinking; thinking, too, was influenced by patterns of speech: in many ways the sentence preceded the word. The Viennese genius Karl Kraus exemplified this obsession, with his brave insistence on what the corruption of rhetoric might mean. By the time of the Second World War the novel—a transitory form of art that had emerged only around 1750—seemed to have run its course. Writers felt that the technique of objective, impersonal narration was nonsense; that with the dissolution of society the traditional subject of the novel, the conflict between personal aspirations and the demands of society, was disappearing; that, indeed, in the age of the atom bomb fact had become stranger than fiction. Many of them went on downward on the inward path, toward fantasy and poetry, becoming more and more incomprehensible: given the cultural situation, this hurt them little. Some of them recognized that the novelist's and the historian's tasks were closer than people were accustomed to think, since both of them are engaged in the same endeavor of reconstructing the past. Out of this eventually a new literary form will emerge, the outlines of which we cannot clearly see as yet.

The meaninglessness of letters may be, however, a transitory phenomenon. There is a countervailing element: the slowly rising consciousness of the meaningfulness of the past, which may create a new appetite for a kind of literature that is engaged in imaginative reconstructions of things that we have once known.* It is an appetite that, because of their very nature, other media of communication are unable to fill. So far as authorship goes, movies and television are indirect media; because of the artificial complexity of their production, their products are the results of the cooking or of the freezing of the writer's material. So far as readership goes, neither of them evokes the kind of imaginative mental construction that lends a dimension comparable to the pleasures of reading. Again, possibly only for a small minority, a new rediscovery of meaning in letters may be ahead: for those who take a high pleasure in reading will probably do this more intensely than the present majority of readers, scanning the print with nervous and superficial speed.

* See below, pp. 213–216.

The senselessness of the arts 12

How the highest refinements of artistic consciousness have degenerated into primitivism with astonishing speed.

Few people realize how relatively recent, and transitory, the concept of the *artist* has been. Like literacy, it was a product of the bourgeois period. There were no artists, as such, before the eighteenth century. The painter, the sculptor, the architect, the musician were simply craftsmen. In many European languages, including English, artist and artisan meant the same things. This does not mean that, like many of the stonemason-sculptors and cathedral builders of the Middle Ages, they were anonymous; far from it: they lived at a time of the greatest individuality, in the eighteenth century, when not even two pieces of furniture were the same. The carpenter, the cabinetmaker, the painter of ceilings, the painter of portraits were, all, artisan-artists, in one way or another. Their work was appreciated by the people who used them. Beyond that, there were connoisseurs of refinement but there was, as yet, little or no theorizing about aesthetics—which, indeed, seems to be absent in great ages of art.

During the nineteenth century this was beginning to change, on different levels, for a variety of reasons. Romanticism was breaking through to a new dimension in the recognition of consciousness, including aesthetic imagination. The inflation of society made more and more people consumers of art. The mass production of things by machines, of furniture, for example, led to an increasing separation of the world of the artist from the world of the artisan—an odd development, when one considers that this was happening at the time when society was becoming more democratic, not less. (Eventually, in the twentieth century, the artisan would disappear while the artist, like the snob, remains with us.)

But perhaps the most important change was the evolution of self-consciousness that some artists were realizing through their work. Thus, for example, the Impressionist painters recognized that an objective representation of external reality was impossible, that external reality was to a great measure formed from the inside of the viewer, that the object of his observation was not independent from the observer. In this respect they were the forerunners of the greatest revolution of our consciousness in four hundred years, running ahead of the discoveries of some of our greatest physicists in the twentieth century, though they, the Impressionist painters, were seldom aware of the meaning of what they were doing.

They were, however, among the greatest artists of all time, these votaries of light and color, Monet, Pissarro, Utrillo, Sisley and their, by no means inconsiderable, English and American contemporaries, including their forerunner Turner. The quality of their art is alone sufficient to redeem the reputation of the entire Bourgeois Age. The shimmering beauty of their pictures lets us glimpse an earthly paradise, no matter how elusive: and this happens, paradoxically, through a recognition of the limits of our senses. Something like this happened to their contemporaries, the Impressionist and Symbolist poets, who rose to heights of poetic suggestiveness precisely through their recognition of the limits of speech. The same thing was true of the Impressionist musicians, Debussy and Ravel who, proceeding from the limitations of melody (but not of melodiousness), made harmony—the most difficult and yet the deepest and most suggestive of the three basic elements of music (rhythm, melody, harmony)—into the main element of their compositions. They, too, reached heights of suggestive beauty that would touch the hearts, perhaps even more than the ears, of some people at a depth that no music reached either before or after.

These were shimmering, insubstantial pinnacles of art, not broad and sunlit plateaus of recollection and rest where now disciples could gather to build a new epoch. They were profoundly revolutionary and nontraditional. Their followers would be revolutionary rather than profound, and antitraditional rather than nontraditional. The badge of the artist now was the rejection of all that was bourgeois—paradoxically, at a time when artists were treated better by the bourgeois than ever before and when some of them had become very much bourgeois themselves, though of course they would not admit this. What Péguy said around 1910 in *Notre Patrie*—"It will never be known what acts of cowardice have been motivated by the fear of not looking sufficiently progressive"—may be more applicable to certain famous artists of the time than we care to admit. Instead of austerity, the breakup of the old forms was leading to primitivism which was beginning to have a fatal appeal. We can see this in the evolution—or, rather, in the devolution—of Cézanne, Van Gogh, the young Picasso. In any event, by 1910 what people, rather inaccurately, call "modern art" was in full growth. Abstract painting, cubism, expressionism, vorticism, futurism, they appeared, they flourished in the years immediately preceding the outbreak of the Great War. Around 1912 Ezra Pound wrote, quite rightly, that "the artist is the antennae of the race." More than in any other field of life, it was in the world of art that a concert of explosions signaled the end of a certain world and the coming of the catastrophe in 1914. Some artists certainly sensed this, though they did not know it: they knew not what was happening, indeed, they knew not what they were doing. Still they were "the antennae of the race"—though not for very long.

❖

Ever since 1910, artists remained revolutionaries, with diminishing results. This had much to do with the increasing fusion of the world of art with the world of the intelligentsia. On the one hand the respectable bourgeois went on, sustaining and supporting art, including the revolutionary pretensions of certain artists, with a kind of indulgence that was characteristic less of generosity than of conformism, of a fatal lack of self-confidence, again the fear of not looking sufficiently progressive. The consumers of art would go along with everything, dependent as they were on artistic opinion rather than on their own tastes. This alone was catastrophic, since even bad taste is preferable to no taste at all. On the other hand, artists were becoming dependent less on money than on publicity. They depended on the intelligentsia; they joined it, including its opinions. The effect of this was a disaster, in more than one way. By becoming synonymous with progress, revolution, innovation, art lost much of its meaning. Eventually even its spirit of innovation was drying up. In 1913 the first large American show of modern art, in the New York Armory, had created much excitement: for the first time the avant-garde of Paris was shown, while outside philistines howled, scarcely restrained by the police. In 1963 the fiftieth anniversary of this event was celebrated in the same place, but now all the philistines were inside. In 1913 the avant-garde had been really revolutionary; there had been a world of difference between 1863 and 1913, between Delacroix and Cézanne (or, at that, between Brahms and Ravel), whereas there was virtually no difference between Picasso and Picasso (or between the Stravinsky of 1913 and the Stravinsky of 1963), the so-called progress in the arts having become a mechanical crawl. I say "mechanical" because much of the art of the twentieth century became primitive to the point of impersonality and interchangeability. Fakery was now dominant, not only in the manufacture of publicity for art and artists, but in the manufacture of art itself. Whereas even extraordinary craftsmen have found it impossible to copy or to fake the painters of the past with anything resembling perfection, the style of most painters in the mid-twentieth century could be reproduced by people with little talent to the point where no one would know the difference.

In the end some of the artists with the most revolutionary pretensions proved to be the most commercial and conformist ones. The recent history of sculpture, architecture, music followed essentially in the same way. The once inspiring breakthrough to functional forms very soon gave way to machinelike buildings that, in spite of the white ferroconcrete and the glassiness of their materials, proved astonishingly impermanent, soulless and dirty. The "modern," and "ageless," buildings (and also the furniture) of the twentieth century were peeling and aging more rapidly than had huts of peasants in the Middle Ages; they became, also, much more rapidly uninhabitable. Even more significant was what happened to music. After the War of 1914 certain serious musicians tried to liberate themselves from the limitations of the traditional framework of the octave scale, of the—admittedly cumbrous—traditions of musical notation, and of tonality. But this liberation, again, led them to primitivism where composition and performance became more complicated, while the result of their sounds became more monotonous. Here, too, the intellectualization of art contradicted the very development of democracy. In spite of their avowed radicalism, the "serious" world of the musical intelligentsia and the increasingly widespread world of popular music grew more and more apart. For a while the latter showed some genuine promise, through the American development of what was called jazz, in which simple melodies could be extraordinarily enriched through complex and sophisticated harmonies that were continuously applied to them by their performers who, thus, after centuries were cultivating the art of musical improvisation anew. But, this, too, would not last: by the late 1940's intellectualization was corrupting jazz to the point where it was ceasing to be popular. Thereafter the vogue of what was called rock and roll was to signal the proletarian and barbarian advance of the coming Dark Ages with its monotonous and pervasive rhythm, cries and sounds, performable by people with hardly any knowledge of music whatsoever. Their popularity suggested that the end of the road was near, that the peoples of the West were obsessed with a passion for self-hatred.

By the 1960's, during what was otherwise a vast movement of crumbling and dissolution, the single cohesive symptom that was typical of all forms of art was a cult of ugliness. This was very different from the representation of ugly prostitutes as they had been painted by Rouault in 1903–1904, a massive outcry by a sensitive artist against the false standards of bourgeois security and beauty at that time. Behind the pursuit of ugliness in the 1960's stood the empty face of the masochist, the negative death-wish. This cult of ugliness spread from fashions to music through the public lettering, the shapes and forms and electric sounds of which had, however, run dry of imagination; they would do little else but reproduce the bizarre shapes of art nouveau and of the Wurlitzer colors of the Chicago World's Fair of 1933. On the one hand it seemed as if democracy had finally arrived to take over forms of art, that the proletarian Beatles were the antennae of the race. On the other hand this cult of primitivism showed few signs of imagination or even of genuine strength. Its popularity was the result of a most complicated publicity, and its sounds the results of a most complicated technological cookery, raucous twangs made by instruments plugged into electrical circuits, banshee wails produced by indifferent owlish technicians manipulating electronic tapes into artificial sounds.

❧

Thus it is in the arts that the breakup of the Modern Age has been most complete. At the same time something quite novel has happened: the artists ceased to be the antennae of the race. Having become absorbed by the intelligentsia, their minds, too, absorbed the hopelessly antiquated ideas of progress, especially since this kind of vacuousness was now profitable and easy: no artist was starving, no artist had much to fight against. Abdicating their responsibilities, relinquishing the self-demands of their craft, artists became the squarest of the squares, a multitude of little Mondrians. Their claims of revolt and of independence were now entirely hollow. The virtues of abstract art were being proclaimed at the very time when people's lives were stultified by the abstract figures clicked out by the mechanical cerebrations of bureaucrats and computers. Abstract art would fit perfectly to decorate the corridors of the Pentagon, the American Ministry of War; it fitted them even better than the military oils of a Meissonnier would fit the halls of, say, the French Ministry of War a century ago. The validity of nonrepresentative art was propounded at the very time when it was said that art had finally come about to represent what the artist really felt. Absurdity became the hallmark of art at the very time when meaninglessness was dissolving interior communications, when it should have been the task of artists, more than before, to infuse new meaning into the world. Instead they became the respectable salesmen of the commerce of chaos. Nonrepresentative painting, nonmusical music, non-house house, these were not at all the ultimate results of a brave breakthrough to new forms that had begun a century ago with anti-naturalist painting, anti-melodic music, anti-homey architecture: they were the ultimate results of the—probably transitory—reign of abstract intellectuality.

But something else, too, was beginning to happen. Abstract painting, for example, began to fulfill a function that had not been the principal function of painting for centuries: it became mere decoration. A sequence of colors, a jumble of colorful forms could be agreeable on the walls of a room, far more than on those of a museum. For the first time in centuries music was coming together with dancing: if it could not be listened to, at least one could dance to it, and millions did. The modern idea of the artist was dying out: art was not. Nearly fifty years ago Huizinga wrote about the "waning of the Middle Ages": at that time "the connections between art and fashion were closer than at present. . . . The amazing extravagance of dress during the last centuries of the Middle Ages was, as it were, the expression of an overflowing aesthetic craving, which art alone did not suffice to satisfy."* We can see something of this now.

* *The Waning of the Middle Ages* (New York, 1956), p. 55.

The question now is this: are new forms starting to crystallize or does the broken wreckage of old forms mean, simply and squarely, a return to primitivism? There is, after all, not much that is agreeable in the prospect that a hundred years from now abstract paintings and sculptures would predominate in concrete cottages, or that people would stomp and shake to electronic shrieks of rhythm much as they do now. This, of course, is a strong possibility. Yet at the same time things have developed in the very opposite ways in which they had been projected. Technology did not kill our craving for art; far from it. The invention of photography, for example, had very little to do with the revolt of painters against naturalistic representation (that could be seen in the work of certain painters even before the fruition of the labors of Niepce and Daguerre). The pictorial art had a far greater effect on photography than the reverse; eventually the best photographers were fiddling with their cameras and materials in order to produce artistic effects. The disinterest of artists in technology was probably one of their more genuine attitudes. Less than a century ago the shapes of locomotives and ships would still engage the inspiration of a Monet, while artists now show no interest at all in jet planes or spacecrafts. We have seen that their rejection of the present has been regrettably schizophrenic and incomplete since they could not liberate themselves from the revolutionary illusions of an adolescent futurism. Eventually some of them will overcome this, by recognizing that human creativity, as human communication, is not altogether boundless, that it is wholly dependent on things that we already know. Those artists who have anything new to say or to show will, too, have to turn to the past. The Renaissance, after all, had come out of a rediscovery of Antiquity. A new rediscovery of another portion of the past may still be ahead of us.

Of course this cannot happen in the same way as it happened before. Not only does history not repeat itself: our sensitivities, together with our very habits of perception, have changed. It is true that, again somewhat like at the end of the Middle Ages, the sense

of sight is now predominant for us, which is again "closely connected with the atrophy of thought."* But sight has become the
most intellectual of our senses: it will not remain satisfied, for long,
with the atrophy of thought.

* Huizinga, *op. cit.*, p. 284, about the end of the fifteenth century in France
and in the Netherlands: "Thought takes the form of visual images. Really to
impress the mind a concept has first to take a visible shape. The insipidity of
allegory could be borne, because the satisfaction of the mind lay in the vision."

The destruction of nature 13

How, in transforming nature, human civilization has discovered that it may be destroying itself.

For nearly a thousand years the landscape of Europe remained largely the same. Cities grew, villages expanded, others burned down, forests retreated, the land was tilled first one way, then in another, fields were beginning to be enclosed in the west, a few canals were dug, a few new roads were built, west of the Elbe and the Danube the wolves disappeared after 1700, but there were no great changes. Except for the habitations and for the few roads maps registered no man-made features but the marks of nature. During the eighteenth century in England, during the nineteenth century on the Continent, industry began to alter the face of the earth. It also transformed the habits of people, especially after they left their rural habitations. Much of the so-called Industrial Revolution was evolutionary, it was revolutionary only in its consequences —the opposite of political revolutions which are revolutionary in their immediate effects, and often not in their consequences. Much of these consequences has been described for us, usually by first-rate novelists and by second-rate historians. We are only now beginning to be aware of the enormity of some of these consequences, that man cannot for long tamper with nature with impunity. Elements of life, air and water, which men could take for granted since the beginning of time, have become polluted by the works of men themselves. One hundred years ago this was visible but in a few select hellholes, in the constituencies of satanic mills; by now this kind of pollution affects millions even in the suburbs and in the countryside.

At least for a century or so there were great compensations for this. Between one hundred and fifty years ago the everyday lives of large masses of peoples of the white race were beginning to change for the better. Eventually they changed more than they ever had before or after. Very few of our ancestors had enjoyed constant heat, running water, ample light one hundred years ago. All of these amenities—central heating, indoor plumbing, electric lighting—were invented during the nineteenth century; they were available to the majority of our ancestors as early as fifty, sometimes as early as one hundred years ago. I have written about this earlier. The great breakthrough occurred before the Great War, not after.* In the beginning of the nineteenth century Napoleon could progress from the Seine to the Tiber no faster than could Julius Caesar two thousand years before: by the end of the century one could travel from Rome to Paris in twenty-four hours in a comfortable sleeping car. The locomotive, the steamship, the motor car, the submarine, the airplane, the radio, the telegraph, the telephone, were all invented and put into practice before 1914. The inventions of the last fifty years changed our everyday lives much less.

Even before industrialization our attitude toward nature was beginning to change. For a long time nature had been regarded as the enemy of man. It had to be eliminated, pushed back, those portions of it which could be made useful for man had to be trimmed and tamed. The fact that the Romantic movement and the Industrial Revolution sprang forth at the same time, around 1800, was an amazing coincidence, perhaps even a providential one. There were now people who preached reverence for nature, for all of nature—an inclination largely unknown in the Orient, all of its

* See above, pp. 73–74.

animisms notwithstanding. At its best, this attitude reflected a deepening of historical consciousness. People wished to preserve not only profitable land but also the beauties of the natural landscape, of which they discovered more and more variants—mountains, for example, which before 1800 had been regarded as dangerous and horrid. At its worst, a senseless naturalism would contribute to the elimination of the sense of man's uniqueness: this is indeed what happened, and still happens, when professional naturalists and scientists are but two of a kind. The more naturalists and scientists abounded among us, the more the destruction of nature went on. Still people became more aware of the condition that industrial progress was threatening nature, increasingly so. Eventually the very idea of technical progress was beginning to lose its earlier unquestionable appeal—the consequence of atom bombs and of industrial pollution.

※

No historian has yet attempted to sketch the story of this progressive destruction of nature. It would be instructive to know, if even approximately, the answer to questions such as these: How, and when, did the air in cities such as London and New York change? What was the difference in its components, say, in 1950, 1930, 1910, 1890, 1870? When did the quality of municipally pumped water, once the pride of cities such as Vienna, Philadelphia, Budapest, begin to lose its relative pureness and clearness? When did the accumulation of traffic begin to slow down the routine progress of the transportation of persons and of goods from one place to another? When did the peak of industrial diseases occur, when of respiratory illnesses? When were local vegetables beginning to disappear, when were frozen fish and frozen meat beginning to replace fresh fish and freshly butchered meat and poultry in the markets of this or that metropolis? What were the stages of the chemical and industrial pollution of the great rivers of America and Europe? Many of these statistics are available (some of which are to be handled with caution, since they represent the backward projections of ecologists)* in specialized or municipal libraries; they ought to be brought together. They would illustrate the increasing difficulties and even hazards to life in the great cities of the Western world; indeed, the passing of the urban and urbane era in Western civilization. During the nineteenth century, all of the terrible crowdedness of the industrial tenements notwithstanding, for many people city life was still preferable to country life, not only because of the civic and cultural advantages of the city but also because of such things as the quality of city water, its sewage facilities, its sanitary standards, its medical services. But by the middle of the twentieth century many of these advantages were gone: not only the quality of life but the services—mail, telephone, trains, police protection—in the cities began to deteriorate, especially in the United States. Their deterioration followed those millions who were fleeing to the suburbs.

Much has been written, especially in America, about our insensate destruction of nature. I need not and, at any rate, I cannot sum up the findings and writings of experts, some of whom have put us in their debt because of their serious efforts of warning people about the consequences of the destruction of the natural environment. Yet many of these experts, too, were not exempt from the customary failings of intellectualism: because of the self-imposed captivity of their minds within "scientific" categories, they were simply projecting the continuation of what seemed to be going on. Take, for example, the hue and cry about the so-called "population explosion." Few people recognize that the destruction of nature has been proceeding fastest in those regions of the earth where the growth of the population has been the slowest (in Western Europe and in the urban regions of the United States); that the highest living standards still exist in these very regions where the density of people is the highest, too. The most extensive and senseless practices of destroying the landscape occurred in the United States which, compared to Western Europe, is an underpopulated country. Only it

---

* Let us not forget, for example, the widespread marketing of unhealthy and adulterated food during the nineteenth century.

does not give this impression because of the extraordinary impermanence of its habits of settlement, because of the constant movement of its population. This want of permanence, rather than the want of scientific foresight, threatens the natural environ‹ ment and the quality of life itself.

It is instructive to consider how impermanent the greatest achievements of material progress have proved to be, sometimes in a surprisingly short span of time. Consider the greatest engineering achievements of the nineteenth or of the early twentieth century: the Suez Canal, the American transcontinental railroad, the Trans-Siberian railroad, the Panama Canal. These marvels of engineering have not only changed the face of the earth, they involved the destinies of entire continents. Less than one hundred years after their completion what happened to them? The Suez Canal is wrecked and impassable; the last transcontinental trains in the United States are going out of existence; air transport is replacing the railroad even in the wastes of Siberia; the Panama Canal loses its importance for American shipping and for the American navy every year. But, then, these things were created not at all by the inexorable march of progress. Their engineering followed in the wake of political and social calculations of progress, by what people *thought* was progress: and the future has seldom conformed to the projections of this kind of calculation.

Consider the automobile, for example. It has been a principal instrument of the piecemeal destruction of cities, and later of the countryside. During the twentieth century it also revolutionized warfare. Yet it is a prototypically nineteenth-century means of transportation, as well as a nineteenth-century kind of social status symbol.* The presence of millions of *individual* vehicles was suitable to the century of individualism, not to that of mass production and mass transport. Had the automobile (whether gas- or steam-

---

* A traffic count in Paris showed that during the Second Empire, characterized as it was by prosperity and by social inflation, the number of vehicles increased at a fantastic rate: on the Rue de Rivoli from 1851 to 1869 from 8,000 to 21,000 a day. Had the automobile not been invented, we would in all probability face the same kind of traffic jam in every great city of the Western world—facing not clouds of gasoline but mountain ranges of horse droppings.

propelled) been invented before the railroad, it would surely be on the way to extinction now.

I write about these things to insist upon the truism that The March of Science or of Technology is not inexorable or inevitable or even mechanical or automatic. It is nothing but the outcome of ideas of men—at times of their outdated ideas. History is governed not by logic; rather, it is logic—and especially scientific logic—that is governed by history. It is because of this condition that so much of the massive engineering and building of the twentieth century becomes so rapidly dispensable: Rockefeller Center will not last one hundred years, let alone a thousand.

The destruction of nature, in any event, results in unexpected and unpredictable consequences. For one thing, nature comes back at you, as the entomological consequences of DDT suggest: the destruction of one kind of insect eventually results in the rise of a more fierce and more resistant species, and at what cost! It is not only that concrete is being poured where once fields and forests stood. The reverse, too, happens, sometimes with astonishing results. In those green interstices between suburban developments where agriculture had been abandoned but where houses do not yet stand a kind of jungle reappears in a few years, of a kind as has not been seen in Eastern America for centuries. For the savagery of nature responds to human savagery. Since about 1950 our essential maps are road maps. Unlike in the past, the main features on the map are no longer nature-made but man-made. But maps now are good for only a few years, at the most, and not only for the automobile public: the face of the land and the marks of the landscape are transformed every few years, without cease. There is much wisdom in the contemporary American witticism that a tolerable place in which to live nowadays must be a depressed area—where the pace of change is reduced, not because of the "backwardness" of the people but because of the very absence of interest by builders and by social planners in their profitable modernization.

We must "Cultivate well projected Inventions" that would put "the World in much better circumstances than it is in. We try for Machines to render the Wind as well as the Water Serviceable to us; and extend our Empire into all the Elements." Extend our Empire into all the Elements! This was written not by Benjamin Franklin but by Cotton Mather, in 1723. (Puritanism, proclaimed people from Mencken and Clarence Darrow to Professor Hofstadter, was supposed to have been antiscientific, anti-intellectual, anti-progressive. The very opposite was true.) The answer to this Puritanism, of course, was the Johnsonian one: man's principal business is his knowledge of man, rather than that of his environment, his mastery of himself rather than that of his environment. But we, two hundred years later, cannot rest content with this, as we realize that man's destruction of nature is involved with his destruction of himself, and not necessarily in a sequential order.

❧

That man's destruction of nature may lead to his destruction of himself has now become rather evident. What is less evident is that the degeneration of his self-knowledge may be the cause, and not the consequence, of his destruction of nature. For the self-knowledge of man was not only an intellectual endeavor: it involved the progress of the science and of the art of medicine. There, too, the greatest breakthrough occurred fifty to one hundred years ago, not after. In the most advanced nations of the Western world life expectancy rose by fifteen years during the fifty years after 1875: during the last fifty years it inched forward, adding another five or eight years at the most. Infant mortality, on the average between 20 and 30 percent around 1865, dropped to about 6 percent by 1914 and to about 3 percent by 1965. The great general progress of medicine included anesthetics, the elimination of pain that had been so frequent an intruder in our ancestors' lives. By 1914, for the first time in the history of mankind, it was possible for a European or an American to live through long stretches of decades without ever experiencing acute pain in any form. This was all to the good. After 1945, however, it began to appear that the practice of medicine, too, was not exempt from the general degeneration of progress. The family doctor, especially in the United States, was disappearing; the personal contact between patients and physicians became, like hospital care, routine, mechanical, impersonal, often breaking down. Together with the advance of specialization the ethics of the medical practitioners decayed. Against this were stacked up the claims of wonder drugs, and wondrous transplantations of entire noses, toes, and hearts. These rare achievements were comparable to the Men on the Moon: wondrous things, without much effect on the ordinary lives and tribulations of mankind. In the past the surgeon had been on the bottom rank of the medical profession; until about 1880 in some places he could practice without a degree. By 1880 he was properly in the center; thereafter he moved to the top, the master mechanic in the body shop, typical of a way of thinking where man was but a thing among things and where even the popular language reflected this.*

At the same time the doctor (whose name had originally meant "teacher") of medicine became the priest of modern men and women. People went to his office (for he would seldom visit them) in order to seek assurance. For every person who was sitting in these offices because he was seeking relief from racking pain, there were five or ten who came in search of a certain term, a definition, a category: they wanted to be told what was wrong with them. This, then, was another evidence of "internalization." The physical and psychical symptoms of patients were overlapping. Those specialists who prattled about "psychosomatic" diseases, like those who spoke about "extrasensory perception," missed the point, as usual. They ought to have recognized that most diseases are psychosomatic to some extent, just as every kind of human perception is to some extent extrasensory. But let us not philosophize about this further. Physically speaking, men and women and children during the twentieth century in the Western world were healthier than ever before. Mentally speaking, they were more disturbed than ever before. I am not merely referring to the increasing curve of mental diseases. Even those who had never visited a psychiatrist were

---

* The first locomotives were sometimes called iron horses. By 1925 in America successful businessmen were sometimes called the spark plugs of the organization. This reflected a dimming sense of reality. Whereas the first gaunt engines looked like iron beasts, human beings do not look like spark plugs.

aware of their mental problems, far more than before.

This kind of awareness was increasing. Again there was more to this than the result of the mental confusion that accompanies the breakdown of a once customary civilization. It marked another step in "internalization," though few people recognized it, including the star surgeons and transplantationists. This "internalization" involved the breakdown of our still traditional, and largely unquestioned, notion of causes and effects. I shall try to explain this as simply as I can.

Illness, like suffering, may be a result of external or of internal causes, or of both. The greatest, and the unexceptionable, triumphs of modern medical science involved finding the causes and the symptoms and the cure of the "external" group. We know how to treat a wound, a break, an external infection, a parasitic contamination far better than before. This is not only due to progress in medical techniques. The therapy succeeds because we know *the causes* (the etiology)—all of them physical and external—as well as *the symptomatic development* (the pathogenesis) of these diseases. Thereby they can also be prevented. Yet far the largest incidence of ailments—whose number is growing—belongs to another group, to that of "internal" causes.* For example (and it is a relatively primi-

Group of illnesses:	A (External)	B (External/Internal)	C (Internal)
Etiology (Their causes):	Known	Unknown	Unknown
Pathogenesis (Their symptomatic development):	Known	Known	Unknown
Preventability:	Yes	No	No
Therapy (Their cure):	Etiological (causal)	Pathogenetic (developmental)	Symptomatic (temporary)

* There is yet a third, smaller, group, that of "external/internal" causes: this in-between group includes mostly malfunctions of secretioning hormones. In this passage I have drawn on the article by Arthur Jores, Professor of Internal Medicine in the University of Hamburg, from *Orientierung* (Zurich, June–July 1967), translated in *Mérleg* (Vienna, October 1967). Jores sums up his very telling article in a table which I translate and reproduce here, adding a few explanatory variations for the sake of an English-speaking readership:

tive example), modern medicine can alleviate the symptoms of a headache, or the pains caused by an ulcer. It can also remove the latter: but it cannot do much, if anything, about its cause. Most of the patients now crowded in doctors' offices and hospitals are suffering from this "internal" group of ailments, the prevalence of which is increasing and which—a significant observation, this!—seem to be unique to the human species.

In any event, their causes are neither "purely" external nor "purely" physical. We know little or nothing about their causes; consequently we can do little or nothing to prevent them. They are often involved with a person's existential condition. This does not mean that psychosomatology is the wave of the future, or that persons suffering from chronic headaches or ulcers are hypochondriacs: but it means that it is more and more senseless to consider a person's "physical" condition in isolation, apart from the development of his existential personality. The intrusion of mental factors into the structure of physical events is no longer something esoteric or merely relevant to telepathy. It is a palpable reality in everyday life, encountered each day by thousands of physicians who recognize its existence, and by many more thousands of physicians who slur over it, even though they ought to know better.

One hundred years ago Taine wrote: "Renouveler la notion de cause, c'est transformer la pensée humaine"—the renewal of the notion of the cause would amount to the transformation of human thought. We can no longer escape this task. We have to recognize the existential causality of human life, the relationships of human causes and human effects which are different from the mechanical relationship of causes and effects that have been monopolizing the concept of causality for at least three hundred years now. Their categorical presumption has been that a cause must always precede its effect, and that the same causes must necessarily produce the same effects, a presumption which Freud himself was incapable of transcending. Yet for human beings the very process of thinking, on the conscious and also on the subconscious level, complicates, disturbs and transforms the relationship of causes and effects, whereby this relationship becomes far more complex than the primitive mechanical relationship of causes and effects in the outside world. Moreover, in human life the cause of something may not always lie in the past but in a vision of the future. Almost all of human unhappiness, and much of human suffering, exists when there is little or nothing to look forward to. Human life always involves the wanting of more life: when this wanting ceases, life flickers out: it has to have some kind of purpose, no matter what. This kind of purpose/cause exists in the future, not in the past. In any event, it resides within us, within our organism, of which our mind is an integral, and not a separable, part. The kind of science that is incapable of thinking in other categories than in those of mechanical (and therefore predictable and calculable) causes and effects, that has eliminated the notion of purpose from the world, has not much more to tell us; indeed, it is the principal agent of the destruction of nature and of man.

The decay of science

14

How, at the time of their greatest triumphs, scientists have found that their basic principle of objectivity has proved to be an illusion.

In the past the main instrument in the destruction of nature was nature itself—its pestilences, swarms of insects, storms, floods, earthquakes—now it is mostly the result of the applied science of man.

Science is not an external system of reality but a human product. The universe and nature were earlier than man, but man was earlier than the science of nature and of the universe—a common-sense truth that is, alas, much obscured nowadays. The so-called scientific method, together with our view of the universe, is not much more than three hundred years old. From Copernicus through Kepler and Descartes to Newton people discovered that their traditional notions of nature were inaccurate, that the earth was not the center of the universe, that it indeed moved around the sun, that life was governed by laws of motion the mechanics of which could be ascertained through objective methods of mathematical calculation. All of this made little difference for a long time.* It may have contrib-

* Much of this makes little difference even now. Whether the earth really goes around the sun, or the sun around the earth—now, really, what difference does it make?

uted to the irreligiosity and to the agnosticism of certain thinkers whose God-belief was wobbly anyway. The vast majority of mankind, even those in the Western world who were ignorant of these discoveries, were unaffected by them for hundreds of years. It is even conceivable that much of the so-called Industrial Revolution could have occurred without them. The Romans and, some people say, the Chinese, had invented engines and machines without ever having heard about objectivity or the laws of gravity.

Still the categories of the modern view of nature and of the universe would eventually catch up with the work of the lowliest tinkerer. For the scientific revolution of the seventeenth century was a great event, one of the greatest in the history of mankind since the coming of Christendom. But—and this is a fascinating paradox—its motive force, at least for a while, was man's increase of self-knowledge, rather than his increasing knowledge of the external world. This increase in man's self-confidence led to the discoveries of science, not the other way around. The prestige of science was but an extension—admittedly a very large extension—of man's capacity to know. Thus for a long time the word "scientist" simply meant "man of knowledge," a broad meaning that still lives on in the German word *Wissenschaft*. During the second half of the nineteenth century, then, the prestige of natural science began to outrace the rest—reasonably so, since at that time the applications of natural science were beginning to transform the world, including the everyday lives of our ancestors, for the better. By 1900 the meaning of "scientist," in the English-speaking nations, narrowed down to mean "natural scientist" (most of the claims of the hobbling "social sciences" notwithstanding). "Scientist" was now something closer to an engineer or a technician than to a historian or a philosopher. Most people and, of course, virtually all scientists, now took it for granted that science would further improve not only the material conditions of life on earth but the operations of the human mind. Many scientists said, and professed to believe, that it was only a question of time before the rigorous pursuit of scientific objectivity and the extensive application of scientific instruments would produce the answers to the few remaining questions about the nature of universal phenomena and about the nature of human life that were still "unsolved." Many people still believe this, regrettably so.

There were always a few people, including some of the greatest minds in the civilization of Western Europe, who entertained profound doubts about the claims of objective science from the beginning. They include Descartes's contemporary Pascal who was not only a religious thinker but a scientist and a mathematical genius, and who instantly recognized the big hole in the categorical postulate of objectivity, of that fundamental principle in the development of modern science: Pascal instantly saw that the separation of object from subject was insufficient. During the eighteenth century few people read Pascal: still, not only religious thinkers but all kinds of humanists would agree with Pope that the proper study of mankind was man, or with Dr. Johnson who said much of the same thing, more amply and sonorously so. During the nineteenth century, however, Benjamin Franklin was the best seller, not Samuel Johnson. The ways of the humanists and of the scientists were now beginning to part, though for a while their vested disinterest in God would provide for a kind of intellectual fraternity between some of them. Belief in science, at any rate, was now becoming more universal than belief in God, for entire populations who otherwise knew nothing about science at all. In the United States the two beliefs coexisted in the minds of millions, ranging from the faith of Christian Scientists to the American Catholic priest whose sermon this writer had the privilege of hearing as he called God the master mechanic of the Universe, no doubt an American improvement of Voltaire's God who was the clockmaker of it all.

Still the elements of a popular disillusionment with science were beginning to appear, especially after 1945. For the first time there was a triumphant invention of science—the atomic bomb—of which most people wished it had not been invented at all. For another thing, some people recognized how the horrors of mass killings during the Second World War would not have been possible without the methods of modern science, that Hitler's Third Reich was not merely something reactionary but something super-modern. The stainless steel image of progress became gradually tarnished. The most spectacular branch of science was no longer applied physics, it was biochemistry. When its publicity-conscious practitioners announced that they had found The Key to Life, there was no universal outburst of joy, rather, the contrary. Their further predictions to the effect that soon they would be able to produce human beings out of test tubes were sufficiently chilling news for most people to try to dismiss it from their minds. Pessimism about the future of unbridled applications of science was no longer the self-conscious monopoly of poets or traditionalists: it was beginning to spread widely. This kind of incipient anti-scientism was now the result of experience as well as of premonition, altogether different from the superstitious opposition to science in pre-scientific centuries and among pre-scientific populations.

Much of this disillusionment had to do with scientists as well as with science. People were still accustomed to think of "science" as the great external system of nature. The recognition that science does not exist apart from scientists, that the history of science is the history of scientists and nothing else, was not yet sufficiently realized: but at the same time the earlier notion of the objective and impartial scientist was beginning to go by the board. People were beginning to realize that scientists, too, were out for their own good, no more and no less. During the First World War the German scientists who perfected poison gas were national heroes no less than those of their colleagues who produced ingenious chemical substances by the distillation of air. During the Second World War other German scientists conducted murderous experiments at the expense of the health of prisoners; but it is also a matter of record how certain American scientists, liberals and inscribed Democrats, jumped and shrieked with joy when they saw the first atom bomb burst in the dark dawn of the New Mexico desert. Research followed politics, not politics science. Had the Germans not persecuted the Jews, the United States would not have had its atom bomb before anyone else. During the 1950's certain scientists argued that the fallout from atomic tests was a hazard to health; other scientists denied this. The first were Democrats, the second Republicans. The applied scientific (and, therefore, political) advocacies of Scientific Heroes such as Dr. Oppenheimer reflected the prevailing climate of opinion among the American intelligentsia: liberal in the early Thirties, fellow traveler in the late Thirties, an anti-Fascist Democrat in the early Forties, a One-Worlder in the Forties, a chastened liberal in the Fifties—chapter headings of the history of American intellectuals, Professor's Progress, 1932–1957. (Few scientists were conservatives or reactionaries: most of them were liberal fellows, amateurs of things such as chamber music or even modern art, ever ready to sign petitions against censorship or in favor of abortion, respectable things to do.)

This was even truer of the practitioners of the so-called social sciences. In most cases the results of the researches of most political scientists, sociologists, psychologists, anthropologists, economists were predictable from their personal preferences: they were exemplifications of the ideas that were currently respectable. As a matter of fact, this was usually true not only of the results but of the very subjects of their research. The desire for intellectual respectability (or, more accurately, for respectability among intellectuals) was reflected, for example, in the very "scientific equipment" of their bibliographies. On the one hand they would go to great lengths to cite all kinds of names and titles of books that were currently respectable. On the other hand, instead of falsifying evidence or suppressing writings that were contrary to their thesis, they would simply ignore them. Their very bibliographies, no matter how padded, would be highly selective, as would be their scientific vocabulary, conveniently stretched to include the terminology of the time, usually at the expense of thought.

The so-called lay public would seldom be aware of the character of these tricks, though it was beginning to suspect that something was not quite on the up-and-up. Uneasy attitudes began to emerge, even in the United States. One hundred years ago The Scientist, in the popular image, was a benefactor of humanity, a kind of benevolent priest of Reason. In the popular culture of the 1960's—movies, comic strips, stories—the figure of the Bad Scientist was as frequent as that of the Good Scientist, perhaps even more so. Not too many young people were attracted by a scientific career, for a variety of reasons (not all of them respectable): at any rate, this went counter to the earlier projections according to which majoring in science would eventually replace the humanities. Indeed, science, which only recently seemed to have been the most exciting thing in the world, developed into something of a bore. It is significant that this happened at the very time when the achievements of applied science were touching the fantastic, as for example on the occasion of the landing on the moon. The intelligentsia, for example, played numb and dumb when it came to these extraordinary achievements (perhaps because they could not identify themselves with the enormous governmental machinery and the kind of technicians who perfected it: had Fidel Castro landed on the moon instead of Neil Armstrong their attitude might have been different). More important, the landing on the moon aroused the imaginations of common people far less than, say, Lindbergh's first flight across the Atlantic. Far fewer people turned out for the ticker-tape parade of the astronauts in 1969 than for Lindbergh in 1927. The fact that they could watch the moon landing on television was not a sufficient explanation for this. More probably all kinds of people had all kinds of mixed feelings about this kind of thing, whether they admitted this to themselves or not.

Thus, on the one hand, more and more people were beginning to have second thoughts about the promises of science. On the other hand they were, as yet, far from ready to question its principal claims. It would be premature to say that the disillusionment with science has become sufficiently widespread, or even recognized, to the point where it would emerge on the surface of events and influence the development of society and of politics. The President of the United States, for one, greeted the landing on the moon as the greatest event since the Creation—having overlooked Jesus Christ, perhaps to the temporary dismay of his golfing partner the

Reverend Billy Graham. Even among people who ought to know better a schizophrenic attitude toward science existed—a kind of selective schizophrenia rather than an equilibrium.* In one part of their minds people feared the Orwellian world of 1984. In the other part they were looking forward to a Huxleian Brave New World. Between these two parts of their minds there was an iron curtain— or, rather, a barrier of Styrofoam. Thus, for example, the same kind of person who was (or who, at any rate, claimed to be) deeply upset by the damage that American bombs were doing to the ecology of Vietnam was at the same time an enthusiastic advocate of compulsory sex education, preferably starting in kindergarten. Opponents of atomic testing were proponents of biological experimentation. Men and women who would profess to despise people such as Dr. Teller, the self-avowed Father of the H-Bomb, would profess their admiration for people such as Buckminster Fuller, an ancient New England faker, who pushed for the building of colonies for millions at the bottom of the sea. Others, in the name of higher humanism, would abolish the teaching of history from schools and substitute sociology or anthropology instead. Cybernetics, computerization, structural linguistics, quantification in the social sciences, including history—their attraction suggested the enduring prestige of science, or, rather, the enduring attraction of vocabulary as a substitute for thought.

This was so because few people could, as yet, free their minds from the binds and shackles of scientistic (rather than scientific) thinking, including its primitive concept of mechanical causality.

---

* The attitudes of the so-called rebellious youth reflected this schizophrenia. Having turned toward a (fake) mysticism they did not really reject scientism. Their professed interests in Buddhism and astrology coexisted in their minds with their fascination with super-modern drugs and foods, with the world of Batman and Superman, with electronic flick-tricks and Indian chants performed on high-voltage instruments. Fifty years ago an American humorist made justifiable fun of an American steel magnate who had sat in his Renaissance mansion on a priceless Renaissance chair, reading the *Saturday Evening Post*. Fifty years later another generation of so-called rebels were listening to raucous songs making fun of American industrialism and its gadgets—on their stereo-tape sets, sprawling in their sports cars.

Still we were approaching, no matter how slowly, a turning point: for the once single-minded belief and trust in the ability of science to create an earthly paradise existed no longer.

❖

Some of the greatest scientists of the twentieth century had known this all of the time. Some among them discovered something else, too: that the modern ideal of objectivity was but a relative thing, full of holes. For a long time it was believed that sooner or later physicists would be able to find and isolate the basic component of all elements, the building stone of the entire universe, the atom—or, if necessary, the basic component of the atom. During the 1920's it began to dawn on some of them that perhaps this was not possible at all, no matter how powerful the atom-smashers were or might become. They kept finding smaller and smaller particles of the atom, labeling these with great enthusiasm, until eventually they ran out of names. Something more important was dawning upon them—in any event, upon some of them—too. The German physicist Heisenberg discovered that the objective observation of atomic particles was an impossibility, the very nature of atomic particles being such that the very act of observation was interfering and altering, instead of fixing and preserving, the object. This was, of course, something that certain poets had declaimed through the ages, and that certain philosophers such as the Spaniard Ortega were preaching since 1914; but now this was a fact, proven by scientific experiments themselves. This discovery of indeterminacy in the basic substances of the material world was a far greater milestone in the evolution of human thought than was Einstein's theory of relativity. It meant that the modern scientific method, resting on Descartes's separation of the world into subjects and objects, and that the modern view of the universe, dependent upon Newton's mathematical mechanics, were but a limited system, valid only under certain conditions; that they were an invention of the human mind, not less but not more true than, say, Ptolemy's view; that they were the products of an age that was now passing. Few people, including most scientists, realized the profound implications of this discovery, perhaps because they, like Einstein, did not want to. For another thing, the applications of Newtonian science still worked in everyday life, indeed, sometimes fantastically so. Some of the same physicists who accepted (albeit reluctantly) the new principles of quantum physics went on to build atomic bombs with the technology that still depended on Newtonian mechanics and Franklinian publicity.

Eventually the decay of Newtonianism and of Cartesianism will affect the lives—and, what is more important, the minds—of more and more people. But this is a slow process; I cannot tell when. The hold of old ideas is still strong. The intellectual stagnation is part of the deadening slowness with which ideas—especially new ideas—during the twentieth century move. The trust in recognized experts is still strong, even though more experts are proven more and more wrong in their projections, in more and more fields, for the relatively simple reason that I mentioned more than once (simple in its essence but complex in its consequences): they are simply predicting the continuation of whatever seems to be going on.

Still the beginning of disillusionment within certain applications of science will make more and more people question the very validity of scientific objectivity. In an increasingly truthless and loveless world they will recognize that the ideal of objectivity is limited indeed, that even more important than the antiseptic separation of the scientific observer from the matter or person that he is observing is the purpose and quality of his interest; that the purpose of human knowledge is understanding rather than accuracy; that the very quality of observation is inseparable from human participation; that the method of the scientist is inseparable from his purpose. This recognition of the function of purpose will be a great event. It will mark the final stage in the decay of the determinism of modern science, of this once triumphant achievement of the Western mind, which, paradoxically, has one fundamental thing in common with the fatalism of the most primitive of peoples: the notion that man is a product, that everything that he does, thinks or feels is determined by external forces, that the freedom of his will is nothing but an illusion.

I need not illustrate where this kind of irresponsible narrow-mindedness has led us. It is still governing the minds of millions, including their leaders, teachers, and authorities. Thus it is by no means certain that the acceptance of a more chastened, more realistic, more moral view of science is around the corner, that it will set in before the destruction of much of the world occurs. For meanwhile, through our pursuit of transforming the world, modern civilization moves toward death like a massive and ever-growing monster. Few people read the Apocalypse nowadays, perhaps reasonably so. For what we have to face is not an Apocalypse loosened down over us by an angry God but an apocalypse created by men themselves. We are now capable of destroying most of the world. Suddenly, after one thousand years, the end of the world is coming into sight again, though in a very different way from that in which people thought of it during the Middle Ages. Perhaps all of this has an unconscious attraction for us. It is no longer farfetched to see in every new "triumph" of science a manifestation of the death-wish of modern men. The principal mystery of our participation in the universe remains what it has always been: Where do we come from? Where are we going? Now, when people can tamper with the creation of life and with its extension, they have come close to eliminating the meaning of human life itself. They have made man a thing among things, in a maddening scientific man-made universe in the middle of which hundreds of millions live in a truthless void. There are reasons to believe that the modern world, like modern man, is actually propelled by its own desire of self-annihilation. If this continues unabated, the end of the Modern Age and the end of the world may be one.

The faithlessness of religion

How the updating of religion has led to a flight of faith from the churches.

We have now come to the end of this series of topics; I am to write about what people believe. This is difficult. History is the result, surely in the long run, and sometimes in the short run, too, of what people think and of what they believe: but the evidences of these things are difficult to grasp. (For this very reason they are so easy to prattle about: there are no proofs.) We know, to some extent, what a person said or what he did; we know to a much lesser extent what he thought, and even less what he believed. There is an additional difficulty when it comes to religion. The importance, the significance, the meaning of people's beliefs about other people, and about all kinds of worldly things, are to some extent ascertainable from their acts; a person's belief in God may have no worldly consequences at all. This has always been so. But these difficulties are further compounded when it comes to large numbers of peoples in democratic times, when there is yet another gap: beyond the usual discrepancy of what people may say and what they really think, there is the other one, superimposed by democratic conformity, between what they say they believe and what they really believe.

Still let me try. During the last few centuries, especially in West-ern Europe, medieval faith was dying out, its cult was replaced by modern reason. This was a long process, this dissolution of religion, for a long time far less successful than what the votaries of the Enlightenment would have had us think. Centuries had to pass before the new discoveries of the scientific universe would filter down to the minds of the masses of people who no longer felt the need for the presence of God to explain the world, including their own existence, for them. Long before Nietzsche there were men such as the Marquis de Sade or eccentric English prophets of Rea-son who proclaimed the Death of God, but few people were listen-ing. Still the great erosion of religious beliefs that had begun in the eighteenth century spread wider during the nineteenth. By 1900 only a minority of men and women of the white race were regular churchgoers. Belief, of course, is not a matter of statistics: if in one place twice as many people are found in church on Sundays than in another place this does not necessarily mean that the people in the first place are twice as religious (and not even that they are twice as pious) as those in the second. Still the external acts of people reflect their inner dispositions to some extent. The place of God in the minds of most people was weakening—or, rather, emptying. This is what Nietzsche, a little less than a century ago, would call "the death of God," not at all in a triumphant mood. But this was the end of something, not the beginning. By 1950 less than 5 percent of Scandinavians were churchgoers, something that had been pre-dicted by Kierkegaard a century earlier. By 1960 the erosion of religious practice, something that had affected mostly the Protestant populations, began to affect many of the traditionally (but perhaps only traditionally) Catholic peoples of the world, too, an event to which I am coming in a moment.

❈

There were significant and, on occasion, important exceptions to this long decline. History is never of one piece: there were the personal dramas of conversions or of reconversions of some of the finest minds and characters, remarkably frequent at times even during the twentieth century. Also, from the point of view of sheer numbers, during the nineteenth century the greatest movement of conversions took place, when entire populations were converted to Christian religions by missionaries in Africa, Asia, Oceania. Within Western civilization the decline of churches was uneven; it was transformed on occasion by revivals of faith. People would grow sick and tired of prolonged troubles: having been tormented by the misdeeds of their fellow men, they would be disillusioned with their promises, they would rediscover the solaces of religion and of some kind of belief in God. On two occasions, approximately from 1780 to 1825, reaching its peak after the ravages of the French Revolution and the Napoleonic wars, and again between 1940 and 1960, reaching its peak after the Second World War, these renewed waves were general phenomena involving much of the Western world. (Oddly enough, no such religious revival followed the First World War, perhaps because that war was less typical of the inhumanity of man than of the inhumanity of society.)

There was another thing, too: the condition of democratic conformity. The most astounding thing that foreign visitors found in the early United States was the fact that its many churches were prospering. In reality this should have been no more astounding than the behavior of millions of Italian Communist voters who have their children baptized in the local Catholic church: a certain minimum of religious observance was deemed necessary for a certain minimum of social respectability. In the United States church and state may have been separate, whereas society and religion certainly were not. Elsewhere church and state were not separate but this did not make much difference at all. Members of the churches, their priests and pastors, craved, on the average, respectability and acceptability; indeed, good Christians were taught to be good patriots. Agnostic and atheist rulers, from Jefferson to Stalin, eventually discovered that the churches were less dangerous than what they had thought, that they would give the state little trouble, though sometimes they should have been responsible for the conduct of certain recalcitrant individuals. Almost all of the German cardinals, bishops, pastors and priests under Hitler restricted religion to religion; they said nothing about the misdeeds of the state, not to speak of its misdeeds against non-Christians par excellence, such as the Jews.

Still, during the Second World War and after, sincere and thoughtful ex-Protestants, ex-Jews, ex-atheists were sufficiently inspired by the teachings of Roman Catholicism, exemplified as these had been by the acts of certain Catholics, to become converts. This was part and parcel of the last wave of a revival of religion which, for a moment, seemed to have come close to reversing the tendency toward general irreligion in the Western world. For a few years the churches were filling up again. In the United States, for example, circa 1952, for the first time in its history it was a decided advantage to be known as a Catholic, especially for government positions, since this was seen as the surest proof of one's Americanism and anti-Communism. In Western Europe, for the first time in a century, certain presidents and prime ministers were believing Catholics, some of them daily communicants. In Eastern Europe certain bishops and cardinals were national heroes. The respectability of religion affected even intellectuals; they would admit into their ranks entire departments of religious philosophers; thus came into being the Theological Section of the Atheist International. As late as 1958 the funeral of Pope Pius XII developed into a world spectacle such as had not been seen before even in Rome: among the dignitaries of the world the American Secretary of State arrived early and stayed late, inquiring into the chances of certain candidates for the Papacy whose election would have been particularly agreeable for the American government, a task before which his harsh Presbyterian ancestors would have coiled up in horror.

And now, less than twelve years later, all of this suddenly seems very long ago. At a time when Protestantism was on its last legs, when atheism was becoming disreputable even among the intelligentsia, when the Age of Reason seemed little more than a past chimera, when the Catholic Church seemed more powerful and prestigious than virtually at any time since the Reformation, it let down the gates, it proclaimed its willingness to come to terms with the modern, indeed, with the super-modern world. Gradually it appeared that the external strength of the Roman Catholic Church, too, was deceptive, that this image of a turreted cathedral still standing, rather resplendent, in the middle of a vast emptying religious plain, was a mirage. The reality was rather that of the crumbling baroque churches of Rome, in the middle of crowded streets, surrounded and pressed by the modern world on all sides. The old and simple patriarch, Pope John XXIII, whose peasantlike humanity inspired millions outside of the Church, may have known this better than had others when, suddenly, he proclaimed a call for the renovation of the Church, for a new Council, the first in nearly a century, in the spirit of *aggiornamento*. That word was probably a mistake. *Aggiornamento* meant opening the windows in Italian; in other languages the somewhat superficial impression was that a call had been issued for modernization, for the updating of the Church and for religion itself. The large and majestic windows of the Roman Catholic Church were indeed opened, to them rushed all kinds of ambitious people, waving white flags that quickly soiled in the polluted air, while others, including members of the Theological Section of the Atheist International, were clamoring for control of the mimeographing machines.

I must not be sarcastic, I believe in the verity of the marvelous Portuguese proverb: God writes straight with crooked lines; I cannot pretend to evaluate the meaning of the Vatican Council in the 1960's. But I can say that many of its outcomes reflected an astonishing extent of psychological ineptitude on the part of its churchmen. They did not realize that by opening the windows they were letting in neon light rather than sunlight, gasoline fumes rather than fresh air, the din of publicity rather than the harmonies of nature, while on the porches of their churches the money-changers of belief were gathering anew, so that their interiors seemed no longer those cool and silent places of repose; they seemed less and less inviting, fewer and fewer people from the outside were now coming in. They did not see that whether the Church was relevant or not relevant to the modern world had nothing to do with its attraction, the eventual strength of which existed for the best precisely when the Church seemed untouched by the temptations of the modern world. Now it became apparent that the modern image of a stern and self-confident body of religious men and women corresponded to reality only in part, that the erosion of self-confidence deeply affected them, that they desired to be part of the world. Only now their aspiration was not so much to bring the Church into accord with the state, it was to bring it into accord with modern society. They sought conformity not with nationalism but with progressivism. Thus they would eliminate many traditions, Latin, high language, the profoundest of passages from the Mass (including the last Gospel of St. John), much ceremony from the liturgy. With it went much of the inspiration and, perhaps, much of the innocence of millions, too.

In the middle of the Council Pope John died. The work of the Council went on, eventually dying out in chatter. Much good work may have been done by the present Pope and still much good may come from the Council's renovation of the Church. What it did not produce was the renovation of faith. Perhaps this work was the unconscious preparation for the dismantling of an external edifice whose very monumentality now belonged only to the past. Perhaps, unconsciously, the Church was readying itself for the new Dark Ages. Still in the short run what happened was a mass crumbling even among those people who had been more or less unaffected by the erosion of religion before: Dutchmen, Catholic Americans, for example. Thus, less than one hundred years after Nietzsche, the Death of God argument became bread and butter for all kinds of theologians and journalists; and it began to penetrate the minds of people, few of whom realized (though many of them probably sensed) that the Death of God did not mean a Triumph of Reason. Even fewer knew that what Nietzsche had meant was the death of the ancient notion of an external God who rules the universe outside of us (and that perhaps with the evolution of consciousness there could arise a deeper, inner God-belief). People now saw that their church was, after all, not very different from any other institution: and those priests who were rather desperately trying to keep up with the times only showed how the inflation of society and the dissolution of traditions affected them, too. Thus the strength of the faith of large populations was undermined, among other things, by the behavior of the visible church itself. All of this happened at a time when young people, far from being rationalist atheists, were shakily poking around for some kind of faith: but no longer were they attracted by the Christian churches, no longer by the Catholic Church.

❖

There remain the Jews, this most extraordinary minority in history. Nietzsche wrote one hundred years ago that anyone who wanted to understand the then future of Europe had to keep two new elements, the Jews and the Russians, in mind. (He left America out, a big omission all right.) Contrary to the sometimes lingering belief, Nietzsche was not an anti-Semite; he was, indeed, an anti-anti-Semite. But he was among those who foresaw trouble if the influx of Jews from Russia to Europe would continue for long without cease. This migration of Jews out from the western provinces of the old Russian Empire into the rest of the world was one of the most extraordinary and consequential events of the nineteenth century: no historian worthy of this story has yet arisen. The Jews were about the only people who migrated not only from the countryside to the cities, or from the Old World to the New, but from one nation to another. Within a few decades, sometimes within a few years, their numbers would rise from 1 to 4 or 5 percent of certain national populations, from 10 to 30 percent of the populations of certain cities, from 10 up to 50 percent of certain professions. They would naturally prosper in the capitalist and early-capitalist societies of the nineteenth century. They became assimilated, civic-minded, determined to be patriotic; they would soon intermarry with the Christian bourgeoisie, sometimes with the aristocracy. All of this evoked a great deal of envy, and the modern phenomenon of racial anti-Semitism that, in many ways (though not in all), differed from the ancient, and largely religious, Judaeophobia. The liberal world believed that this was a temporary reaction, that with the assimilation of the Jews it would disappear. This was quite wrong. The popular hatred would rise against the assimilated Jews even more than against their poor benighted brethren and relatives who still lived in ghetto-like quarters, murmuring their outlandish prayers and wearing their outlandish habits. It was the successful newcomer, prospering within the society of the nation, who was envied. Few people understood the consequences of this. Among them were the Zionists and Hitler. The first, at the opening of the twentieth century, proclaimed that after two thousand years the Jews should declare that they are a separate people and return to Palestine. The second believed that this would not happen, and that the presence of Jews in the midst of non-Jewish peoples was the chief instrument of the decay and eventual disaster of the latter. This was the core of his philosophy, since Hitler, unlike most other racists, was an anti-Semite first, and a racist only second. He believed that, had it not been for Jewish influences, the Western democracies would not have declared war on him in 1939. He consequently decided that even if he couldn't win this war he would accomplish the elimination of the Jews from Europe. His obedient cohorts, with the aid of certain less disciplined but more enthusiastic Eastern European auxiliaries, succeeded in liquidating a little less than half of all of the Jews of Europe. Still the ultimate result of this was something unprecedented in the extraordinary history of this extraordinary people, something that was also without precedent in the history of Europe, indeed, of Western civilization. By 1950 most of the Jews of the world lived in the Western, not in the Eastern Hemisphere, in the lands of the New World, not in those of the Old.

Most of them were citizens of the two Superpowers. In the United States they were first-class citizens; indeed, they rose to dominate most of American intellectual and cultural life, with remarkably little opposition from the good-natured people of the United States. In the Soviet Union where an externally disguised but nevertheless prevalent official anti-Semitism corresponded with the vile popular prejudices against them, Jews were, for all practical purposes, second-class citizens, full assimilation as well as emigration having been largely closed to them. The third largest conglomeration of Jews in the world, in the new, proud and self-assertive state of Israel, had to fend and fight for themselves, surrounded as they were by a large group of hostile Arab peoples. Even there the erosion of traditional religion went on. The typical Jew of the late twentieth century may not have been an atheist but he was probably an agnostic. On the other hand, the more than century-old process of his assimilation was coming to an end. Few Jews, after 1950, were attracted to Christianity. Indeed, some of them were beginning to assert their Jewish identities, trying to transmute their Jewishness into a positive and recognizable element of their consciousness. Whether this was yet another last attempt to come to terms with oneself at the end of the Age of Reason or whether it suggested the beginning of a new search for faith was difficult to tell.

At any rate, Nietzsche was right: the history of Western civilization of the last one hundred years could not be understood without considering the presence of Jews and the contributions of Jewish prophets such as Marx or Freud in our midst. But Hitler was not only wrong because of his evil deeds; he, and other anti-Semites, were most probably wrong, too, in their belief that the Jewish spirit was the fatal infection, that these Jewish influences were the most powerful solvents of Western civilization and morality: for this belief rested on the assumption that except for the influx of Jews and the pervasiveness of their spirit the nations of the white race would have remained full of health and Christian in spirit. This was not much more than an illusion. Still it is unarguable that the last phase of the Modern Age corresponded with the rapid rise of Jews in the world—which is probably why few of them could liberate their restless and powerful minds from its intellectual categories: for men such as Freud and Einstein were revolutionary thinkers only in a superficial sense, their minds belonged in the nineteenth not in the twentieth century, they were the last of the positivists.

An Age of Reason succeeded an Age of Faith; faith in reason replaced the faith in faith; faith in man was the promise that followed faith in God. But now when the Age of Reason is gone, when faith in reason is broken up, when faith in man has collapsed, what now? Are we on the threshold of another Age of Faith? Yes: and no.

Yes: because there is a strong fideistic*—fideistic rather than religious—element in the new and pervasive cults of young people, for one thing. They are groping for a new faith, ready to believe almost anything that seems wholly new. There is not much that is good in these primitive, irrational and hallucinatory aspirations for spirituality. The very fact that they are so widespread in the United States suggests both the social superficiality of certain American religious traditions and the fatal attraction of savagery that may be the curse left by the Indians on this most prosperous land. The interest in Oriental forms of religions, together with the cult of drugs, reflects a tendency to fatalism and to unreason that go not only against the cult of reason but against the very grain of Western Christianity and of European humanism. After all is said, fatalism and determinism are but two sides of the same coin. Both of them deny, explicitly, the existence of free will, the notion that men are free moral agents, responsible for their acts, which, after all, was the fundament of our morality and civilization. They signify a devolution, not an evolution, of consciousness, a regression toward primitivism, since both determinism and fatalism teach us that man, including his senses, is a product of outside impulses and forces. The IBM engineer and the hippie have boxed themselves into the same box, where they are rather uncomfortably together, having left little or no room for imagination.†

* Fideism: the emphasis of faith over all other elements of belief (hope and charity). This is typical of many Oriental religions but not of the West where it is a heresy, though no doubt often dominant in popular religious attitudes.
† The sense-hallucinatory practices induced by drugs have nothing to do with the cultivation of imagination: for imagination is nourished by more-or-less conscious sources from our personal past, whereas hallucination is the very

Still the signs for the groping for a new faith are inescapable. Yet this should be no source of comfort, as it wasn't even for Belloc, surely an ardent believer, who wrote in 1924, the year when both Wilson and Lenin died: "What I think will spring out of the new filth is a new religion. I think that there will arise in whatever parts of Christendom remain, say, 200 years hence . . . some simplified, odd, strong code of new habit, comparable to the sudden code of habit which Arabia constructed on the ruins of Christian doctrine in the East . . . a new religion, because human society cannot live on air. . . . This conception of a new religion (and, therefore, an evil one) arising out of the rottenness of the grave of truth, seems today at once fantastic and unpleasant. Unpleasant I admit it is; fantastic I do not believe it to be."*

There exist other signs, too. By 1970 the cold and rigid atheism of the cast-iron materialists of the turn of the century is dead. The hatred and the contempt for the clergy, too, have died away. Perhaps this is because the clergy are no longer powerful. But there may be more to this: the contemporary criticism of the churches, including of the Pope, for their relative failures in not having spoken or acted clearly enough during the last world war, is not a mark of indifference or even of contempt: it is a sign, rather, of high expectations. The present generation cannot comprehend the inaction of churchmen, they say they would have expected more of them. . . .

But here we arrive at a most important point. This kind of dissatisfaction concerns itself with the worldly function of the churches, with their failures of not having fought enough against

---

opposite of memory: oriented toward a nonexistent future, it wishes to blot out personal reality, unlike memory which is inspired by the deepening of it. Dependent upon external stimulants, hallucination is fundamentally passive, whereas imagination is fundamentally active.

* More than ten years ago I wrote: "I, for one, am often tempted to see in our times many symptoms suggesting the eventual probability of a rapid, and sometimes brutal, transition from an age of reason to an age of faith—by which I mean not at all a return to traditional Christian religiosities but an increasing willingness, by masses of people, to believe, if necessary, at the expense of thinking: perhaps the inescapable ultimate consequence of our interregnal condition of moral and cultural chaos."

injustice. The churches and the religions of the Western world have become extremely sensitive in this regard. This is certainly true of most Protestant churches, while the spirit of the Vatican Council and of Roman Catholicism in the 1960's, too, has been suffused by the vocal insistence of some priests and nuns and theologians to join the first ranks in the world fight against injustice. This may be a not unreasonable adjustment of one's tasks in the short run: but I believe that it is a catastrophic adjustment of sights in the long run. Our world has come to the edge of disaster precisely because of its preoccupation with justice, indeed, often at the expense of truth. It is arguable, reasonably arguable, that there is less injustice in this world than a century ago. Only a vile idiot would argue that there is less untruth. We are threatened not by the absence of justice, we are threatened by the fantastic prevalence of untruth. Our main task ought to be the reduction of untruth, first of all—a task which should have been congenial to intellectuals who, however, failed in this even more than had the worst of corrupt clerics. Of justice and truth the second is of the higher order. Truth responds to a deeper human need than does justice. A man can live with injustice a long time, indeed, that is the human condition: but he cannot long live with untruth. The pursuit of justice can be a terrible thing, it can lay the world to waste—which is perhaps the deepest predicament of American history.

Thus we might not pass into another Age of Faith, at least not for a while. This false priority preoccupies us; we attempt to satisfy our consciences with the thin gruel of worldly justice, limited and rather hopeless as it is. For this preoccupation with justice is often only a reflection of the fear of encountering injustice. Behind it looms the terrible predicament of modern man, his fear of death, which paradoxically, helps to propel him toward death. I am not arguing in religious terms; I am not appealing to the traditional specter of consolation which the belief in immortality has provided. For most of my readers are not believers; moreover, the image of this consolation can be exaggerated in retrospect. Anyone with more than a superficial knowledge of the Middle Ages will know how strong and pervasive was the fear of death then, all of the belief in immortality and the brutishness of daily life notwithstanding. At the end of the Modern Age, too, our grim preoccupation with life is but the reflection of our fear before the specter of death, in more than one way now.

The mutation of morality 16

How the emancipation of women has led to the pursuit of their degradation.

During the Middle Ages morality was not separable from religion. This inseparability lasted for a long time. Eventually morality survived the disappearance of religion, especially in certain Protestant nations. During the Second World War, for example, peoples among whom practitioners of religion were now a very small minority (Scandinavians, English) behaved better than many others among whom a far larger proportion were regular churchgoers, not to speak of Germans and Austrians on whom certain pagan and tribal appeals had a strong hold. This enduring decency of the English-speaking and also of other northwestern European peoples was not, however, the result of the kind of atheistic humanism that existed elsewhere in Europe, the virtues of which intellectuals had preached, believing that this higher kind of man-made morality would simply succeed the disappearance of Christianity. There is reason to believe that the relatively moral behavior of the English, for example, was the, often unconscious, result of tradition rather than of cerebration, that there remains to this day a deep religious undercurrent in the consciousness of these people who were, after all, only superficially affected by the intellectual categories of a Cult of Reason.

Still at the time of this writing this is scant consolation. The kind of moral consciousness that had its origins in a religious upbringing —whether in the life of peoples or in the life of a single person— may survive the decay of religious belief for a surprisingly long time, but surely not forever. The English, the American, the Scandinavian peoples may yet have to drink the bitterest cups and swallow the dregs of despair. Moreover, the high standards of morality among these peoples were, all, effective in their civic, social, public lives: they reflected a concern with injustice, rather than with untruth. Fairness, rather than honesty, is the great English virtue. At this point I must say that in our critical situation this is no longer enough.

The great moral crisis of our time has penetrated to the innermost core of human beings; it is even more personal than it is social. The profoundest problems of morality involve, after all, what people do (and how they think) with their own selves: in other words, what people do privately (or, rather, what they think of their own acts). It is therefore that the problem of sexual, that is, of carnal morality is at the center of the moral crisis of our times; it is not merely a marginal development. The overwhelming majority of its commentators of course say (though they do not always think) the contrary. They believe that the newly found freedom in sex is only a long overdue consequence of the broader realization that the old forms of tradition and society no longer serve. They could not be more wrong.

❧

After about 1890 the bourgeois morality of the nineteenth century was breaking up. The prime result of this in the first decades of the twentieth century was what people, rather euphemistically, would call the emancipation of women. Legally, politically, socially, women were now to enjoy all of those privileges that had been, by and large, the monopoly of men. Some of these reforms were overdue and reasonable. Most of their results were extremely confusing since they involved ultimately not so much the legal or the social as the sexual situation of women. The earlier ideals of virginity, of chastity, of the indissolubility of marriage faded. Women would now bare their legs in public, perhaps for the first time since the fall of Rome, fifteen hundred years before. These, seemingly revolutionary, changes in mores and fashions burst forth during the half-decade after the First World War, approximately between 1919 and 1924. Compared to this the so-called fashion revolution of the Sixties amounted to little. On the other hand this revolution was not as thoroughgoing as most people believed. Women were still torn between their desire to dress and to undress. Virginity may no longer have been much of an ideal, especially in the Protestant nations: but giving birth out of wedlock was still a kind of social catastrophe, paradoxically because of the democratization of society.* Divorce was now acceptable; but the more-or-less open practice of adultery became slightly less common than before while the institutions of the mistress and the gigolo were disappearing. Most important, there was an inherent contradiction in the results of the sexual emancipation. The idea (it was a masculine idea, for this surely was not written on the countenances of Miss Pankhurst's suffragettes) of elevating women from sexual objects to sexual partners simply failed. No matter how they wriggled their clothes down to bikinis or miniskirts, girls on the beach, secretaries in offices, lonely women on vacation could not wriggle out of the feminine chrysalis of expectant passivity: they could choose in theory, not in practice; indeed, their act of choice narrowed down to refusal or consent. The cunning art of sexual choice in which women had excelled through centuries degenerated. The whole idea of sexual partnership did not get off the ground, indeed, it hardly got into bed. Women were now sexual objects more than before; they were back where they started from.

---

* As late as 1900 in many peasant villages not only of Eastern but of Central Europe illegitimate birth was not regarded as much of a social stigma: but as the social standards of these peasants rose, they acquired lower middle-class attitudes.

These are, however, serious matters. They should not be treated with frivolity. For the liberal prophecies were, as usual, wrong. Their baneful consequences abide with us. The emancipation of women has not led to a more harmonious understanding between the sexes. Prostitution has not disappeared; venereal diseases went on fluctuating; illegitimacy rose rather than fell. The free discussion of sexual matters, together with the enormous vogue of Freudian psychoanalysis, solved little; as a matter of fact hordes of men and women were now unhappy and troubled with their sexual lives. This phenomenon is of the greatest importance. For one thing, it demonstrates how the publicizing of certain acts actually stimulates their occurrence, the very opposite of what the liberal purveyors of pornography have been preaching. More important, it points to a function of causality that is still far from being adequately understood. This is that the anticipation of something may indeed be the cause of it, whereby the mechanical relationships of causes and effects are often reversed. It is certainly arguable that the principal "cause" of divorces in the twentieth century was that the categorical possibility of divorce existed, that at least one of the causes of sexual frustration was the knowledge that sexual frustration (like a "nervous breakdown") existed as an admissible, recognizable, analyzable, curable social category. Again we meet my principal theme: the increasing intrusion of mental factors into the structure of events, very much including those personal events that, according to Dr. Freud, are the results of our "deepest" drives. People speak, rightly, of the enormous hypocrisies whereby these drives had been suppressed during the Victorian era. At the same time there is not the slightest evidence that our minds are less preoccupied with sex than were those of our ancestors: the opposite is true. Our lives are inundated with sexual allusions and sexual imagery. Sexual freedom, increasing nudity, and the legalization of pornography have not made our daily lives easier: far from it.*

* Note that I did not add "uninhibited speech": for, in reality, the habitual user of obscene words is full of inhibitions. Quite apart from the condition that the habitual use of these words amounts to the cheapest kind of self-

But this massive assault of sexual imagery and suggestiveness from the outside is only one element in our condition. There is something that is more important. The present preoccupation with sexuality may reflect the recognition that sexual acts include, after all, perhaps the last residues of a mysterious privacy that no longer exists in a standardized and mechanical world. I write "sexual acts," not "the sexual act" because there seems to be occurring yet another very important mutation in the evolution of our consciousness. We are beginning to be aware that the act of coitus is not the ultimate, not the deepest, or even the acutest, kind of experience of human flesh. Let me explain what I mean. There are reasons to believe that by 1970 many people in the Western world behaved in bed differently than had their ancestors. For one thing, in 1870 people made love without saying much at all. By 1970 they were talking to each other, before and sometimes even during the sexual act—surely a sign that the intense awesomeness of it was no longer the same. Its meaning became different—therefore it *was* different. For another thing, women and wives were now told and taught that they were to reach the same peaks of sexual satisfaction that were previously supposed to have been the monopoly of their men and husbands. This was another imbecile outcome of primitive propaganda parading in the disguises of sophistication. It caused a lot of trouble, as women were told to forget that their satisfaction is of a different, though by no means less deep, nature than that of men, for a number of reasons, not all of them anatomical (while a man can use a woman as a sexual object, a woman cannot so use a man). Women would eventually recover their senses: girls would not. Last but not least, men and women were beginning to recognize some-

---

assertion, their constant employment merely fulfills a verbal (and mental) vacuum by a ready-made and, therefore, thoughtless expression. The result is a language that is not only vulgarized but impoverished.

Still the habitual employment of obscene words, as indeed of any kind of word, tells us something about the society and the people who use them. In this respect it may be worth noting how the now widespread and printable "f—— (you)" suggests not the sexual act but the contempt and the harm that one person wishes to inflict on another.

thing that Freud had missed, though his epigone Adler, who invented (or, rather, reinvented) the inferiority complex, came closer to the truth: that even more important than the actuality of the sexual act was the imaginary relationship of the partners.* Therefore the imaginations of men and of women, rebelling instinctively against the abstract notion of sexual equality, began to be attracted by different forms of degradations, by ugly variants of these two ugly words sadism and masochism. In plain English, the sexual act, which for centuries meant the ultimate goal, the full culmination of romantic desire, was now something too plain. Out of this came a mass indulgence in the practices of perversions and of degradations.

This kind of human realization is something sadly and frighteningly tragic. It corresponds to the surfeit of affluence, to the spoiled and corrupt state of our societies. At first sight all of this is nothing but the typical reaction of a sick society to the approaching end of the world. This is largely true: but there is also something more to this than the exaggerated reactions of anti-Puritanism or than the excrescences of idle minds consumed with boredom. It reflects, too, an expansion—or, rather, the wish for an expansion—of the imagination of ordinary men and women, a mutation, perhaps a quantum jump, in the internal evolution of consciousness. It is a beginning of the spreading realization that the sexual act may not be the end of an aspiration but the beginning of a relationship. Women have always known this, in one way or another. For men Byron's immortal platitude remained valid, at least until recently: love, all of woman's world, was but part of man's existence. Going through the lonely, neon-lit darkness of their days men were now discovering their enormous inner need for love. For many sensitive young men in 1970 Byron's essentially traditional and feudal apophthegm of 1810 was no longer true. In a loveless, meaningless, and untruthful world love was becoming more than a portion of their existence,

* The best thing that Freud ever wrote (late in his career) was that the sexual act meant the forming of a community of two; but he failed to explore the consequences of this: that, for example, a community is not a solution but a process, not an end but a means, it exists not through the disappearance but through an equilibrium of tensions.

more than a response to a merely transitory need. This increase in imaginative sensitivity, probably even more than the insensitive personal responsiveness of modern women, may explain at least partly the extraordinary extent of homosexuality, especially in the English-speaking countries. It became far more widespread than Lesbianism, men being more imaginative than women; for homosexuality is only rarely the result of hereditary hormonal imbalance: it is a disease not of the flesh but of the spirit, not of the body but of the imagination.

We have now entered a world where love is becoming, curiously enough, more and more necessary and even practical. Among us there exist a happy few whose internal lives will be marvelously safe from much of the terror and loneliness of the new Dark Ages. They will have discovered that love, like inspiration, cannot be conceived as a gift of the Gods, a divine breath of bliss coming from without.* They will have learned that, like inspiration, love must come from within: that, like imagination, it is a flower that must be cultivated with constancy, beyond its first bloom so that it will eventually grow into the kind of profound respect that constitutes the very dignity of human love. A little more than one hundred years ago Tolstoy (who had a Puritan and barbaric streak within him) began *Anna Karenina* with this most sentimental and philistine sentence: "Happy families are all alike; every unhappy family is unhappy in its own way." In our times the opposite is rather true. Thus some people learn that even temporary happiness is not something coming from the outside, that it is not the result of divine intervention or of body chemistry or of sexual mechanics but that it is a human creation—a minority, with sufficient inner resources, who, unlike a

---

* As late as during the eighteenth century women (very much including married women) in the very sophisticated and considerably corrupt societies of Venice, Naples, Rome considered love as a happy occurrence coming from the outside, an accident of destiny (even the English term "falling in love" faintly suggests this). French travelers to Italy were amused to record that it was the custom of these Italian ladies to closet themselves in their houses on such an occasion, refusing to receive anyone; their servants would solemnly announce: "La Signora é innamorata," "Milady has fallen in love." Our corruptions are different.

century ago, will not be pitied or superficially respected but admired and secretly envied by the most sophisticated among their neighbors because of their fidelity to their spouses and because of their loyalty to their families. (The seal of virginity, too, may rise in popular esteem as a rare thing, marking the inviolate integrity of the desirable best.) All of this will not signify a return to an older morality which was, at any rate, full of holes; it will signify, rather, another stage in the "internalization" of the human condition, in the evolution of human history which may be, after all, summed up as *the slow spiritualization of the flesh.*

The growing recognition that our imaginative needs are passing beyond the act of coitus *in depth* as well as *in time* is part of this evolution.* By *depth* I mean recognition of the condition that the momentary carnal union of two persons is but another step to a further deepening of their relationship; by *time* I mean the recognition that the sexual act may not be the end but the beginning of something in their lives, the quality of which depends on its endurance as much as its endurance depends upon its quality.

Let us not be carried away with high hopes! Such people now exist, the salt of the earth; they will be living among us until the end of time. How much their example will mean to others is quite another question. For meanwhile the dissatisfied frenzy of the sexual preoccupation of minds goes on. Leaving all moralizing aside, it does not take much insight to discover in the crowding manifestations of this frenzy, very much including its fascination with degradations, not merely the despair of millions of hopeless and lonely people but the existence of a death-wish of an entire civilization. I am not indulging in apocalyptic theologizing. I am pointing at the desire to fuse the moment of the culmination of carnal pleasure and the moment of spiritual death into one. For women the culmination

* It is only now that many people are beginning to recognize how, for example, the acutest of carnal experiences, the erotic moment of climax, occurs not in their groins but in their minds. This recognition does not mean the thinning intellectualization of sex, it means more than that: it is part of a thickening crystallization of the evolution of human consciousness, of the slow spiritualization of the flesh.

of sexual desire has often carried with itself a sense of annihilation. That, of course, is a temporary sensation. But just as a moment of our lives may be the microcosm of our entire life, this kind of death-wish, more and more typical in contemporary aspirations of men and women in the West, may reflect the death-wish of its peoples.* Propagated under the false and superficial auspices of sexual libera-tion, this now spreads like an oil-slick over millions of formerly untouched lives, besmirching and covering large areas of the con-sciousness of peoples. The desire to be raped and overwhelmed by brute primitive force from the outside becomes the goal of the pursuit of pleasure, especially for people who no longer trust, or even know, their own capacity of being able to create their own happiness. Carnally speaking—or, rather, *thinking*—far more people in this world wish to be dominated than to dominate. This is where the half-baked idea of the legalized "pursuit of happiness"—with all the respect due to the moderate wisdom of the American Founding Fathers, perhaps the emptiest phrase ever written in a declaration of *independence!*—has eventually led us.

* This is probably why pornographic literature and pornographic spectacles are now full of images of a white woman submitting to her brutal domination by Negro men, and virtually never with the reverse image of a white man raping a Negro woman. (In the days of slavery this was different: the imagery of lust, involving the domination of one person by another, was sustained by the condition that the Negro girls abused by their white masters were *slaves*.)

III

BEGINNING

The New Dark Ages

17

How, at the end of an age, some of its beginnings appear again.

The end and the beginning of life are two extreme conditions. Their symptoms are similar in some ways. As senility progresses, more and more of its symptoms resemble the helplessness of infancy. At two separate points of their lives an old man and a child may be equally feeble, physically speaking, but there is one great difference: the weak body of the child contains the element of his potential strength, the weak body of the old man no longer does. The feebleness of mind, too, in a state of advanced senility may resemble the feebleness of the mental operations of infancy: but the old man's potentiality for knowing, unlike his potentiality for doing things, is actually greater than that of the child's because of the very large accumulation of his memories. On the other hand an old man may no longer want to activate many of his memories, especially the more recent ones: his memory is more and more drawn toward his childhood, a phenomenon observable in many old people who remember accurate details of their early years that they seem not to have recalled before.

179

We ought not apply biological rules to civilizations: this is where Spengler went wrong. Still there exist similarities, though not analogies, between the history of a single human being and the history of a human aggregation. A civilization, too, has its youth and its old age, and it shows symptoms that may be described in human terms. Thus a civilization, in its last stages of decay, shows symptoms of primitivism and of infantilism which reappear from within, tendencies of its early rude childhood. We do not know much about this, principally because we know more about historical decay than about historical infancy. (We know nothing about the birth, and very little about the infant phase of Rome, for example: we know much more about its decline and fall.) Yet we know some things about the birth and infancy of our, Western or European, civilization during the Dark and later in the Middle Ages. We have a frail basis for some comparisons.

We are, moreover, beginning to recognize the appearance of symptoms of its decay. Multiplying before our very eyes are astonishing compounds of things very old and very new, of primitiveness and sophistication. Even in these times of instant, superficial, parajournalistic history it is too early to write this history—a history not of the ending of the Modern Age but of the beginning of something new. One may, however, detect some of its elements, one of which is the attraction for certain medieval forms of thought in the minds of millions during the late stage of the Modern Age.

❧

It would seem that the further away we were from the Middle Ages the more the Middle Ages were dead and buried in our minds. This has not been so. The Middle Ages had, on the whole, a better reputation during the nineteenth than during the eighteenth century; more significantly, they were also more *interesting* for many people. This had much to do with the rediscovery of History by the Romantic movement. Still the adjectives "dark" and "medieval" remained largely pejorative; indeed, they were synonymous in the minds of many people, well into the twentieth century.

There came, then, a chapter in the history of the twentieth century, full of significance: a revolt against the bourgeois spirit and against the institutions of the Modern Age; a mass movement, yet one which came from the "Right" rather than from the "Left." This movement, usually called the "Fascist" period, lasted from about 1920 to 1945. (Its accepted name has been inaccurate and misleading: for "Fascism" was an Italian thing, whereas this trans-European movement was at least as German as it was Italian in its inspiration. Mussolini wanted to re-create new Renaissance attitudes, not medieval ones.) What happened in Europe after 1920 was, in any event, a reaction against the ideas of the Enlightenment, of the French Revolution, of the ideology of the Modern Age. This reaction was both revolutionary and conservative, conservatives and Nazis were involved in it until they parted company; it was shared by millions who knew something of the past and by others who were brutal futurists; it was historical and anti-historical at the same time.

Much of the foregoing is applicable to the mind of Hitler who, for a moment, in 1940, seemed to have triumphed over Europe, somewhat like a new Diocletian. A few days before the fall of Paris, Reynaud, the little, intelligent, dapper bourgeois Premier of France, broadcast to his people: if Hitler wins this war, he said, "it would be the Middle Ages again, but not illuminated by the mercy of Christ." This was largely correct, though it did not help Reynaud a bit. In 1940 certain aspects of the Middle Ages had a strong appeal for millions of people, not only for the triumphant Germans but also for many of their enemies. For a moment it seemed that the swift German victory over France meant a return, politically speaking, to the days of the Holy German–Roman Empire, a Europe dominated by Germans, North Italians, Spaniards, with England excluded from Europe, France divided, or reduced to her shape before 1500, the Netherlands, Artois, Flanders, perhaps even a reconstituted Burgundy incorporated into the empire. But there was more to this than political shapes. In 1940 Du Moulin de Labarthète, a sensitive observer of the early Vichy period, recorded in his memoirs "this kind of return to the Middle Ages, this 'instinctive

medievalization,' something that Berdyaev* hasn't foreseen at all."
In 1940 the defeat of France seemed to have marked the end of the
entire era of bourgeois civilization: of the preponderance of Western over Central Europe, of parliamentary liberalism, of finance
capitalism, of the Age of Reason, of France; all of this seemed to
have come to an end. A Europe pullulating with German *Lands-
knechten*, with mercenary soldiers in the service of an imperial
ideology, it signaled something of a new order, this German-Spanish
Europe with Jews restricted, Freemasonry disappearing, capitalism
replaced by a new social order, corporations and guilds and the
family exalted anew as the basic unit of society—it was reminiscent
of a Europe around 1500, before the Modern Age began.

This reappearance of the Middle Ages did not last. It did not
survive the Germans' defeat; it did not even survive the high noon
of their triumphs. For one thing, we have seen that the medieval
inspiration was alien to some of Hitler's allies, including Mussolini
and other Fascists. More significantly, the medieval side was but
one facet of Hitler's mind, albeit an important one. Widespread in
the attitudes of the Nazi hierarchy was a kind of nihilistic egotism,
super-modern and pagan-primitive at the same time. The medieval
adjective would not fit this attitude, no matter how broad and
superficial its application might be.

On June 18, 1940, on that crucial day in the history of the twentieth century, Churchill's phraseology may have been not only more
inspiring but more correct than Reynaud's. Churchill evoked the
specter, not of a return to the Middle Ages, but of a lurch into the
Dark Ages. If we fail, he said, "then the whole world, including the
United States, including all that we have known and cared for, will
sink into the abyss of a new Dark Age, made more sinister, and
perhaps more protracted, by the lights of perverted science."

❖

There was, and there still is, another medieval element in the
making and in the unmaking of the modern world. This is to be

---

* This philosopher, whose neo-Christian writings in the 1930's enjoyed a
certain reputation, contrasted the shining virtues of the Middle Ages with the
gloomy decay of the bourgeois spirit; see below, p. 193.

found in the United States. Millions of people came to America straight from medieval parts and portions of Europe; they became American before (and, sometimes, without) becoming modern, enlightened, bourgeois. There are Americans who have medieval faces, notwithstanding their modern glasses and teeth. The faces of the grim couple portrayed in Grant Wood's archetypal antimedieval picture, "American Gothic," are definitely German, not Anglo-Saxon. But among the Anglo-Saxons, too, the Puritans, all of their middle-classness, all of their incipient capitalism notwithstanding, were not bourgeois people. In many important ways their minds were medieval minds. They hankered after many of the patterns of thought of the Middle Ages, and even for some of the institutions of the Middle Ages. Their revolt was largely a revolt against the spirit of the Renaissance, in more than one sense. On the other hand this attraction for the Middle Ages was dominant only in one part of their minds, in the other half of which they were progressives, not reactionaries. In 1705 the city fathers in Philadelphia outlawed fornication, simply and squarely, which was a rather medieval thing to do—and added a clause that the innocent spouses of the guilty parties had the right to sue for divorce, something that was super-modern, very American, by no means typically European or bourgeois. This kind of dualism has marked many American aspirations and institutions from the beginning, perhaps until the present day.

American religiousness had a medieval facet throughout its history. It was reflected in the fundamentalism of many American Protestants; it showed in the arguments of William Jennings Bryan at the Tennessee "monkey trial" in 1925, whose mind was a compound of the medieval and of the modern American, full of the convictions of a John Hampden and of a Henry Ford. Most of the attitudes of American Catholicism, too, have been far more Byzantine than Jansenist.* In 1955 one of my freshmen wrote: "America is

* The attribution of "Jansenism" to the Irish influence in American Catholicism is a shibboleth, almost entirely devoid of sense and meaning. It is true that many of the refugee Irish and English seminarians in the seventeenth century were trained in northern French seminaries where the teaching was often Jansenist. But those priests stayed in France, few of them returned to Ireland, even fewer came to America. The Jansenist tradition, in France, was

closer to the middle ages because we kept our religion while the Europeans are not really religious"—a not untypical assertion by a student generation among whom I found another freshman who thought that "Western civilization" meant civilization west of the Mississippi. In 1957, when the first American space rocket was launched, priests blessed a St. Christopher medal which was inserted in its tip; and it was recorded that some of the mechanics said rosaries in order to stop gremlins from causing trouble with the complicated engines. This happened in the same year when the American Institute of Management had completed a "management audit" of the Catholic Church, giving it an *A* rating for "management efficiency," a computed grade of 88, whereby the entire Roman Catholic Church was rated only slightly below the Standard Oil Company of New Jersey: the American Catholic press greeted this news with considerable satisfaction. Elements of medieval populism that had not been seen in Europe for centuries lived on in the United States. Where else in the world would people speak with such familiar ease of "St. Pete" and "St. Joe"; where else could one see, as I once saw in the yearbook of a Catholic high school, the picture of a football player, stopping in the chapel on his way to the football field, with the caption: ". . . saying a reverent 'hello' to Christ"?

This tendency to the popularization of the sacred is something very different from the somber calculations of bourgeois religiosity; it is different, too, from the vulgar childishness that appears sometimes in the religious processions of, say, southern Italy; it is primitive and complicated at the same time. There is a Byzantine streak in the super-American character. The Byzantines had summarized the classics and the New Testament to make them easier reading; one thousand years later the super-Americanized magazine editor Edward W. Bok asked Lyman Abbott for "a short and snappy life of Christ." There is a medieval facet to American economic life: we have seen, in an earlier chapter, that whereas in a typical capitalist

---

characterized by an extreme kind of intellectual scrupulosity, something that was (and is) not very characteristic of the American Catholic clergy.

society income and social function depended on property, in the United States property depended increasingly on income which, in turn, issued from the reward of social functions. Horace Greeley spoke of our "Gothic race," with its "resistless tendency . . . toward the sand of the mighty Pacific sea." He meant the Northern masses but there was a Gothic facet to the American South, too, evident in the forms of their superstitions and of their steamboats, in the dark sweetness of their potions as well as in their ceremonies, including the Byzantine-medieval Klan, with its penitential oaths and hoods, with its Gothic cult of the letter "K," Klans, Kliglapps, klaverns, Kleagles. Even more Gothic than the neo-Gothic cathedrals financed by businessmen in the nineteenth century were their cathedrals of commerce, their Gothic iron factory halls, the cupolas of their mansions, their fascination by the mastodon and by the spirit of Barnum. There is a medieval facet to the American Constitution, whose Congress is in many ways more like a medieval assembly than it is like a bourgeois parliament, the speeches and the debates on its floor being less important than are the practices of its committees and of their investigations: judicial bodies, as in the Middle Ages, having the power of hauling people before them to "testify." There are many other medieval facets of American politics: consider but the Breughelesque spirit of the party conventions, with their overwhelming imperative to shout, in the end, a proclamation of unanimity. There is a medieval facet to the American presidency: for the President, perhaps especially in the twentieth century, is something like an elected monarch; and there is ample evidence suggesting the inclinations of millions of Americans toward an elective monarchy of a particular family or a clan. There is a medieval streak in American conformity and also in certain social inclinations, in a country where more than half of its emancipated womanhood marry before they are twenty-one years old. The American popular imagery is full of medieval symbols: consider the names of American gangs in one single city, where these were recorded in 1958: Chaplains, Bishops, Dukes, Templars, Scorpions, Crusaders, Lords, Demons, Dragons. Demons and Dragons have, in any event, a powerful hold on the American popular imagination.

Aren't Superman and Batman, after all, super-modern versions of medieval archangels?

In one very important way these medieval characteristics of the American spirit are but the results of what happens to extremes: when people draw the extreme consequences of an idea they are bound to arrive at its very opposite. There are many Americans who, having drawn some of the extreme consequences of the materialist categories of the Age of Reason, arrive at their cultivation of a faith. There was, in any event, a kind of unrestrained spiritualism on the bottom of the American mind from the beginning. But what I am arguing is not that America "remained" to some extent medieval from its very beginnings; my argument is that this peculiar coexistence of medieval with super-modern habits of mind has been typically American; and now I am no longer speaking of its compounds but of the condition of this kind of coexistence. For Americans have been, generally speaking, both unable and unwilling to recognize the peculiar coexistence of their, often evidently contradictory, mental categories—*and this kind of inability was in itself a medieval habit of mind.* "The Middle Ages were the era of the split mind par excellence," wrote Arthur Koestler in *The Sleepwalkers;* more accurately, and perhaps more profoundly, C. Delisle Burns wrote in *The First Europe:* "The medieval world was unwilling to face the fact [I would have written "condition"] that contradictory statements could be found in equally authoritative sources."* Probably even the great Jakob Burckhardt was, for once, wrong when he said that *all* proponents of leveling, and of enforced equality, were natural enemies of the Middle Ages.† What Huizinga wrote about the medieval mind is far more applicable, indeed, it is applicable with astonishing accuracy, to the modern American mind. "A too systematic idealism," Huizinga wrote, ". . . gives a certain rigidity to the conception of the world . . . men disregarded the individual qualities and fine distinctions of things, deliberately and of set purpose, in order always to bring them

---

* *The First Europe* (London, 1947), p. 667.
† *Historische Fragmente* (Stuttgart, 1957), p. 38.

under some general principle. . . . What is important is the impersonal. The mind is not in search of individual realities, but of
models, examples, norms." "There is in the Middle Ages a tendency
to ascribe a sort of substantiality to abstract concepts."* All of this is
as true of the Puritan divine as it is of the Professor of Sociology, of
Disneyland as well as of the State Department, of Superman as of
the Public Relations man. It was surely true of the American national philosophy of anti-Communism as late as in the 1950's, on
every level of its manifestations.

Still one facet of a people does not amount to a full profile.
During the Middle Ages "every notion concerning the world or life
had its fixed place in a vast hierarchic system of ideas, in which it is
linked with ideas of a higher and more general order, on which it
depends like a vassal on his lord. . . ." There is nothing American
in this, not at all.

※

A German victory in 1940 would have brought back, at least
temporarily, something resembling the late Middle Ages. The
United States would not have been unaffected by this, as its people
were indeed affected by the attractions of the pseudo-religious faith
of anti-Communism a decade later. One can detect something of
this kind of recurrence elsewhere, too. The Bolshevik Revolution has
been an enormous lurch for Russia—backward, for in many ways
Lenin and his cohorts forced her back to her state before Peter the
Great. By 1940 even this resemblance ceased: evidently the reversion went further back; for the tyranny of Stalin was reminiscent of
the tyranny of Ivan the Terrible, not of Peter the Great. With the
end of their empires the Spanish, the Dutch, the British, the French,
too, came back to their places in Europe where they had been four
or five hundred years ago—profound dislocations which were not
merely external in their import and in their consequences.

But to stretch this argument further would be misleading. Those
conservatives, in Europe or in America, who were hoping for some

* *The Waning of the Middle Ages* (New York, 1956), pp. 215–216, 218.

kind of return to an Age of Faith, some kind of re-medievalization, in order to save what they (often quite unhistorically) con-
strued as the traditional order of Western civilization, failed to see
that the decay was more advanced than that. They proceeded from
the illusory assumption that their peoples were still Christian *au
fond,* deep down. But the peoples were not interested. Many things,
especially after 1960, showed a reversion to barbarism. What were
reappearing were some of the tendencies and habits of the Dark
Ages, not the institutions of the Middle Ages. Tribal gang warfare,
widespread nomadism, the abandoning of the cities, sexual anarchy,
drug culture, the meaninglessness of letters, Dragons, Demons,
finally the incipient breakdown not only of law and of order but of
many of the comforts and services of material civilization—these
things were reminiscent not of medieval Europe but of the Dark
Ages. Within the Catholic Church, too, the reformers propagated no
longer re-medievalization (which used to be their stock in trade),
they rediscovered the virtues of the early Christians—without having given this much thought at all; for what the harsh and often
cruel puritanism of a Tertullian or of an Orosius has to offer to
these people is difficult to imagine.

By 1970 Western civilization was in a much more advanced stage
of decay than in 1940. There was a latent danger in the comparabil-
ity of this condition alone, to which I referred, in passing, earlier:
the danger that soon generations might arise who may look back at
Hitler as a potential savior of civilization, deploring the event of his
defeat. We need not, however, fear a restoration of Hitlerism; and
there is still little evidence to suggest that (perhaps except for England) a new Puritan reaction might be around the corner. It is more
likely that hordes of young nomads might camp in the ruined cities
and on the ruined shores of civilization, young men and women
reminiscent of the Berserkers* and Vikings and Vandals and Goths
to whose habits and to whose appearance the more and more

---

* The Berserkers were so called because of their cultivation of a hairy and
bear-like appearance, including vestments: they were wild and unpredictable:
thence the word "berserk."

numerous forerunners of these new nomads seem to be fatefully attracted.* "They let the hair and beard grow long as soon as one has come of age." They like to dye their hair and even parts of their bodies. "None of them has home, land or business of his own." Even in times of peace they respect not the privacy and the property of the old. "They are prodigal with the goods of others, they care nothing for their own." "They are so strangely inconsistent. They love indolence, but they hate real leisure." This is Tacitus on the early Germanic tribes.

Still the transition in which we now live is full of contradictory elements. Nothing disappears completely, and few things disappear overnight. Many of the institutions, even more of the habits, and very many of the forms of thought that have grown up during the Modern Age remain with us. They have become the, sometimes fateful, mental inheritance of our children. Perhaps it is because of this continuous inheritance of an evolving consciousness that each of the great periods of transition has been shorter than the previous one: the emergence of medieval Europe lasted twice as long as its passing. Each transition is more complex than the preceding one: each, too, keeps more of the preceding age. Two hundred years after

---

* This attraction—subconscious rather than conscious—exists for things that are Nordic, all of the present anti-Nordic ideology and the cult of African and Asian things and styles notwithstanding. The defeat of Germany in 1945 did not mean the victory of the Latin or of the Southern peoples. In the anti-Puritan reaction of British and Scandinavian, Dutch and American youth there is something wild and racial in inspiration: the long lank hair, the Amazonic character of women, the emphasis on physical handsomeness and on a kind of hirsute virility reflects a tendency for something that is far from being "Leftist," intellectual, international: it is, rather, tribal, barbarian, youthful, narrow-minded and proud. It reflects the appetite for a new roving Vikingism. (In America not the square Prussian crew cut of the Fifties but phenomena such as the Hell's Angels and of the Iron Crosses worn by the hordes of surfers are symptomatic of the rise of barbarian Vikingism in the West.) The Jews in Israel, too, incorporated national and military attitudes whose styles are German and English. The violent self-assertion of Negroes in the United States, too—all of the fads of African hair styles, etc., notwithstanding—are at least partially Northern in character. The Southern Negro was soft and sweet in character, music, diction. The Detroit and New York Negro, in being rude, destructive, cunning and violent, tries to assert himself by showing that he is capable of the violence of the Nordic white.

the fall of Rome, around 700, Roman beliefs and habits had largely disappeared, or they survived only in transformed and artificial forms. Two hundred years after the discovery of America, around 1700, there were still many medieval institutions, habits, forms of thought that had been current in Europe in 1450. There is reason to hope that the New Dark Ages may not last hundreds of years; and there is reason to believe that their darkness will not be uniform.

The bourgeois interior

Why the most maligned characteristic of the Modern Age may yet be seen as its most precious asset.

The Modern Age, or Modern History, are now misnomers. They were farsighted misnomers centuries ago, when they were coined and put into intellectual currency by our ancestors who were overoptimistic in this regard; they took the growing and sprouting landscape of new trees for a perennial forest opening up around them. They are shortsighted misnomers now. Sometime in the future the now closing period of history will receive another name. This giving of names is the kind of intellectual exercise that ought not preoccupy us at this time. Yet I must say something about a principal characteristic of this so-called Modern Age that is still with us, because of its protean manifestations, many of which will, I am sure, survive into the New Dark Ages or whatever comes next.

I am thinking of the bourgeois spirit. In writing about this I must break through an amorphous intellectual obstacle. "Bourgeois" and "bourgeoisie" are not English words. (From my experience with examination papers I suspect that probably the majority of the three hundred million people whose native language is English cannot spell them without one mistake or two.) The reason for this is that the phenomenon of a bourgeoisie was largely peculiar to the continent of Europe. In England and in the United States large middle classes have existed: and the term "bourgeois" has been considered as if it were their French equivalent. But this virtual equation of bourgeois and middle class has been wrong. They were not, and are not, the same things. Every society has a class that is situated in the middle, between the upper and the lower classes. Not every society had, or has, a bourgeoisie. The existence of a middle class is a universal, a sociological phenomenon. The existence of the bourgeois, on the other hand, has been a particular phenomenon, a historical reality.

The difficulties of the word "bourgeois" have been compounded by its reputation. For more than a century now it has been a bad word: it suggested not only "middle-class" but also "unimaginative," "pedestrian," "philistine." There was a romantic and an aesthetic element in this attribution of vileness to the bourgeois. The self-professed artist, sometime after 1820, especially in France, claimed to be an aristocrat of the spirit, and even the brummagem aristocracy of the bohemians professed to be the very antipole of the bourgeoisie. Ridiculed by aristocrats as well as by radicals, during the nineteenth century the bourgeois were hated by the extreme Right and Left alike.

This nineteenth-century, sometimes snobbish, and later Marxist, usage of the term was, in reality, narrow and inaccurate. Marx equated, in effect, the bourgeois with the capitalist spirit. He was wrong. Anti-Marxists, such as the German social thinker Werner Sombart in his monumental *Der Bourgeois* (1911), made the same mistake, from a different angle. They did not consider sufficiently that one could be a bourgeois without being a capitalist which was true of many people in the rising professions; or that, conversely, one could be a capitalist without being a bourgeois; that in many instances rich people were excluded from the ranks of the bourgeois for all kinds of reasons. In America Charles A. Beard wrote that the United States has only one large class, "the petty bourgeoisie—despite proletarian and plutocratic elements which cannot come under that classification . . . the American ideal most widely expressed is the *embourgeoisement* of the whole society—a universality of comfort, convenience, security, leisure, standard possessions of food, clothing and shelter." Standard possessions of food, clothing and shelter? These are middle-class aspirations, not bourgeois ones. The philosopher Berdyaev, in *The Bourgeois Mind* (1934), again equated the middle class with the bourgeois: the bourgeois mind, he wrote, is both materialist and smug, "self-satisfaction is one of his characteristic traits." This is nearly nonsense. The principal criticisms one might level against the bourgeois mind are its caution, its calculation, its cowardice, its seeking refuge in conformism: the kind of thoughtless self-satisfaction of which Berdyaev writes was more characteristic of the European aristocracies than of the bourgeoisie.

After the Second World War certain discriminating writers, especially in France, recognized that the meaning of "bourgeois" was not so simple, after all. Pierre Gaxotte suggested, in passing, that it meant something more than a social class.* In one of his aphoristic essays Jean Dutourd had some rather intelligent things to say about the term "bourgeois": "It is one of those ambiguous and inconstant terms that change at every turn of history. In spite of Molière's mockeries that anticipate Flaubert's, the word means something different at the time of the Fronde and under Louis XV, during the reign of Robespierre and of Napoleon III, for the Communards of 1871 and for the surrealists under the reign of André Breton. . . ." "Flaubert himself, so violently anti-bourgeois, heartily approved the suppression of the Commune, regretting only that too few of the workers had been executed. . . ." "In our days the bourgeois have abdicated. In fact the bourgeois democracies of the second half of the twentieth century are socialists. To apply their old discredited name to them is nothing but hypocritical propaganda."† In a thoughtful book, *Métamorphose du bourgeois,* Professor Jacques

---

* In his *Histoire des Français,* esp. Vol. II (1951).
† Dutourd, *Le fond et la forme,* I (Paris, 1958), 22–25.

Ellul has tried to come to terms with this fluidity of meaning. "The bourgeois is Proteus himself," he writes. "A grotesque weakling and a man of iron, an imbecile and a powerful executive, a cold-hearted egotist and a founder of philanthropies, a Milquetoast and an adventurer, a lecher and a family man. . . . who is the bourgeois?"* The question evokes the most extreme and contradictory answers. "Was there ever an enterprise greater than the Industrial Revolution? . . . Strangely enough, we admire that revolution and we despise the bourgeois who invented it and put it into effect."† He goes to a fashionable contemporary dictionary where he finds that "bourgeois," "thinking bourgeois," "seeming bourgeois" is defined as "vulgar." This dictionary (the *Robert*) uses certain selective citations to buttress its point. Flaubert: "I call a bourgeois anyone who thinks low" (". . . quiconque pense bassement.") Gide: ". . . there are bourgeois workers and bourgeois nobles. I recognize the bourgeois not by his habits and not by his social level but by the level of his thinking. The bourgeois . . . hates everything that he cannot understand." This is not much help.

Professor Ellul is quite right when he criticizes some of these "definitions." He, too, insists that the institution of private property is not necessarily characteristic of the bourgeoisie. Yet his book, too, is unsatisfactory on an important point. Obsessed as he is with the protean and changing forms of the "bourgeois," Ellul in effect equates him throughout with "modern man."

Bourgeois: modern. Let me now try to sort out what I have in mind.

※

Instead of the Modern Age we *could* speak of the Bourgeois Age. Those who talk of the age of aristocracy before the First World War, or before the War of American Independence, do not know what they are talking about. The aristocracies may have kept their social, and in certain countries their political leadership, but by the

---

* (Paris, 1967), p. 10.
† *Ibid.*, p. 12.

eighteenth century in most of Europe the prevailing ways of thought were bourgeois. A sociography of the principal thinkers, writers, artists, poets, inventors of the last three hundred years would show that their vast majority came from a bourgeois background—no matter how many of them may have attacked the bourgeoisie.

The mathematicability of reality, the cult of reason, free trade, liberalism, the abolition of slavery, of censorship, the contractual idea of the state, constitutionalism, individualism, socialism, nationalism, internationalism—these were not aristocratic ideas. For bourgeois means something more than a social class: it means certain rights and privileges, certain aspirations, a certain way of thinking even more than of living. Note that I write "ways of thinking" rather than "frames of mind": for the bourgeois standards and habits of thought were constantly changing; and what was characteristic of them was not their fixity *but the way in which they have been changing*. (Had the aristocracies had their way there would have been little change.) The bourgeois spirit—and this is its least admirable characteristic—has been too conformist, not sufficiently independent. The bourgeoisie tried to conform to the powers that prevailed. With a few inspiring exceptions the European aristocracies during the entire Modern Age have done the same: they, perhaps even more than the aspiring bourgeoisie, knew how to adapt themselves to new rulers, new powers, new times; they did this a trifle more gracefully than most of the bourgeois: that was all.

There was a difference nonetheless. The aristocracies would conform indifferently. The bourgeois would conform with a kind of nervous energy. The behavior of the former conformed more than had their minds. The minds of the latter conformed as much as had their behavior. (The idea-mongering philosophers and writers of the nineteenth century, including Dostoevsky, missed this: obsessed with their ideological discovery of what ideas can do to men they overlooked the more complex problem of what men can do to ideas.)

The Middle Ages were marked by the domination of aristocracies: but during the Modern Age democracy was not yet dominant. True, the ideas of popular government became more current
and finally respectable: but democratic standards were not wholly
translated into practice, not even in the English-speaking nations,
until literally our very times. Typical of the bourgeois era was the
coexistence of democratic ideas with aristocratic standards. The half-
thousand years from about 1450 to 1950 were no longer an age of
aristocracy and not yet that of democracy: in many places of the
Western world it would not be altogether wrong to designate them
as the Bourgeois Age.

❖

Free citizens: this was the original aspiration of a bourgeoisie
whose emergence, in Europe, long preceded that of capitalism. "The
first mention of the word [bourgeois] occurs in France in 1007"
(Henri Pirenne). It had nothing to do with capital: it had very
much to do with the city. "Bourgeois," "Bürger," "burgher," "bor-
ghese" meant city dweller. For the European city as it grew during
the Middle Ages was different from the Greek *polis* and the Roman
urbs as well as from the modern American city. It had walls which
provided for security. They made for a sharp physical separation of
the city from the surrounding countryside. This lasted for hundreds
of years. There was a definite distinction of citizen from country-
man. It was a privilege to belong to the community of the city.
"Stadtluft macht frei," some Germans were wont to say: the city air
makes you free. This was true at least in a metaphorical sense.
Citizenship meant a real community, not an artificial one. The
otherwise rich Russian language, for example, has no word that is
the equivalent of bourgeois: the nearest word means "city dweller,"
devoid of the implications of civic and political rights, of an urban
community, of permanence of residence. But Russian cities, with
few exceptions, had no walls separating them from the surrounding
land. The walled portion of the city, as the Kremlin in Moscow, was
there to keep the rulers apart from the rest of the people, as in
China.

In England, too, with few exceptions (and, of course, in America) cities had no walls. In the English-speaking countries the rights acquired by the gentry, by the yeomanry, by the merchants, by these developing classes in the middle of the social structure were not predominantly urban. On the other hand the controlled confluence of democracy and aristocracy was the special strength of English civilization: the social attraction of certain aristocratic standards marked the prevalence of an English kind of civility which, except perhaps for a brief period, could not be properly called bourgeois, while it was certainly patrician.

The great achievements of European civilization during the last half-thousand years were predominantly patrician in their inspiration, urbane in their manners, urban in their spirit. This kind of urban civilization, with its liberties, had little in common with those of ancient Athens or Rome and not much in common with the liberties that had been extracted by the nobility from their weak kings during the Middle Ages. This kind of "urbanization" was different, too, from the external spreading of cities with the subsequent disappearance of all distinctions between city and country, from that enormous suburbanization of everything that has set in during the twentieth century and that people who should, but don't, know better, mistakenly call the "urbanization" of the world. The monstrous conglomerations of a Tokyo or a Los Angeles are not at all urban in the traditional sense. They have much to do with the enormous swelling of a middle class: they have little to do with the bourgeois spirit. In a country such as Japan we can speak of a swelling middle class, we can even speak of the swelling of capitalism, but not of a bourgeoisie in the older European sense, just as the "Westernization" of Japan (as also of many other countries) means, simply, Americanization.

The transition from an aristocratic to a democratic era, or the increasing admixture of aristocracy with democracy, explains the bourgeois spirit only in part. The Greeks and the Romans experienced the former without ever being bourgeois. Their thinking was different from that of our closer ancestors. Their consciousness was different, as their aspirations were different. The bourgeois kind of

"urbanization" was a later phase in the evolution of human consciousness, it marked the beginning of the "internalization" of the
human condition, to which I have been referring throughout this
book, probably at the cost of irritating many of my readers with this
kind of repetition.

❖

Free, and also secure: these were marks of the bourgeois spirit.
Not for nothing did satirical draftsmen and writers depict the
bourgeois wearing a nightcap, tucking himself under a large com-
forter on a rainy or wintry night. When we think of a bourgeois
scene, we seldom think of nature outdoors; we usually think of
something that is human, comfortable, cozy. We seldom think of a
bright glittering morning; we think of an afternoon or evening. Is it
thus true that the bourgeois epoch was the long autumn afternoon
of Western civilization, following, say, the glorious dawn of Antiquity and the glorious noon of the Renaissance? This is what thinkers
such as Spengler tell us, insisting even that there were bourgeois
colors such as brown. But there is something else that Spengler did
not understand: that the increasing "interiority" of the bourgeois era
was involved with the increasing "internalization" of the human
condition in the West.

All of its spiritual aspirations notwithstanding, the medieval
civilization was strongly external, "all things in life were of a proud
or cruel publicity" (Huizinga). The bourgeois era of European
civilization, on the contrary, was marked by the internal deepening
of human consciousness of which Erasmus, Montaigne, and even
disillusioned aristocrats such as La Rochefoucauld were early prime
examples. As the exploration of the external world accelerated, at
the same time our ancestors became more and more aware of the
interior landscape of their minds.

Words such as *self-love, self-confidence, self-command, self-*
esteem, self-knowledge, self-pity; other words such as *disposition,*
character, ego, egoism, conscience, melancholy, apathy, agitation,
embarrassment, sensible, sentimental, appeared in English or

French in their modern sense only two or three hundred years ago. And as their appearance marked the emergence of something new in the minds of peoples, something new appeared, too, in their daily lives. As the self-consciousness of medieval people was spare, the interiors of their houses were bare, including the halls of nobles and of kings. The interior furniture of houses appeared together with the interior furniture of minds.

There are many potential illustrations of this. One may suffice, from the extraordinary book of our contemporary French historian Philippe Ariès, translated into English under the title *Centuries of Childhood*. He reminds us that in paintings before the end of the fifteenth century interior scenes are extremely rare.

But from that century on, they become increasingly common. The gospel-writer, hitherto placed in a timeless setting, becomes a scribe at his desk, with a quill and an erasing-knife in his hand. At first he is placed in front of an ordinary ornamental curtain, but finally he is shown in a room where there are shelves lined with books: we have come from the gospel-writer to the author in his room, to Froissart writing a dedication in a book. In the illustrations to the text of Terence in the Palace of the Doges, there are women working and spinning in their rooms with their maidservants, or lying in bed, not always by themselves. We are shown kitchens and inn rooms. Love scenes and conversations are henceforth set in the enclosed space of a room.

The theme of child-birth makes its appearance, the birth of the Virgin providing the pretext. Maidservants, old women and midwives are shown bustling round St. Ann's bed. The theme of death appears too: death in the bedchamber, with the dying man fighting for his life.

The growing practice of depicting rooms corresponds to a new emotional tendency henceforth directed towards the intimacy of private life. Exterior scenes do not disappear—they develop into the landscape— but interior scenes become more common and more original, and they typify genre painting during the whole of its existence. Private life, thrust into the background in the Middle Ages, invades iconography in the sixteenth and above all in the seventeenth century: Dutch and Flemish painting and French engraving show the extraordinary strength of this hitherto inconsistent or neglected concept.*

* *Centuries of Childhood* (London, 1961), pp. 346–347.

Even in the richest and noblest houses before the seventeenth century there were hardly any rooms which served for specific purposes since the notion of privacy scarcely existed. Much of the furniture, including even beds and tables, were collapsible and, therefore, portable. "In the same rooms where they ate, people slept, danced, worked and received visitors."* In the seventeenth century this was beginning to change. The collapsible beds, for example, became permanent pieces of furniture, even though for a while the bedroom remained a public room, but the beds were now curtained off. (Later the bedroom becomes *the* private room: the only room in the house that will be called not *salle* but *chambre, camera.*)

What is involved here is far more important than the history of furniture: it involves the history of the family and of the home. Domesticity, privacy, comfort, the concept of the home and of the family: these are, literally, principal achievements of the Bourgeois Age. How wrong it is to believe, for example, that the German insistence on the patriarchal family, surviving into the twentieth century, was medieval in inspiration! The idea of the family in the Middle Ages was much weaker than we are accustomed to think. In any event, it was much different from ours.† In the Middle Ages the lives of children were separated from those of their parents; this practice endured for a long time, especially among the aristocracy and among the poor. The idea that children were full-fledged human beings, that they were entitled to a kind of protected equality within the family, this, too, was the result of the bourgeois spirit. By the seventeenth century it ceased to be customary to

* *Ibid.,* p. 394.
† Ariès, *op. cit.,* p. 364: "It may be that the family was weakened at the time of the Germanic invasions, yet it would be vain to deny the existence of a family life in the Middle Ages. But the family existed in silence: it did not awaken feelings strong enough to inspire poet or artist. We must recognize the importance of this silence: not much value was placed on the family. Similarly we must admit the significance of the iconographic blossoming which after the fifteenth and especially the sixteenth century followed this long period of obscurity: the birth and development of the concept of the family."

entrust children to strangers. As Ariès puts it: "This return of the children to the home was a great event: it gave the seventeenth-century family its principal characteristic, which distinguished it from the medieval family. The child became an indispensable element of everyday life, and his parents worried about his education, his career, his future. He was not yet the pivot of the whole system, but he had become a much more important character."

It was only then that, through the bourgeois insistence on privacy, the family became the most important unit of society. Not thus in the admittedly Christian Middle Ages when the idea of the house or the home was still weak. "The concept of the home is another aspect of the concept of the family." Between the eighteenth century and 1950 "the concept of the family hardly changed at all." It grew: it extended further and further through society. As late as a century and a half ago medieval habits of family life, including the absence of the children from the home, still prevailed among the poor of many a nation. But finally family life "embraced nearly the whole of society, to such an extent that people have forgotten its . . . [largely bourgeois] origins."*

⁂

The family: the home. If we, in our situation, have any kind of nostalgia at all, it is for this: for the security, and for the freedom, of the Bourgeois Age, for its *inner* security, and for its *inner* freedom, for a kind of life that some of us have once known and that others among us can still imagine. . . . The very word *nostalgia* in Greek meant, literally, homesickness, a painful longing for a place like home, for something that we have once known. Thus we ought to abandon our superficial and sentimental (and, therefore, false) nostalgia for the chivalry of the Middle Ages, because that is a nostalgia for a world that we have not known: it represents an interest in a past that is ideal, not real—unlike our occasional longing for some of the verities of the Bourgeois Age, still so familiar to us.

* Ariès, *op. cit.*, p. 404.

How curious this is! At the end of the Modern Age millions of people become attracted to bourgeois things. Certain bourgeois scenes have now become idyllic to our minds. This would have surprised the Romantics: they would have revolted against the very notion of it. And yet it was they, the Romantics who, having made a breakthrough in the direction of consciousness, provided for the development of this rich and still interiority, all of their aristocratic and neo-medieval pretensions notwithstanding. The bourgeois were once the deadly enemies of the Romantics. Or, rather, they only seemed to be. Now we know that the Romantics were bourgeois, and that the bourgeois were Romantics, to a considerable extent, far more than we (and, of course, than they themselves) were accustomed to think. These are not abstract or literary speculations: we can understand them historically. The zenith of Romanticism was the period around 1820. That was the beginning of the bourgeois zenith, of the Modern Age, too, before the enormous smoky swelling of cities, before the revolutions of 1848, before even in Eastern America Jacksonian democracy set in. Characteristic of the architecture and of the furniture before the 1830's was a kind of patrician, rather than aristocratic, elegance, something that evokes in us a real nostalgia: for we could live in those rooms ourselves, unlike in the glittering, coldly magnificent rooms of the eighteenth century. Not only the rooms and the houses, the landscapes of the period around 1820 breathe a kind of comfort to which we instantly respond because, to some extent, they are still familiar and comprehensible for us. The idyllic component is real, not merely Arcadian. Perhaps this interior stillness reflected a momentary state of high equilibrium, the peak achievement of an age. The spirit, even more than the style, of bourgeois interiority suffused the landscape, and it penetrated the minds of millions even in countries and places where a bourgeois class hardly existed at all.

Here is an example: *Stille Nacht,* "Silent Night," the song that is probably known by more people in the world than any other. It was composed by a village priest in 1818, in the Austrian Tyrol. At that time the Tyrol was one of the more backward mountain provinces of the still largely feudal Habsburg Empire. The common ways of life in the Tyrol of 1818 were close to the seventeenth century. The Tyroleans wore the clothes of the past, their towns were isolated, apart; they would not encounter many bourgeois even in the somnolent provincial capital of Innsbruck where the *Bürger* were few, mostly artisans, members of guilds, a few teachers, a few bureaucrats. Even now the childlike simplicity of *Stille Nacht* suggests to us a pastoral (if not *the* pastoral) scene: the village church in a mountain valley, the snow, the silent night. Even people who know little history associate it with a faraway, feudal and pastoral, premodern past.

And yet the success, indeed, the spirit of *Stille Nacht* was not feudal, it was bourgeois. For our cult of Christmas is a bourgeois phenomenon, more recent than we are inclined to think. During the Middle Ages, and for centuries afterward, the principal holy event of the year was Easter, not Christmas, in accord with the Christian theology of the supremacy of the Resurrection, Christ becoming God being an event even greater than His coming to earth. This habit lasted for a long time in Russia, Spain, Ireland, nations that have been touched but little by bourgeois humanism. In Puritan New England, too, and in many places in Scotland Christmas Day was an ordinary workday as late as a century and one-half ago. But during the nineteenth century the cult of Christmas began to spread. Eventually Christmas became associated with commercialism and with publicity, much of which reflected the prevailing need of most people for the kind of sentimentalism that Oscar Wilde, wittily and quite correctly, designated as the Bank Holiday of cynicism.

And yet there is more to this. Christmas has an element of interiority that Easter does not have. Beyond the growth of middle-class sentimentality, beyond the transitory revival of the respectability of religion that occurred during the first quarter of the nineteenth century, this evolution of the cult of Christmas in the lives of people reflected the evolution of "internalization." The growing cult of Christmas was involved with the rise in the cult of the child, indeed, with that of the family whose origins, as we have seen, were less feudal than they were bourgeois. The central figure of the child, God coming to Earth, the giving of gifts, the element of peace and warmth in the middle of winter—this modern cult of Christmas responded to some of the deepest aspirations of the bourgeois spirit. So did *Silent Night.* Its appearance marks the zenith of the Bourgeois Age, in some ways like the words of Goethe's *Wanderers Nachtlied,* expressing the sense of a sublime equilibrium, a sublime stillness. Of all Christmas songs *Stille Nacht* is the simplest and the most childlike; it is not a song for a great choir, it has little of the baroque in it that marks most of our carols even now. Perhaps this was why it had such an attraction for the bourgeois of the world, this *Biedermeyer* melody (for it is far more *Biedermeyer* than folkish) to which the *Bürger* of Vienna, including Protestants and Jews, responded instantly. It traveled thereafter across frontiers and oceans. In the 1950's the Eastern European Communist governments gave up their struggle against the cult of Christmas. In Tokyo "Krismasu" became the greatest feature in the annual program of department stores. I believe that "Silent Night" will be sung one hundred years from now. And thus this final paradox: the most massive survival of a religious cult has been the product of the bourgeois spirit.

❧

We have seen that it is wrong to confuse bourgeois with middle-class, for the latter term is sociological, not historical. It is, also, static, not dynamic. The Bourgeois Age was marked by aspirations, by social ambitions. During the Middle Ages ambition flourished only within the aristocracy; but the Bourgeois Age did not only introduce social mobility, it made a virtue out of it: nobody should rest satisfied with his lot, he should always think of bettering it. For a while "this eagerness to rise in the world" was mixed with the spirit of the Renaissance; it pretended to fulfill something of a heroic ideal: but after the seventeenth century it became involved with the propagation of education. In any event, even after the somewhat compromised heroic ideal was passing, the desire to rise in the world remained strong. The ambitious men and women and adolescents within the new middle classes emulate successful people within their own group. The aspiring bourgeois emulated the classes which still stood above them.

In one sense this led to a social selfishness which was the worst characteristic of the bourgeoisie. In the Middle Ages "people lived in a state of contrast; high birth or great wealth rubbed shoulders with poverty, vice or virtue, scandal with devotion. Despite its shrill contrasts, this medley of colours caused no surprise." But "there came a time when the [bourgeois] could no longer bear the pressure of the multitude or the contact of the lower class." Instead, they cultivated, selfishly, their "homes designed for privacy, in new districts kept free from all lower-class contamination."* This kind of narrow selfishness revolted sensitive people; it still repels us. There gleams a kind of naked selfishness in some of the faces of handsome and successful people, surviving in photographs of an Edwardian Ascot or of the Avenue des Acacias around 1910, that is unappealing, as it reflects a kind of superficial rigidity that may mask something that is either decomposing or already hollow. Certain satirists would capture this better than social thinkers or political philosophers. Saki would record "a garden party in full swing, with smart frocks and smart conversation, fashionable refreshments and fashionable music, and a fevered undercurrent of social strivings and snubbings." The large-spirited and amused Wilde would write of the late-Victorian English bourgeoisie, with "their strange mixture of romance and finance." It is true, of course, that our very sensitivity to such faults of human nature has been the result of our own evolution: we have become more self-conscious of such things, more introspective and, therefore, more critical.

But in another sense the bourgeois aspirations sprang often from a conscious emulation not merely of aristocratic habits but of the classic virtues. These virtues included not only moderation and

* Ariès, *op. cit.*, pp. 414–415.

prudence and a kind of humanism that was cautious in its demophilia; they included the cult of justice, of temperance, and of reason. Such patrician standards of culture and of responsibility were the sources of some of the finest achievements in the civilization of the Bourgeois Age. This is why we should no longer abide by the narrow and distorted Marxist usage of the word "bourgeois": we should recall, instead, its more spacious sense, including its precapitalist suggestion of a free urban citizenry. Beyond this, we should extend its reputation. During the last one hundred years this word has penetrated the vocabularies and the conscious minds of the English-speaking peoples of the world: and it is high time to grant it not only citizenship but to nominate it to a respectable office in the building of the English language which, besides being a means of communication, is a historical building, a living structure of a people's past that has much to say to the present.

But, then, our languages are beginning to reflect this. In the United States, for example, the reputation of "bourgeois" has lately started to rise, at least among cultivated people. Thus the stock of words rises and falls through the years. Their histories are our histories, they both reflect and create the prevailing tendencies of consciousness which are the deepest matters in the histories of peoples. In this stock exchange within our minds "modern" has been falling, "bourgeois" has been rising: a small trend, probably not without some significance.

※

If I could select but one painting by a master of the past five hundred years, for the purpose of illustrating its historical aura, I would probably choose a Dutch or a French master, of the seventeenth or of the late nineteenth centuries, near the beginning or near the close of the age: a Vermeer or a Rembrandt, a Monet, or a Sisley—very different painters who, nevertheless, have one thing in common. Their works exemplify the rich interior lives of our ancestors. By this I do not merely mean their subjects, the rooms painted by Vermeer: this rich interiority shimmers through the trees of Monet. What unites them is their preoccupation with illumination, the attempt of their genius to paint not so much what exists around us as what is visible to us, their understanding of this deepening human recognition that the sense of reality exists within. Their enlightenment is of an interior, not of an exterior nature. Their masterworks embody a human condition to which the word "modern" is too vague and too thin to be properly applicable at all.

This interiority that we are attempting to cultivate and to preserve (for it is a living thing, which cannot be preserved unless it is cultivated) is our bourgeois heritage. It is not merely a cherished image out of the past, a rich knick-knack, an heirloom. It is the most precious heritage of the Western civilization of the last five hundred years.

The consciousness of the past 19

Why our future is our past, to a far greater extent than we are accustomed to think.

A historian must not dabble in prophecy. He, like everyone else, knows nothing of the future. He knows—or, rather, he ought to know—something about the vast and mysterious continuity of human life: that continuity is at least as strong as is change, that nothing disappears entirely, that the end of something is the beginning of something else and that the development of the latter is unpredictable. "History can predict nothing except that great changes in human relationships will never come about in the form in which they have been anticipated," Huizinga wrote in 1935. Who would foresee even as late as 1935 that in a coming Second World War which broke out between Germany and Poland the eventual victors would be the United States and the Soviet Union, dividing Europe between themselves? For a handful of people the construction of atomic bombs was predictable in 1935: that ten years later Americans would cast them on Japanese cities was not. All that a historian may surmise about the future is not what is likely to happen but what is not likely to happen. Not likely to happen is the end of the world: at least not yet. Our potential for physical destruction has grown into something enormous: but we also possess enormous resources of physical reconstruction: again the experience of Europe, and also of Japan after the last world war, demonstrated this.

Even after 1945, however, this reconstruction was not merely the product of technical capacity. It was motivated by the prestige of the liberal democracy and of the industrial productivity whose success seemed to be embodied by the American people, an example which in 1945 could still inspire the energies of millions of people, perhaps especially the defeated and disillusioned former enemies of the United States. Such a conservative-liberal restoration of a world that many of us knew may not happen again.

> How the Great Democracies
> Triumphed,
> and so
> Were Able to Resume
> the Follies
> Which Had so Nearly
> Cost Them Their
> Life

Nearly twenty years ago Churchill wrote this motto for the last volume of his Second World War memoirs. Since that time the beliefs of the peoples of the Western world in the validity of their public institutions weakened further. This does not mean that the majority of these peoples have been addicted to folly. It means that the prospect of civilization is imperiled not only by the material corruption of its institutions: it is endangered by the hollowness of its spirit. Making The World Safe For Democracy, One World, Freedom From Want, International Law, The Welfare State, The Great Society, The Freedom Of The Press, Progressive Education, Sexual Emancipation: they are hollow ideas now. "The ideas of the day," wrote Huizinga in 1935, "demand immediate results, whereas the great ideas have always penetrated very slowly. Like smoke and petrol fumes over the cities, there hangs over the world a haze of empty words."

THE PASSING OF THE MODERN AGE

A generation later behind the increasingly desperate employment of these empty words there looms a desperation with life itself. At the beginning of this century Joseph Conrad, in *Under Western Eyes*, wrote of the Russian mental habit of "a terrible corroding simplicity in which mystic phrases cloth a naive and hopeless cynicism. I think sometimes that the psychological secret of the profound difference of that people consists in this, that they detest life, the irremediable life of the earth as it is, whereas we westerners cherish it with perhaps an equal exaggeration of its sentimental value." The survival of Western civilization, perhaps especially in the United States, depends on whether its way of life will be capable of freeing itself from certain ways of thought that, all superficial appearances to the contrary notwithstanding, now show an alarming similarity to this earlier Russian predicament.

In the Western world the fatal encumbrances of these ways of thought are embedded in the materialist philosophies of human nature whose origins go back for more than one hundred, even two hundred years. They have reduced, rather than elevated, the sense of human nature: they reduced man to a random product, a thing among things, instead of reminding mankind that it was the very creator of its environment. They then compounded this fatal inclination by proposing that man's principal business was not his knowledge of himself but that of his environment: the result was that men gained their mastery over things while they lost their mastery over themselves. They came around to a third, fatal error: thinking as if the science of nature were a reality external to human nature, they began to study man, the most complex organism in the entire known universe, with methods borrowed from their study of man's environment, that is, of less complex and more primitive organisms. The result has been this desperate fatalism, masquerading as a triumphant determinism in the white laboratory robes of modern science, the one-sided belief in which undermined the sense of freedom of the human mind. On top of these ways of thought, then, were piled new mental habits: the more recent influences of a pervasive and, by its very nature, falsificatory publicity, of nearly everything. Through this the always relative and fragile autonomy of indi-

vidual minds and of personal aspirations—in spite or, perhaps, because of the universality of education and of information—has weakened to such an extent that the exercise of private judgment and of
individual integrity has become more and more difficult and, consequently, rare.

᙮

The evolution of human consciousness that I have suggested
throughout this book does not yet seem to be sufficient to counteract
effectively this devolution. There exists, however, a recent development, deeply involved with the evolution of consciousness, which is
full of promise: and this is the growth of the sense of the past in our
minds.

At first sight it seems that nothing could be further from reality.
All around us evidence abounds to the effect that millions, especially the young, regard the past as totally irrelevant, that traditions
are broken and discarded with increasing fervor and speed, that
people wish to extinguish the past from their minds, that God *and*
history seem to have died together.

This overall impression is misleading. The very sound and fury of
this anti-historical rhetoric is a symptom of the ineradicable presence of the past in people's minds: for one cannot discard something that does not exist. Those millions of peasants of past ages
whose lives and minds were bound to a sometimes ageless routine
were not aware that they were traditionalists or conservatives—as
indeed they weren't. "Those who do not know the past are condemned to repeat it." Only we must qualify Santayana's aphorism,
to make its meaning indisputably clear. Our problem is no longer
with people who do not know the past at all. Our problem is with
people who do not want to know the past, their past. Those who do
not want to know their past are no longer condemned by fate; they
are condemning *themselves,* to repeat it. The less they are willing to
confront their past, the more that past weighs upon their existence:
for only by knowing more of the past—our past—can we liberate
ourselves from its burdens.

Increasingly, through the last centuries, knowledge of self has come to mean: know your past, face your past. Our self-conscious-ness has developed together with our sense of the past, no matter how we may have failed to recognize the latter. Even Freud under-stood this, though he did not *know* it: for what else is the essence of psychoanalysis than this: by knowing your past you may free your mind from a painful load in the present.

No one knows all of the past: indeed, we know very little of it: and yet the past is all that we know. As C. S. Lewis once wrote: try to imagine a new color, a new sex, a new monster. You cannot imagine it, save through a new composition of existing colors, sexes, beasts that you already know. This is a common-sense condition the recognition of which is fraught with deep meaning. It means, among other things, that not only knowledge but imagination, too, depends on memory far more than we are still inclined to think. It also means that our knowledge of history and our knowledge of ourselves are not separate matters, since history is not merely the recorded past but the remembered past: and the remembered past is what conscious life is all about.*

Now the recognition of this, too, is a more recent phenomenon than we are accustomed to think. It belongs to the history of history itself. There were chronicles and histories four hundred years ago: but there was little historical consciousness. Even Shakespeare saw nothing wrong in having *Julius Caesar* performed in contemporary Elizabethan dress. Great painters would paint Biblical figures in a contemporary scene. Indeed, the word *contemporary*, as also such words as *primitive, out of date, age, epoch, decade, century, period, anachronism* did not exist; and the very notion of *development*, of *progress* in the dimension of time was either nonexistent or vague. But about three hundred years ago the consciousness of the dimen-sion of history emerged in the minds of people in Western Europe: and this was one of the least recognized, yet most important, achievements of the European mind in the Modern Age.

It had all kinds of consequences. One of them was the emergence

---

* Readers who wish to pursue these matters further may read about them in my book *Historical Consciousness.*

of history as a specialized field of study, eventually with its own professionals. Another, more important, consequence was the emergence of the historical form of thought, applicable to every kind of human experience or knowledge, including science. The interest in history was widening, until it assumed large popular proportions even among the supposedly nonhistorical masses in the twentieth century, including many people in the Soviet Union. At this time of writing, in the year of the moon landing, and a mere fourteen years away from 1984, popular histories outsell popular fiction, and popular historical magazines outsell fiction magazines in most countries of the Western world. In addition to this literary development, the respect, indeed, the appetite, for things that are old is astonishing: old-fashioned objects are avidly sought by all kinds of people, as if they were by nature durable, valuable, beautiful. Perhaps for the first time in the history of mankind the conservation of the older products of man, and of nature formed through man, including cityscapes and landscapes, has become more and more popular: not only conservatives but radicals have become conservationists. Nothing like this existed at the end of the Roman world or at the time when the Middle Ages were waning.

All of this goes against the prevalent assumption that we have entered a post-historic age, that Western man has now become post-historic man, that because of revolutionary technology and revolutionary thinking we have broken away from history, from the past, once and for all. To the contrary: the past lives on in our minds, ever deeper, no matter whether we admit this or not. For those who admit this—who, literally, *admit,* and *welcome,* the presence of the past in their minds—there are at least two consequences. The first is a kind of interest for the history of a period—say, Europe before 1914, or the United States before 1945—that is still within hailing distance in their minds. But this kind of historical interest is no longer merely nostalgic: for the word "nostalgia" contains the element of homesickness and of pain, whereas this kind of interest includes an element of mental, that is, intellectual *and* imaginative, pleasure.

It can give people a mental connection with reality which is one of the few things nowadays that the historical form of reconstruction can give. This is the second consequence, this recognition of the reality of the past. For the past is not like death; it is not irrevocable; it lives on in the present, in our minds. In this respect, too, our transition is different from the great transitions of the past. It is true that the Renaissance was stimulated by a rediscovery of the past, and that indeed some of the modern notions of history grew out of the Renaissance. But five hundred years ago the humanists rediscovered not Aquinas but Seneca, not Abelard but Plato, not Notre Dame but the Pantheon; as Montaigne wrote, "we know the Roman Capitol before we know the Louvre, and the Tiber before the Seine." This is not so now: we are not inclined to jump *two* steps back, over the centuries of the Modern Age to the epoch of the Middle Ages. Our historical interest is rather lodged in the age now passing. We know Napoleon better than we know Julius Caesar, and Churchill rather than Cicero; we are also more interested.

This is not merely a temporary phenomenon. Our consciousness of history has grown to the extent where the historical form of thought envelops not only the legendary past but portions close to the present, because they are *real*—while our more remote ancestors cultivated a vision of the past that was *ideal*.

All through history the heralds of better things and times to come, reformers, prophets, the bearers and champions of renaissances, restorations or *réveils,* have always pointed to past glories and urged a return to and a retrieval of ancient purity. The Humanists, the Reformers and the moralists of Roman times, Rousseau, Mohammed . . . ever had before their eyes the haunting vision of an illusory past of finer quality than the gross present. And it was to this past that they exhorted mankind to return.*

We, on the other hand, "know: a general going *back* is out of the question." Yet this knowledge is not only the result of the modern concept of progress: it happens because of the reality of the past in our minds. One of the very few people who recognized this pro-

* Huizinga, *In the Shadow of Tomorrow* (New York, 1936), pp. 26–27.

foundly important difference between a past that is ideal and a past that is real was the young Ortega y Gasset; his genius made a precise stab at this phenomenon already in 1914, in his *Meditations on Quixote*.

"The theme of the epic," he wrote,

is the past as such: it speaks to us about a world which was and which is no longer, of a mythical age whose antiquity is not a past in the same sense as any remote historical time. . . . The epic past is not *our* past. Our past is thinkable as having been the present once, but the epic past eludes identification with any possible present . . . it is not a remembered past but an ideal past.

Many of us now think of the past as something substantial and even as something real—even though we may not be quite conscious of this condition of our thinking. And this tendency is involved not only with the decay of modernism but also with that of futurism.

Each transition, as we have seen, keeps *more* of the preceding age. This is why the New Dark Ages will be a compound of darkness and light, during which many habits and things of the recent past will not merely survive but will be cultivated by many people. The meaning—indeed, the presence—of this kind of coexistence of the old with the new will escape many people: still it may be even more widespread than was the coexistence of medieval with modern habits and things five hundred years ago, about which Huizinga wrote that "the transition from the spirit of the declining Middle Ages to humanism was far less simple than we are inclined to imagine it."[*]

The work of this fine historian, whom I have often cited in this book, exemplifies my argument. A book such as *The Waning of the Middle Ages*, written around 1920, reflects a historical consciousness that is more sensitive, more steeped in historical imagination than

---

[*] *The Waning of the Middle Ages* (New York, 1956), p. 323: "Accustomed to oppose humanism to the Middle Ages, we would gladly believe that it was necessary to give up the one in order to embrace the other." This was not so. "Humanism was a form before it was an inspiration. On the other hand, the characteristic modes of thought of the Middle Ages did not die out till long after the Renaissance."

the great works of Gibbon, Macaulay, Ranke, of the nineteenth and late eighteenth centuries. This comparison has little to do with the accumulation of research, with the fact that a historian in the twentieth century could draw on so much more material than could his forerunners. It has much to do with the deepening of our historical consciousness, with our real and growing *telepathy* with the past.*

❊

At the best, therefore, the possibility exists that entire peoples, turning inward, may discover the vital advantages of their roots: as E. M. Forster made Margaret Schlegel talk already in 1910, in *Howard's End:*

"Because a thing is going strong now, it need not go strong for ever," she said. "This craze for motion has only set in during the last hundred years. It may be followed by a civilization that won't be a movement, because it will rest on the earth. All the signs are against it now, but I can't help hoping, and very early in the morning in the garden I feel that our house is the future as well as the past."

All the signs are against it now. Still the consciousness of the past will most probably live on, submerged beneath the waves of a new barbarism: sooner or later it will come to the surface, unless the world, or a large portion of it, is destroyed forever.

All the signs are against it now: in 1970, unlike in 1910, indeed for the first time in centuries, we can imagine the end of the world.†

---

* On the other hand, since Huizinga's time (he died in 1945) the profession of historianship, too, has shown that it is far from immune from certain habits that make for the dissolution of the Western tradition of intellect. Its ranks have been inflated, and its standards have begun to rot. Yet history has become such a serious thing that it may not be left to professional historians: it may yet be carried on without and beyond the unimaginative pretensions and the vested interests of the majority of a bureaucratic guild.

† "Perhaps the Darwinian notion of human life on this earth has been wrong on both ends. At the one end Darwin and his scientific followers fantastically elongated the history of man on this earth, pushing its beginnings back from the Biblical version of a few thousand to hundreds of thousands of years, as they point at the bones of what they call Java or Peking man. On the other end their presumption also involved the future, reflecting their basically

Still, I have been writing not of the end of the world about which we know little but of the passing of a certain civilization about which we know something.

At the worst, then, farewell, not to life but to civilization! Let us not forget that the very word, the very concept of *civilization* is relatively recent; yet another product of the historical consciousness of the Modern Age. If, by some miracle, we could travel to ancient Greece or Rome, we would be appalled by the dirt, the cruelty, the primitivism of so many things: unlike the idealists of the Renaissance, we would find them barbarian. . . . For the civilization of the Modern Age in the West is the only civilization that we really know.

This passing, while not devoid of certain promises, is full of misfortunes. "But if happiness is to be found in our misfortunes," Burckhardt wrote one hundred years ago, "it can be only a spiritual one: to be turned facing the past so as to save the culture of former times, and facing the future so as to give an example of the spiritual in an age that might otherwise succumb entirely to the material"— or, rather, I should add, *to the idea* of the material.

In a fragment from his diary, Bernanos: "Le temps passe, passe, et rien de ce que nous attendons n'arrive jamais. C'est peut-être parce que ce que nous attendons est déjà arrivé, mais Dieu ne veut pas que nous le sachions." Time goes on and on and nothing that we expect ever comes about. This is perhaps because what we expect has already come; but God does not want us to know it.

---

nineteenth-century scientific optimism, since according to their time scale Homo sapiens would have a long history of progress ahead of him. Yet, in our present historical situation, the question arises whether this still makes much sense. When these words are written, in the 1960's, we certainly have a different view (*and a different feeling*) about the end of history than even a generation ago. Because of many events (and especially because of the "progress" of science and of technology) the end of the world, through *our own* capacity of destroying all human life, has become, for the first time in history, a reasonable possibility. It is, therefore, no longer unreasonable to assume that the span of human history on this earth may be far shorter than what Darwinism and scientism have been implying, and that it may indeed come to an end a few thousand years after Christ." *Historical Consciousness* (New York, 1968), pp. 271–272.

Index

"Acquisitive" society, 97–8
Adams, Henry, 23
Adolescence, 10, 77 ff., 105 ff.
Aesthetics, 125
"Affluent" society, 97–8
Africa, 51, 60 ff.
"American Gothic," 183
Americanization, 23 ff., 66 ff., 196
Antiquity, 11, 100, 196 ff.
Apocalypse, 154
Ariès, Philippe, 86, 101 ff., 199–201, 205
Aristocracy, 31 ff., 42, 192, 195 ff.
Aristotle, 41
Armstrong, Neil, 150
Arnold, Matthew, 111
Art (artist, artisan), 116, 125 ff.
Austria-Hungary, 45, 101
Australia, 56, 60

Balzac, Honoré, 122, 123
Beard, Charles A., 192–3
Belgium, 51
Belloc, Hilaire, 165

Berdyaev, Nicholas, 182, 192
Bernanos, Georges, 38, 217
Berserkers, 188
Bismarck, Prince Otto von, 20, 61
Blake, William, 16–7
Bourgeois, 23, 32 ff., 71 ff., 144 ff., 169, 191 ff.
Bowra, C. M., 119
Brahms, Johannes, 128
Brittany, 51
Brooks, Van Wyck, 115
Bryan, William Jennings, 183
Burckhardt, Jakob, 186
Bureaucracy, 32, 36 ff., 52 ff., 216n.
Burns, C. Delisle, 186
Byron, Lord George Noel Gordon, 122, 173
Byzantinism, 184–5

Caesar, Julius, 135
Canada, 51
Castro, Fidel, 39, 64, 150
Causality, 98, 142–3, 151–2, 171, 210–11

Centralization, 36 ff.
Cézanne, Paul, 127–8
Childhood, 80 ff., 108 ff., 200 ff.
China, 8, 45, 56, 146
Christianity, 56, 154 ff.
Christmas, cult of, 203–4
Churchill, Winston, 182, 209
Civilization, concept of, 3 ff., 21, 48, 217
Clausewitz, Karl von, 48, 49
Clemenceau, Georges, 23
Conrad, Joseph, 122, 210
Conservatism, 63 ff., 186–7
Copernicus, 145
Criminal power, 42–3, 53–4
Cuba, 39, 45, 47, 51
Czechoslovakia, 46, 118
Czernin, Count Ottokar von, 23

Daguerre, Louis-Jacques, 132
Dark Ages, 12 ff., 42, 70, 179 ff.
Darrow, Clarence, 140
Darwin, Charles, 23, 216–17n.
Debussy, Claude, 126
De Gaulle, Charles, 22, 25, 45
Degler, Carl N., 82n.
Delacroix, Eugène, 128
Democracy, 31 ff., 63 ff., 196 ff.
Descartes, René, 145, 147, 152
Dickens, Charles, 122
Dictatorships, 37 ff.
Dostoevsky, Fyodor, 122, 195
Duhamel, Georges, 104–5
Dulles, John Foster, 158
Dutourd, Jean, 143

Easter, cult of, 203
Economic Man, 87 ff.
Education, 77 ff., 99 ff.
Einstein, Albert, 152–3, 163
Eisenhower, Dwight, 92
Elgin, Lord, 8
Eliot, T. S., 123
Ellul, Jacques, 121n., 143–4
Emerson, Ralph Waldo, 114
Ensor, R. C. K., 74
Erasmus, 198
Etiology (of illnesses), 142n.
Europe, 15 ff., 44 ff., 51

"Facts," illusion of, 98
Families, 68, 72 ff., 200 ff.
Fiedeism, 164
Flaubert, Gustave, 123, 193, 194
Flemish (of Belgium), 51
Ford, Henry, Sr., 183
Forster, E. M., 216
France, 17 ff., 31, 35, 45, 48, 64 ff., 90, 100, 118, 132, 180 ff.
Franco, Francisco, 67
Franklin, Benjamin, 16, 67
Freud, Sigmund, 77, 143, 163, 171 ff.
Fuller, Buckminster, 151

Gaxotte, Pierre, 193
General Electric, 92
Germany (Germanies), 4, 12, 18 ff., 45 ff., 51, 64 ff., 86 ff., 148–9, 187 ff.
Gibbon, Edward, 11–12, 67, 216
Gide, André, 194
Gissing, George, 115
Goebbels, Josef, 80
Goethe, Wolfgang von, 82n.
Gogh, Vincent van, 127
Gothicism, 183 ff.
Graham, the Reverend Billy, 151
Great Britain, 5, 19 ff., 34, 45 ff., 64, 74, 86, 169
Greece, 48
"Gross National Product," 97n.
Guardini, Romano, 4
Guerrilla warfare, 48–49

Hampden, John, 183
Heisenberg, Werner, 152
Henry IV (of France), 35
Historical thinking (historical consciousness), 124, 208 ff.
Hitler, Adolf, 23 ff., 34, 37, 41, 54n., 64, 80, 88, 92, 147, 162, 181 ff.
Ho Chi Minh, 64
Holy League, 35
Horace, 94
Huizinga, Johan, 10, 79, 131, 132n., 186, 198, 203, 209, 214n.
Hungary, 51, 118
Huxley, Aldous, 151

Imagination, 107 ff.
Impressionism, 120 ff.

Industrial Revolution, 70, 72 ff., 135 ff.
Inflation, 86 ff.
Intellectuals, 26, 33, 47, 111 ff., 120 ff.
"Internalization," 69 ff., 142 ff., 175–76, 198 ff., 201 ff.
"International," 49 ff., 6 ff.
Ireland, 19, 52, 203
Israel, 162–63
Italy, 48, 101

Jansenism, 183n.
Japan, 24, 45, 56–57, 197, 204, 209
Jay, John, 67
Jazz, 129
Jeffers, Robinson, 23
Jefferson, Thomas, 67, 157
Jews, 19, 56, 149, 158, 161 ff.
Johnson, Lyndon B., 47
Johnson, Samuel, 16, 140, 147
John XXIII (Pope), 159–60
Jores, Arthur, 142n.
Jura (Swiss), 51

Kennedy, John, 26, 64, 68
Kepler, Johannes, 145
Kierkegaard, Sören, 156
Koestler, Arthur, 186
Kraus, Karl, 123
Krupp Works, 92

La Rochefoucauld, Duke François de, 198
League of Nations, 51
Lenin, Nikolai, 22–23, 165, 186
Lewis, C. S., 212
Liberal (liberalism), 63 ff.
Lindbergh, Charles, 150
Literacy, 102 ff.
Lloyd George, David, 25

Macaulay, Thomas Babington, 216
Mafia (Sicily), 53
Mann, Thomas, 122
Mather, Cotton, 140
Marx, Marxism, 32–33, 43, 64 ff., 77, 163, 192, 206
McLuhan, Marshall, 121
Medicine, 140 ff.
Meissonnier, Ernest, 131
Mencken, H. L., 140

Metternich, Prince Clemens von, 23
Middle Ages, 10, 11–12, 56, 85, 101–02, 129, 131, 135, 180 ff.
"Middle class," 77 ff.
Middle East, 51
"Modern," 11 ff., 191
Monet, Claude, 126, 132, 206–07
Money, 84 ff.
Montaigne, Michel de, 35, 198, 214
Montesquieu, Baron Charles de, 41
Morgan, J. P., 92
Mussolini, Benito, 41, 54n., 88, 181

Napoleon I, 17–18, 40, 133
Nations, nationalism, 17 ff., 34, 63 ff.
Naturalists, 136 ff.
Negroes, 56 ff.
New England, 115, 203
"New poor," 98
Newton, Isaac, 145, 152–53
New York, 5–8, 114
Niepce, Nicéphore, 132
Nietzsche, Friedrich, 4, 156, 160, 163
Nixon, Richard, 39, 67, 150

Objectivity, 153 ff.
Ohio, 17
Opinions, 119 ff.
Oppenheimer, Robert, 149
Orosius, 188
Ortega y Gasset, José, 116n., 152, 215
Orwell, George, 151
Ottoman Empire, see Turkey

Panama Canal, 138
Pascal, Blaise, 147
Pathogenesis (of illnesses), 142n.
Péguy, Charles, 59, 82, 127
Perception, 108 ff.
Photography, 132
Picasso, Pablo, 127
Pirenne, Henri, 196
Pissarro, Camille, 126
Pitt, William (Lord Chatham), 23
Pius XII, 158
Poetry, 124
Poland, 48
Pope, Alexander, 147
Pornography, 9, 171 ff.
Pound, Ezra, 127

Protestantism, 5, 158 ff., 166
Proudhon, Pierre Joseph, 43
Proust, Marcel, 123
Puritanism, 140, 173–74, 183–84, 188, 203

Races (their relations), 55 ff.
Ranke, Leopold von, 216
Ravel, Maurice, 126, 128
Religion, 146–47, 155 ff.
Rembrandt, 206
Renaissance, 13–14, 101, 198
Reynaud, Paul, 181
Robida, H., 7
Rock and roll, 129–30
Romanticism, 126, 135 ff., 180–81, 202 ff.
Roosevelt, Theodore, 32
Roosevelt, Franklin D., 24, 33, 47, 88
Rouault, Georges, 130
Rumania, 46
Rusk, Dean, 67
Russia (Russian Revolution, Soviet Union), 15 ff., 22 ff., 46, 48, 50, 74, 101, 114, 118–9, 160, 196, 210

Sade, Marquis de, 156
St. John Baptist de la Salle, 101
"Saki" (H. H. Munro), 205
Santayana, George, 5, 211
Science, 145 ff.
Scotland, 51, 203
Scott, Sir Walter, 122
Senility, 179–80
Sexuality, 168 ff.
Shakespeare, William, 212
Sherman, William Tecumseh, 48
Siberia, 56, 138
Sicily, 53
Sisley, Alfred, 126, 206
Smith, Alexander, 7
Socialism (Socialists), 63 ff.
Sombart, Werner, 192
Sorel, Albert, 15
South America, 35
South Tyrol, 51
Soviet Union, see Russia
Spain, 20–1, 48, 64
Spengler, Oswald, 4, 180, 198
Stalin, Josef, 24, 34, 37, 118, 157, 186

Steffens, Lincoln, 23
"Stille Nacht," 203–04
Stravinsky, Igor, 128
Suez Canal, 138
Switzerland, 21, 51, 89

Tacitus, 189
Taine, Hippolyte, 143
Talleyrand, Prince Charles-Maurice de, 23
Tastes, 120 ff.
Taylor, A. J. P., 32
Technology, 6–7, 136 ff.
Teller, Edward, 151
Tertullian, 188
Tocqueville, Alexis de, 39 ff., 53–54, 68, 112
Tolstoy, Leo, 122, 174
"Totalitarianism," 37 ff.
Trans-Siberian Railroad, 138
Turkey, 20 ff., 64
Turner, Joseph, 126
Twain, Mark, 123

Ulster, 51
United Nations, 51
Universities, 103 ff.
Utrillo, Maurice, 126

Valéry, Paul, 4
Vermeer, 206
Verne, Jules, 7
Vietnam, 46, 49, 51, 62, 151
Vikingism, 180 ff.
Voltaire, 67, 147

Wales, 51
Walloons (of Belgium), 51
Washington, George, 23
Waugh, Evelyn, 123
Webb, Sydney and Beatrice, 118–19
Wilde, Oscar, 203, 205
Wilson, Woodrow, 23 ff., 165
Wood, Grant, 183
Wright, Orville and Wilbur, 3

Yugoslavia, 48

Zionists, 162

harper ✦ torchbooks

American Studies: General

HENRY ADAMS Degradation of the Democratic Dogma. ‡ *Introduction by Charles Hirschfeld.* TB/1450
LOUIS D. BRANDEIS: Other People's Money, *and How the Bankers Use It. Ed. with Intro, by Richard M. Abrams* TB/3081
HENRY STEELE COMMAGER, Ed.: The Struggle for Racial Equality TB/1300
CARL N. DEGLER: Out of Our Past: *The Forces that Shaped Modern America* CN/2
CARL N. DEGLER, Ed.: Pivotal Interpretations of American History
 Vol. I TB/1240; Vol. II TB/1241
A. S. EISENSTADT, Ed.: The Craft of American History: *Selected Essays*
 Vol. I TB/1255; Vol. II TB/1256
LAWRENCE H. FUCHS, Ed.: American Ethnic Politics TB/1368
MARCUS LEE HANSEN: The Atlantic Migration: 1607-1860. *Edited by Arthur M. Schlesinger. Introduction by Oscar Handlin* TB/1052
MARCUS LEE HANSEN: The Immigrant in American History. *Edited with a Foreword by Arthur M. Schlesinger* TB/1120
ROBERT L. HEILBRONER: The Limits of American Capitalism TB/1305·
JOHN HIGHAM, Ed.: The Reconstruction of American History TB/1068
ROBERT H. JACKSON: The Supreme Court in the American System of Government TB/1106
JOHN F. KENNEDY: A Nation of Immigrants. *Illus. Revised and Enlarged. Introduction by Robert F. Kennedy* TB/1118
LEONARD W. LEVY, Ed.: American Constitutional Law: *Historical Essays* TB/1285
LEONARD W. LEVY, Ed.: Judicial Review and the Supreme Court TB/1296
LEONARD W. LEVY: The Law of the Commonwealth and Chief Justice Shaw: *The Evolution of American Law, 1830-1860* TB/1309
GORDON K. LEWIS: Puerto Rico: *Freedom and Power in the Caribbean. Abridged edition* TB/1371
GUNNAR MYRDAL: An American Dilemma: *The Negro Problem and Modern Democracy. Introduction by the Author.*
 Vol. I TB/1443; Vol. II TB/1444
GILBERT OSOFSKY, Ed.: The Burden of Race: *A Documentary History of Negro-White Relations in America* TB/1405

ARNOLD ROSE: The Negro in America: *The Condensed Version of Gunnar Myrdal's* An American Dilemma. *Second Edition* TB/3048
JOHN E. SMITH: Themes in American Philosophy: *Purpose, Experience and Community* TB/1466
WILLIAM R. TAYLOR: Cavalier and Yankee: *The Old South and American National Character* TB/1474

American Studies: Colonial

BERNARD BAILYN: The New England Merchants in the Seventeenth Century TB/1149
ROBERT E. BROWN: Middle-Class Democracy and Revolution in Massachusetts, 1691-1780. *New Introduction by Author* TB/1413
JOSEPH CHARLES: The Origins of the American Party System TB/1049
WESLEY FRANK CRAVEN: The Colonies in Transition: 1660-1712† TB/3084
CHARLES GIBSON: Spain in America † TB/3077
CHARLES GIBSON, Ed.: The Spanish Tradition in America + HR/1351
LAWRENCE HENRY GIPSON: The Coming of the Revolution: 1763-1775. † *Illus.* TB/3007
JACK P. GREENE, Ed.: Great Britain and the American Colonies: 1606-1763. + *Introduction by the Author* HR/1477
AUBREY C. LAND, Ed.: Bases of the Plantation Society + HR/1429
PERRY MILLER: Errand Into the Wilderness TB/1139
PERRY MILLER & T. H. JOHNSON, Ed.: The Puritans: *A Sourcebook of Their Writings*
 Vol. I TB/1093; Vol. II TB/1094
EDMUND S. MORGAN: The Puritan Family: *Religion and Domestic Relations in Seventeenth Century New England* TB/1227
WALLACE NOTESTEIN: The English People on the Eve of Colonization: 1603-1630. † *Illus.* TB/3006
LOUIS B. WRIGHT: The Cultural Life of the American Colonies: 1607-1763. † *Illus.* TB/3005
YVES F. ZOLTVANY, Ed.: The French Tradition in America + HR/1425

American Studies: The Revolution to 1860

JOHN R. ALDEN: The American Revolution: 1775-1783. † *Illus.* TB/3011

---

† The New American Nation Series, edited by Henry Steele Commager and Richard B. Morris.
‡ American Perspectives series, edited by Bernard Wishy and William E. Leuchtenburg.
a History of Europe series, edited by J. H. Plumb.
§ The Library of Religion and Culture, edited by Benjamin Nelson.
‖ Researches in the Social, Cultural, and Behavioral Sciences, edited by Benjamin Nelson.
Σ Harper Modern Science Series, edited by James A. Newman.
° Not for sale in Canada.
+ Documentary History of the United States series, edited by Richard B. Morris.
# Documentary History of Western Civilization series, edited by Eugene C. Black and Leonard W. Levy.
Λ The Economic History of the United States series, edited by Henry David et al.
¶ European Perspectives series, edited by Eugene C. Black.
** Contemporary Essays series, edited by Leonard W. Levy.
* The Stratum Series, edited by John Hale.

RAY A. BILLINGTON: The Far Western Frontier: 1830-1860. † *Illus.* TB/3012
STUART BRUCHEY: The Roots of American Economic Growth, 1607-1861: *An Essay in Social Causation. New Introduction by the Author.* TB/1350
WHITNEY R. CROSS: The Burned-Over District: *The Social and Intellectual History of Enthusiastic Religion in Western New York, 1800-1850* TB/1242
NOBLE E. CUNNINGHAM, JR., Ed.: The Early Republic, 1789-1828 + HR/1394
GEORGE DANGERFIELD: The Awakening of American Nationalism, 1815-1828. † *Illus.* TB/3061
CLEMENT EATON: The Freedom-of-Thought Struggle in the Old South. *Revised and Enlarged. Illus.* TB/1150
CLEMENT EATON: The Growth of Southern Civilization, 1790-1860. † *Illus.* TB/3040
ROBERT H. FERRELL, Ed.: Foundations of American Diplomacy, 1775-1872 + HR/1393
LOUIS FILLER: The Crusade against Slavery: 1830-1860. † *Illus.* TB/3029
DAVID H. FISCHER: The Revolution of American Conservatism: *The Federalist Party in the Era of Jeffersonian Democracy* TB/1449
WILLIM W. FREEHLING: Prelude to Civil War: *The Nullification Controversy in South Carolina, 1816-1836* TB/1359
PAUL W. GATES: The Farmer's Age: *Agriculture, 1815-1860* △ TB/1398
THOMAS JEFFERSON: Notes on the State of Virginia. ‡ *Edited by Thomas P. Abernethy* TB/3052
FORREST MCDONALD, Ed.: Confederation and Constitution, 1781-1789 + HR/1396
BERNARD MAYO: Myths and Men: *Patrick Henry, George Washington, Thomas Jefferson* TB/1108
JOHN C. MILLER: Alexander Hamilton and the Growth of the New Nation TB/3057
JOHN C. MILLER: The Federalist Era: 1789-1801. † *Illus.* TB/3027
RICHARD B. MORRIS, Ed.: Alexander Hamilton and the Founding of the Nation. *New Introduction by the Editor* TB/1448
RICHARD B. MORRIS: The American Revolution Reconsidered TB/1363
CURTIS P. NETTELS: The Emergence of a National Economy, 1775-1815 △ TB/1438
DOUGLASS C. NORTH & ROBERT PAUL THOMAS, Eds.: *The Growth of the American Economy to 1860* + HR/1352
R. B. NYE: The Cultural Life of the New Nation: 1776-1830. † *Illus.* TB/3026
GILBERT OSOFSKY, Ed.: Puttin' On Ole Massa: *The Slave Narratives of Henry Bibb, William Wells Brown, and Solomon Northup* ‡ TB/1432
JAMES PARTON: The Presidency of Andrew Jackson. *From Volume III of the Life of Andrew Jackson. Ed. with Intro. by Robert V. Remini* TB/3080
FRANCIS S. PHILBRICK: The Rise of the West, 1754-1830. † *Illus.* TB/3067
MARSHALL SMELSER: The Democratic Republic, 1801-1815 † TB/1406
JACK M. SOSIN, Ed.: The Opening of the West + HR/1424
GEORGE ROGERS TAYLOR: The Transportation Revolution, 1815-1860 △ TB/1347
A. F. TYLER: Freedom's Ferment: *Phases of American Social History from the Revolution to the Outbreak of the Civil War. Illus.* TB/1074
GLYNDON G. VAN DEUSEN: The Jacksonian Era: 1828-1848. † *Illus.* TB/3028

LOUIS B. WRIGHT: Culture on the Moving Frontier TB/1053

American Studies: The Civil War to 1900

W. R. BROCK: An American Crisis: *Congress and Reconstruction, 1865-67* ° TB/1283
T. C. COCHRAN & WILLIAM MILLER: The Age of Enterprise: *A Social History of Industrial America* TB/1054
W. A. DUNNING: Reconstruction, Political and Economic: 1865-1877 TB/1073
HAROLD U. FAULKNER: Politics, Reform and Expansion: 1890-1900. † *Illus.* TB/3020
GEORGE M. FREDRICKSON: The Inner Civil War: *Northern Intellectuals and the Crisis of the Union* TB/1358
JOHN A. GARRATY: The New Commonwealth, 1877-1890 † TB/1410
JOHN A. GARRATY, Ed.: The Transformation of American Society, 1870-1890 + HR/1395
HELEN HUNT JACKSON: A Century of Dishonor: *The Early Crusade for Indian Reform.* ‡ *Edited by Andrew F. Rolle* TB/3063
WILLIAM G. MCLOUGHLIN, Ed.: The American Evangelicals, 1800-1900: An Anthology ‡ TB/1382
ARNOLD M. PAUL: Conservative Crisis and the Rule of Law: *Attitudes of Bar and Bench, 1887-1895. New Introduction by Author* TB/1415
JAMES S. PIKE: The Prostrate State: *South Carolina under Negro Government.* ‡ *Intro. by Robert F. Durden* TB/3085
WHITELAW REID: After the War: *A Tour of the Southern States, 1865-1866.* ‡ *Edited by C. Vann Woodward* TB/3066
FRED A. SHANNON: The Farmer's Last Frontier: *Agriculture, 1860-1897* TB/1348
VERNON LANE WHARTON: The Negro in Mississippi, 1865-1890 TB/1178

American Studies: The Twentieth Century

RICHARD M. ABRAMS, Ed.: The Issues of the Populist and Progressive Eras, 1892-1912 + HR/1428
RAY STANNARD BAKER: Following the Color Line: *American Negro Citizenship in Progressive Era.* ‡ *Edited by Dewey W. Grantham, Jr. Illus.* TB/3053
RANDOLPH S. BOURNE: War and the Intellectuals: *Collected Essays, 1915-1919.* ‡ *Edited by Carl Resek* TB/3043
A. RUSSELL BUCHANAN: The United States and World War II. † *Illus.*
Vol. I TB/3044; Vol. II TB/3045
THOMAS C. COCHRAN: The American Business System: *A Historical Perspective, 1900-1955* TB/1080
FOSTER RHEA DULLES: America's Rise to World Power: 1898-1954. † *Illus.* TB/3021
JEAN-BAPTISTE DUROSELLE: From Wilson to Roosevelt: *Foreign Policy of the United States, 1913-1945. Trans. by Nancy Lyman Roelker* TB/1370
HAROLD U. FAULKNER: The Decline of Laissez Faire, 1897-1917 TB/1397
JOHN D. HICKS: Republican Ascendancy: 1921-1933. † *Illus.* TB/3041
WILLIAM E. LEUCHTENBURG: Franklin D. Roosevelt and the New Deal: 1932-1940. † *Illus.* TB/3025
WILLIAM E. LEUCHTENBURG, Ed.: The New Deal: *A Documentary History* + HR/1354
ARTHUR S. LINK: Woodrow Wilson and the Progressive Era: 1910-1917. † *Illus.* TB/3023

2

BROADUS MITCHELL: Depression Decade: *From New Era through New Deal, 1929-1941* ∆ TB/1439
GEORGE E. MOWRY: The Era of Theodore Roosevelt and the Birth of Modern America: 1900-1912. † *Illus.* TB/3022
WILLIAM PRESTON, JR.: Aliens and Dissenters: *Federal Suppression of Radicals, 1903-1933* TB/1287
WALTER RAUSCHENBUSCH: Christianity and the Social Crisis. ‡ *Edited by Robert D. Cross* TB/3059
GEORGE SOULE: Prosperity Decade: *From War to Depression, 1917-1929* ∆ TB/1349
GEORGE B. TINDALL, Ed.: A Populist Reader: *Selections from the Works of American Populist Leaders* TB/3069
TWELVE SOUTHERNERS: I'll Take My Stand: *The South and the Agrarian Tradition. Intro. by Louis D. Rubin, Jr.; Biographical Essays by Virginia Rock* TB/1072

Art, Art History, Aesthetics

CREIGHTON GILBERT, Ed.: Renaissance Art **
Illus. TB/1465
EMILE MALE: The Gothic Image: *Religious Art in France of the Thirteenth Century.* § 190 illus. TB/344
MILLARD MEISS: Painting in Florence and Siena After the Black Death: *The Arts, Religion and Society in the Mid-Fourteenth Century. 169 illus.* TB/1148
ERWIN PANOFSKY: Renaissance and Renascences in Western Art. *Illus.* TB/1447
ERWIN PANOFSKY: Studies in Iconology: *Humanistic Themes in the Art of the Renaissance. 180 illus.* TB/1077
OTTO VON SIMSON: The Gothic Cathedral: *Origins of Gothic Architecture and the Medieval Concept of Order. 58 illus.* TB/2018
HEINRICH ZIMMER: Myths and Symbols in Indian Art and Civilization. *70 illus.* TB/2005

Asian Studies

WOLFGANG FRANKE: China and the West: *The Cultural Encounter, 13th to 20th Centuries. Trans. by R. A. Wilson* TB/1326
L. CARRINGTON GOODRICH: A Short History of the Chinese People. *Illus.* TB/3015
DAN N. JACOBS, Ed.: The New Communist Manifesto and Related Documents. TB/1078
DAN N. JACOBS & HANS H. BAERWALD, Eds.: Chinese Communism: *Selected Documents* TB/3031
BENJAMIN I. SCHWARTZ: Chinese Communism and the Rise of Mao TB/1308
BENJAMIN I. SCHWARTZ: In Search of Wealth and Power: *Yen Fu and the West* TB/1422

Economics & Economic History

C. E. BLACK: The Dynamics of Modernization: *A Study in Comparative History* TB/1321
STUART BRUCHEY: The Roots of American Economic Growth, 1607-1861: *An Essay in Social Causation. New Introduction by the Author.* TB/1350
GILBERT BURCK & EDITORS OF *Fortune:* The Computer Age: *And its Potential for Management* TB/1179
SHEPARD B. CLOUGH, THOMAS MOODIE & CAROL MOODIE, Eds.: Economic History of Europe: *Twentieth Century* # HR/1388
THOMAS C. COCHRAN: The American Business System: *A Historical Perspective, 1900-1955* TB/1080

ROBERT A. DAHL & CHARLES E. LINDBLOM: Politics, Economics, and Welfare: *Planning and Politico-Economic Systems Resolved into Basic Social Processes* TB/3037
PETER F. DRUCKER: The New Society: *The Anatomy of Industrial Order* TB/1082
HAROLD U. FAULKNER: The Decline of Laissez Faire, 1897-1917 ∆ TB/1397
PAUL W. GATES: The Farmer's Age: *Agriculture, 1815-1860* ∆ TB/1398
WILLIAM GREENLEAF, Ed.: American Economic Development Since 1860 + HR/1353
ROBERT L. HEILBRONER: The Future as History: *The Historic Currents of Our Time and the Direction in Which They Are Taking America* TB/1386
ROBERT L. HEILBRONER: The Great Ascent: *The Struggle for Economic Development in Our Time* TB/3030
DAVID S. LANDES: Bankers and Pashas: *International Finance and Economic Imperialism in Egypt. New Preface by the Author* TB/1412
ROBERT LATOUCHE: The Birth of Western Economy: *Economic Aspects of the Dark Ages* TB/1290
W. ARTHUR LEWIS: The Principles of Economic Planning. *New Introduction by the Author*° TB/1436
WILLIAM MILLER, Ed.: Men in Business: *Essays on the Historical Role of the Entrepreneur* TB/1081
GUNNAR MYRDAL: An International Economy. *New Introduction by the Author* TB/1445
HERBERT A. SIMON: The Shape of Automation: *For Men and Management* TB/1245
RICHARD S. WECKSTEIN, Ed.: Expansion of World Trade and the Growth of National Economies ** TB/1373

Historiography and History of Ideas

J. BRONOWSKI & BRUCE MAZLISH: The Western Intellectual Tradition: *From Leonardo to Hegel* TB/3001
WILHELM DILTHEY: Pattern and Meaning in History: *Thoughts on History and Society.*° *Edited with an Intro. by H. P. Rickman* TB/1075
J. H. HEXTER: More's Utopia: *The Biography of an Idea. Epilogue by the Author* TB/1195
H. STUART HUGHES: History as Art and as Science: *Twin Vistas on the Past* TB/1207
ARTHUR O. LOVEJOY: The Great Chain of Being: *A Study of the History of an Idea* TB/1009
RICHARD H. POPKIN: The History of Scepticism from Erasmus to Descartes. *Revised Edition* TB/1391
MASSIMO SALVADORI, Ed.: Modern Socialism # HR/1374
BRUNO SNELL: The Discovery of the Mind: *The Greek Origins of European Thought* TB/1018
W. WARREN WAGER, ed.: European Intellectual History Since Darwin and Marx TB/1297

History: General

HANS KOHN: The Age of Nationalism: *The First Era of Global History* TB/1380
BERNARD LEWIS: The Arabs in History TB/1029
BERNARD LEWIS: The Middle East and the West ° TB/1274

History: Ancient

A. ANDREWS: The Greek Tyrants TB/1103

ERNST LUDWIG EHRLICH: A Concise History of Israel: *From the Earliest Times to the Destruction of the Temple in A.D. 70* ° TB/128
THEODOR H. GASTER: Thespis: *Ritual Myth and Drama in the Ancient Near East* TB/1281
MICHAEL GRANT: Ancient History ° TB/1190
A. H. M. JONES, Ed.: A History of Rome through the Fifth Century # *Vol. I: The Republic* HR/1364
Vol. II The Empire: HR/1460
NAPHTALI LEWIS & MEYER REINHOLD, Eds.: Roman Civilization *Vol. I: The Republic* TB/1231
Vol. II: The Empire TB/1232

History: Medieval

MARSHALL W. BALDWIN, Ed.: Christianity Through the 13th Century # HR/1468
MARC BLOCH: Land and Work in Medieval Europe. *Translated by J. E. Anderson* TB/1452
HELEN CAM: England Before Elizabeth TB/1026
NORMAN COHN: The Pursuit of the Millennium: *Revolutionary Messianism in Medieval and Reformation Europe* TB/1037
G. G. COULTON: Medieval Village, Manor, and Monastery HR/1022
HEINRICH FICHTENAU: The Carolingian Empire: *The Age of Charlemagne. Translated with an Introduction by Peter Munz* TB/1142
GALBERT OF BRUGES: The Murder of Charles the Good: *A Contemporary Record of Revolutionary Change in 12th Century Flanders. Translated with an Introduction by James Bruce Ross* TB/1311
F. L. GANSHOF: Feudalism TB/1058
F. L. GANSHOF: The Middle Ages: *A History of International Relations. Translated by Rémy Hall* TB/1411
DENYS HAY: The Medieval Centuries ° TB/1192
DAVID HERLIHY, Ed.: Medieval Culture and Society # HR/1340
J. M. HUSSEY: The Byzantine World TB/1057
ROBERT LATOUCHE: The Birth of Western Economy: *Economic Aspects of the Dark Ages* ° TB/1290
HENRY CHARLES LEA: The Inquisition of the Middle Ages. || *Introduction by Walter Ullmann* TB/1456
FERDINAND LOT: The End of the Ancient World and the Beginnings of the Middle Ages. *Introduction by Glanville Downey* TB/1044
H. R. LOYN: The Norman Conquest TB/1457
ACHILLE LUCHAIRE: Social France at the time of Philip Augustus. *Intro. by John W. Baldwin* TB/1314
GUIBERT DE NOGENT: Self and Society in Medieval France: *The Memoirs of Guibert de Nogent.* || *Edited by John F. Benton* TB/1471
MARSILIUS OF PADUA: The Defender of Peace. *The Defensor Pacis. Translated with an Introduction by Alan Gewirth* TB/1310
CHARLES PETET-DUTAILLIS: The Feudal Monarchy in France and England: *From the Tenth to the Thirteenth Century* ° TB/1165
STEVEN RUNCIMAN: A History of the Crusades *Vol. I: The First Crusade and the Foundation of the Kingdom of Jerusalem. Illus.* TB/1143
Vol. II: The Kingdom of Jerusalem and the Frankish East 1100-1187. Illus. TB/1243
Vol. III: The Kingdom of Acre and the Later Crusades. Illus. TB/1298
J. M. WALLACE-HADRILL: The Barbarian West: *The Early Middle Ages, A.D. 400-1000* TB/1061

History: Renaissance & Reformation

JACOB BURCKHARDT: The Civilization of the Renaissance in Italy. *Introduction by Benjamin Nelson and Charles Trinkaus. Illus.* Vol. I TB/40; Vol. II TB/41
JOHN CALVIN & JACOPO SADOLETO: A Reformation Debate. *Edited by John C. Olin* TB/1239
FEDERICO CHABOD: Machiavelli and the Renaissance TB/1193
J. H. ELLIOTT: Europe Divided, 1559-1598 *a* ° TB/1414
G. R. ELTON: Reformation Europe, 1517-1559 ° *a* TB/1270
DESIDERIUS ERASMUS: Christian Humanism and the Reformation: *Selected Writings. Edited and Translated by John C. Olin* TB/1166
DESIDERIUS ERASMUS: Erasmus and His Age: *Selected Letters. Edited with an Introduction by Hans J. Hillerbrand. Translated by Marcus A. Haworth* TB/1461
WALLACE K. FERGUSON et al.: Facets of the Renaissance TB/1098
WALLACE K. FERGUSON et al.: The Renaissance: *Six Essays. Illus.* TB/1084
FRANCESCO GUICCIARDINI: History of Florence. *Translated with an Introduction and Notes by Mario Domandi* TB/1470
WERNER L. GUNDERSHEIMER, Ed.: French Humanism, 1470-1600. * *Illus.* TB/1473
MARIE BOAS HALL, Ed.: Nature and Nature's Laws: *Documents of the Scientific Revolution* # HR/1420
HANS J. HILLERBRAND, Ed., The Protestant Reformation # TB/1342
JOHAN HUIZINGA: Erasmus and the Age of Reformation. *Illus.* TB/19
JOEL HURSTFIELD: The Elizabethan Nation TB/1312
JOEL HURSTFIELD, Ed.: The Reformation Crisis TB/1267
PAUL OSKAR KRISTELLER: Renaissance Thought: *The Classic, Scholastic, and Humanist Strains* TB/1048
PAUL OSKAR KRISTELLER: Renaissance Thought II: *Papers on Humanism and the Arts* TB/1163
PAUL O. KRISTELLER & PHILIP P. WIENER, Eds.: Renaissance Essays TB/1392
DAVID LITTLE: Religion, Order and Law: *A Study in Pre-Revolutionary England.* § *Preface by R. Bellah* TB/1418
NICCOLO MACHIAVELLI: History of Florence and of the Affairs of Italy: *From the Earliest Times to the Death of Lorenzo the Magnificent. Introduction by Felix Gilbert* TB/1027
ALFRED VON MARTIN: Sociology of the Renaissance. ° *Introduction by W. K. Ferguson* TB/1099
GARRETT MATTINGLY et al.: Renaissance Profiles. *Edited by J. H. Plumb* TB/1162
J. H. PARRY: The Establishment of the European Hegemony: 1415-1715: *Trade and Exploration in the Age of the Renaissance* TB/1045
J. H. PARRY, Ed.: The European Reconnaissance: *Selected Documents* # HR/1345
J. H. PLUMB: The Italian Renaissance: *A Concise Survey of Its History and Culture* TB/1161
A. F. POLLARD: Henry VIII. *Introductioh by A. G. Dickens.* ° TB/1249
RICHARD H. POPKIN: The History of Scepticism from Erasmus to Descartes TB/1391
PAOLO ROSSI: Philosophy, Technology, and the Arts, in the Early Modern Era 1400-1700. || *Edited by Benjamin Nelson. Translated by Salvator Attanasio* TB/1458

R. H. TAWNEY: The Agrarian Problem in the Sixteenth Century. *Intro. by Lawrence Stone* TB/1315

H. R. TREVOR-ROPER: The European Witch-craze of the Sixteenth and Seventeenth Centuries and Other Essays ° TB/1416

VESPASIANO: Rennaissance Princes, Popes, and XVth Century: *The Vespasiano Memoirs. Introduction by Myron P. Gilmore. Illus.* TB/1111

History: Modern European

RENE ALBRECHT-CARRIE, Ed.: The Concert of Europe # HR/1341

MAX BELOFF: The Age of Absolutism, 1660-1815 TB/1062

OTTO VON BISMARCK: Reflections and Reminiscences. *Ed. with Intro. by Theodore S. Hamerow* ¶ TB/1357

EUGENE C. BLACK, Ed.: British Politics in the Nineteenth Century # HR/1427

D. W. BROGAN: The Development of Modern France ° Vol. I: *From the Fall of the Empire to the Dreyfus Affair* TB/1184
Vol. II: *The Shadow of War, World War I, Between the Two Wars* TB/1185

ALAN BULLOCK: Hitler, A Study in Tyranny. ° *Revised Edition. Iuus.* TB/1123

GORDON A. CRAIG: From Bismarck to Adenauer: *Aspects of German Statecraft. Revised Edition* TB/1171

LESTER G. CROCKER, Ed.: The Age of Enlightenment # HR/1423

JACQUES DROZ: Europe between Revolutions, 1815-1848. ° *a Trans. by Robert Baldick* TB/1346

JOHANN GOTTLIEB FICHTE: Addresses to the German Nation. *Ed. with Intro. by George A. Kelly* ¶ TB/1366

ROBERT & ELBORG FORSTER, Eds.: European Society in the Eighteenth Century # HR/1404

C. C. GILLISPIE: Genesis and Geology: *The Decades before Darwin* § TB/51

ALBERT GOODWIN: The French Revolution TB/1064

JOHN B. HALSTED, Ed.: Romanticism # HR/1387

STANLEY HOFFMANN et al.: In Search of France: *The Economy, Society and Political System In the Twentieth Century* TB/1219

H. STUART HUGHES: The Obstructed Path: *French Social Thought in the Years of Desperation* TB/1451

JOHAN HUIZINGA: Dutch Civilisation in the 17th Century and Other Essays TB/1453

WALTER LAQUEUR & GEORGE L. MOSSE, Eds.: Education and Social Structure in the 20th Century. ° *Volume 6 of the* Journal of Contemporary History TB/1339

WALTER LAQUEUR & GEORGE L. MOSSE, Eds.: International Fascism, 1920-1945. ° *Volume 1 of the* Journal of Contemporary History TB/1276

WALTER LAQUEUR & GEORGE L. MOSSE, Eds.: Literature and Politics in the 20th Century. ° *Volume 5 of the* Journal of Contemporary History. TB/1328

WALTER LAQUEUR & GEORGE L. MOSSE, Eds.: The New History: *Trends in Historical Research and Writing Since World War II.* ° *Volume 4 of the* Journal of Contemporary History TB/1327

WALTER LAQUEUR & GEORGE L. MOSSE, Eds.: 1914: *The Coming of the First World War.* ° *Volume3 of the* Journal of Contemporary History TB/1306

JOHN MCMANNERS: European History, 1789-1914: *Men, Machines and Freedom* TB/1419

PAUL MANTOUX: The Industrial Revolution in the Eighteenth Century: *An Outline of the Beginnings of the Modern Factory System in England* TB/1079

KINGSLEY MARTIN: French Liberal Thought in the Eighteenth Century: *A Study of Political Ideas from Bayle to Condorcet* TB/1114

NAPOLEON III: Napoleonic Ideas: *Des Idées Napoléoniennes, par le Prince Napoléon-Louis Bonaparte. Ed. by Brison D. Gooch* ¶ TB/1336

FRANZ NEUMANN: Behemoth: *The Structure and Practice of National Socialism, 1933-1944* TB/1289

DAVID OGG: Europe of the Ancien Régime, 1715-1783 ° *a* TB/1271

GEORGE RUDE: Revolutionary Europe, 1783-1815 ° *a* TB/1272

MASSIMO SALVADORI, Ed.: Modern Socialism # TB/1374

DENIS MACK SMITH, Ed.: The Making of Italy, 1796-1870 # HR/1356

ALBERT SOREL: Europe Under the Old Regime, *Translated by Francis H. Herrick* TB/1121

ROLAND N. STROMBERG, Ed.: Realsim, Naturalism, and Symbolism: *Modes of Thought and Expression in Europe, 1848-1914* # HR/1355

A. J. P. TAYLOR: From Napoleon to Lenin: *Historical Essays* ° TB/1268

A. J. P. TAYLOR: The Habsburg Monarchy, 1809-1918: *A History of the Austrian Empire and Austria-Hungary* ° TB/1187

J. M. THOMPSON: European History, 1494-1789 TB/1431

DAVID THOMSON, Ed.: France: Empire and Republic, 1850-1940 # HR/1387

H. R. TREVOR-ROPER: Historical Essays TB/1269

W. WARREN WAGAR, Ed.: Science, Faith, and MAN: *European Thought Since 1914* # HR/1362

MACK WALKER, Ed.: Metternich's Europe, 1813-1848 # HR/1361

ELIZABETH WISKEMANN: Europe of the Dictators, 1919-1945 ° *a* TB/1273

JOHN B. WOLF: France: 1814-1919: *The Rise of a Liberal-Democratic Society* TB/3019

Literature & Literary Criticism

JACQUES BARZUN: The House of Intellect TB/1051

W. J. BATE: From Classic to Romantic: *Premises of Taste in Eighteenth Century England* TB/1036

VAN WYCK BROOKS: Van Wyck Brooks: The Early Years: *A Selection from his Works, 1908-1921 Ed. with Intro. by Claire Sprague* TB/3082

RICHMOND LATTIMORE, Translator: The Odyssey of Homer TB/1389

ROBERT PREYER, Ed.: Victorian Literature ** TB/1302

BASIL WILEY: Nineteenth Century Studies: *Coleridge to Matthew Arnold* ° TB/1261

RAYMOND WILLIAMS: Culture and Society, 1780-1950 ° TB/1252

Philosophy

HENRI BERGSON: Time and Free Will: *An Essay on the Immediate Data of Consciousness* ° TB/1021

LUDWIG BINSWANGER: Being-in-the-World: *Selected Papers. Trans. with Intro. by Jacob Needleman* TB/1365

H. J. BLACKHAM: Six Existentialist Thinkers: *Kierkegaard, Nietzsche, Jaspers, Marcel, Heidegger, Sartre* ° TB/1002

J. M. BOCHENSKI: The Methods of Contemporary Thought. *Trans. by Peter Caws* TB/1377
CRANE BRINTON: Nietzsche. *Preface, Bibliography, and Epilogue by the Author* TB/1197
ERNST CASSIRER: Rousseau, Kant and Goethe. *Intro. by Peter Gay* TB/1092
FREDERICK COPLESTON, S. J.: Medieval Philosophy TB/376
F. M. CORNFORD: From Religion to Philosophy: *A Study in the Origins of Western Speculation* § TB/20
WILFRID DESAN: The Tragic Finale: *An Essay on the Philosophy of Jean-Paul Sartre* TB/1030
MARVIN FARBER: The Aims of Phenomenology: *The Motives, Methods, and Impact of Husserl's Thought* TB/1291
PAUL FRIEDLANDER: Plato: *An Introduction* TB/2017
MICHAEL GELVEN: A Commentary on Heidegger's "Being and Time" TB/1464
J. GLENN GRAY: Hegel and Greek Thought TB/1409
W. K. C. GUTHRIE: The Greek Philosophers: *From Thales to Aristotle* ° TB/1008
G. W. F. HEGEL: On Art, Religion Philosophy: *Introductory Lectures to the Realm of Absolute Spirit.* || *Edited with an Introduction by J. Glenn Gray* TB/1463
G. W. F. HEGEL: Phenomenology of Mind. ° || *Introduction by George Lichtheim* TB/1303
MARTIN HEIDEGGER: Discourse on Thinking. *Translated with a Preface by John M. Anderson and E. Hans Freund. Introduction by John M. Anderson* TB/1459
F. H. HEINEMANN: Existentialism and the Modern Predicament TB/28
WERER HEISENBERG: Physics and Philosophy: *The Revolution in Modern Science. Intro. by F. S. C. Nortrop* TB/549
EDMUND HUSSERL: Phenomenology and the Crisis of Philosophy. § *Translated with an Introduction by Quentin Lauer* TB/1170
IMMANUEL KANT: Groundwork of the Metaphysic of Morals. *Translated and Analyzed by H. J. Paton* TB/1159
IMMANUEL KANT: Lectures on Ethics. § *Introduction by Lewis White Beck* TB/105
QUENTIN LAUER: Phenomenology: *Its Genesis and Prospect. Preface by Aron Gurwitsch* TB/1169
GEORGE A. MORGAN: What Nietzsche Means TB/1198
H. J. PATON: The Categorical Imperative: *A Study in Kant's Moral Philosophy* TB/1325
MICHAEL POLANYI: Personal Knowledge: *Towards a Post-Critical Philosophy* TB/1158
KARL R. POPPER: Conjectures and Refutations: *The Growth of Scientific Knowledge* TB/1376
WILLARD VAN ORMAN QUINE: Elementary Logic *Revised Edition* TB/577
MORTON WHITE: Foundations of Historical Knowledge TB/1440
WILHELM WINDELBAND: A History of Philosophy *Vol. I: Greek, Roman, Medieval* TB/38
Vol. II: Renaissance, Enlightenment, Modern TB/39
LUDWIG WITTGENSTEIN: The Blue and Brown Books ° TB/1211
LUDWIG WITTGENSTEIN: Notebooks, 1914-1916 TB/1441

Political Science & Government

C. E. BLACK: The Dynamics of Modernization: *A Study in Comparative History* TB/1321
KENNETH E. BOULDING: Conflict and Defense: *A General Theory of Action* TB/3024

DENIS W. BROGAN: Politics in America. *New Introduction by the Author* TB/1469
ROBERT CONQUEST: Power and Policy in the USSR: *The Study of Soviet Dynastics* ° TB/1307
ROBERT A. DAHL & CHARLES E. LINDBLOM: Politics, Economics, and Welfare: *Planning and Politico-Economic Systems Resolved into Basic Social Processes* TB/1277
HANS KOHN: Political Ideologies of the 20th Century TB/1277
ROY C. MACRIDIS, Ed.: Political Parties: *Contemporary Trends and Ideas* ** TB/1322
ROBERT GREEN MC CLOSKEY: American Conservatism in the Age of Enterprise, 1865-1910 TB/1137
BARRINGTON MOORE, JR.: Political Power and Social Theory: *Seven Studies* || TB/1221
BARRINGTON MOORE, JR.: Soviet Politics—The Dilemma of Power: *The Role of Ideas in Social Change* || TB/1222
BARRINGTON MOORE, JR.: Terror and Progress—USSR: *Some Sources of Change and Stability in the Soviet Dictatorship* TB/1266
JOHN B. MORRALL: Political Thought in Medieval Times TB/1076
KARL R. POPPER: The Open Society and Its Enemies *Vol. I: The Spell of Plato* TB/1101
Vol. II: The High Tide of Prophecy: Hegel, Marx, and the Aftermath TB/1102
HENRI DE SAINT-SIMON: Social Organization, The Science of Man, and Other Writings. || *Edited and Translated with an Introduction by Felix Markham* TB/1152
JOSEPH A. SCHUMPETER: Capitalism, Socialism and Democracy TB/3008

Psychology

LUDWIG BINSWANGER: Being-in-the-world: *Selected papers.* || *Trans. with Intro. by Jacob Needleman* TB/1365
HADLEY CANTRIL: The Invasion from Mars: *A Study in the Psychology of Panic* || TB/1282
MIRCEA ELIADE: Cosmos and History: *The Myth of the Eternal Return* § TB/2050
MIRCEA ELIADE: Myth and Reality TB/1369
MIRCEA ELIADE: Myths, Dreams and Mysteries: *The Encounter Between Contemporary Faiths and Archaic Realities* § TB/1320
MIRCEA ELIADE: Rites and Symbols of Initiation: *The Mysteries of Birth and Rebirth* § TB/1236
HERBERT FINGARETTE: The Self in Transformation: *Psychoanalysis, Philosophy and the Life of the Spirit* || TB/1177
SIGMUND FREUD: On Creativity and the Unconscious: *Papers on the Psychology of Art, Literature, Love, Religion.* § *Intro. by Benjamin Nelson* TB/45
J. GLENN GRAY: The Warriors: *Reflections on Men in Battle. Introduction by Hannah Arendt* TB/1294
WILLIAM JAMES: Psychology: *The Briefer Course. Edited with an Intro. by Gordon Allport* TB/1034
MUZAFER SHERIF: The Psychology of Social Norms. *Introduction by Gardner Murphy* TB/3072
HELLMUT WILHELM: Change: *Eight Lectures on the* I *Ching* TB/2019

Religion: Ancient and Classical, Biblical and Judaic Traditions

C. K. BARRETT, Ed.: The New Testament Background: *Selected Documents* TB/86

MARTIN BUBER: Eclipse of God: *Studies in the Relation Between Religion and Philosophy* TB/12
MARTIN BUBER: Hasidism and Modern Man. *Edited and Translated by Maurice Friedman* TB/839
MARTIN BUBER: The Knowledge of Man. *Edited with an Introduction by Maurice Friedman. Translated by Maurice Friedman and Ronald Gregor Smith* TB/135
MARTIN BUBER: Moses. *The Revelation and the Covenant* TB/837
MARTIN BUBER: The Origin and Meaning of Hasidism. *Edited and Translated by Maurice Friedman* TB/835
MARTIN BUBER: The Prophetic Faith TB/73
MARTIN BUBER: Two Types of Faith: *Interpenetration of Judaism and Christianity* ° TB/75
MALCOLM L. DIAMOND: Martin Buber: *Jewish Existentialist* TB/840
M. S. ENSLIN: Christian Beginnings TB/5
M. S. ENSLIN: The Literature of the Christian Movement TB/6
HENRI FRANKFORT: Ancient Egyptian Religion: *An Interpretation* TB/77
MAURICE S. FRIEDMAN: Martin Buber: *The Life of Dialogue* TB/64
ABRAHAM HESCHEL: The Earth Is the Lord's & The Sabbath. *Two Essays* TB/828
ABRAHAM HESCHEL: God in Search of Man: *A Philosophy of Judaism* TB/807
ABRAHAM HESCHEL: Man Is not Alone: *A Philosophy of Religion* TB/838
ABRAHAM HESCHEL: The Prophets: *An Introduction* TB/1421
T. J. MEEK: Hebrew Origins TB/69
JAMES MUILENBURG: The Way of Israel: *Biblical Faith and Ethics* TB/133
H. H. ROWLEY: The Growth of the Old Testament TB/107
D. WINTON THOMAS, Ed.: Documents from Old Testament Times TB/85

Religion: Early Christianity Through Reformation

ANSELM OF CANTERBURY: Truth, Freedom, and Evil: *Three Philosophical Dialogues. Edited and Translated by Jasper Hopkins and Herbert Richardson* TB/317
MARSHALL W. BALDWIN, Ed.: Christianity through the 13th Century # HR/1468
ADOLF DEISSMANN: Paul: *A Study in Social and Religious History* TB/15
EDGAR J. GOODSPEED: A Life of Jesus TB/1
ROBERT M. GRANT: Gnosticism and Early Christianity TB/136
WILLIAM HALLER: The Rise of Puritanism TB/22
ARTHUR DARBY NOCK: St. Paul ° TR/104
GORDON RUPP: Luther's Progress to the Diet of Worms ° TB/120

Religion: The Protestant Tradition

KARL BARTH: Church Dogmatics: *A Selection. Intro. by H. Gollwitzer. Ed. by G. W. Bromiley* TB/95
KARL BARTH: Dogmatics in Outline TB/56
KARL BARTH: The Word of God and the Word of Man TB/13
WHITNEY R. CROSS: The Burned-Over District: *The Social and Intellectual History of Enthusiastic Religion in Western New York, 1800-1850* TB/1242
WILLIAM R. HUTCHISON, Ed.: American Protestant Thought: *The Liberal Era* ‡ TB/1385

SOREN KIERKEGAARD: The Journals of Kierkegaard. ° *Edited with an Intro. by Alexander Dru* TB/52
SOREN KIERKEGAARD: The Point of View for My Work as an Author: *A Report to History.* § *Preface by Benjamin Nelson* TB/88
SOREN KIERKEGAARD: The Present Age. § *Translated and edited by Alexander Dru. Introduction by Walter Kaufmann* TB/94
SOREN KIERKEGAARD: Purity of Heart. *Trans. by Douglas Steere* TB/4
SOREN KIERKEGAARD: Repetition: *An Essay in Experimental Psychology* § TB/117
SOREN KIERKEGAARD: Works of Love: *Some Christian Reflections in the Form of Discourses* TB/122
WOLFHART PANNENBERG, et al.: History and Hermeneutic. *Volume 4 of Journal for Theology and the Church, edited by Robert W. Funk and Gerhard Ebeling* TB/254
F. SCHLEIERMACHER: The Christian Faith. *Introduction by Richard R. Niebuhr.*
Vol. I TB/108; Vol. II TB/109
F. SCHLEIERMACHER: On Religion: *Speeches to Its Cultured Despisers. Intro. by Rudolf Otto* TB/36
PAUL TILLICH: Dynamics of Faith TB/42
PAUL TILLICH: Morality and Beyond TB/142

Religion: The Roman & Eastern Christian Traditions

A. ROBERT CAPONIGRI, Ed.: Modern Catholic Thinkers II: *The Church and the Political Order* TB/307
G. P. FEDOTOV: The Russian Religious Mind: *Kievan Christianity, the tenth to the thirteenth Centuries* TB/370
GABRIEL MARCEL: Being and Having: *An Existential Diary. Introduction by James Collins* TB/310
GABRIEL MARCEL: Homo Viator: *Introduction to a Metaphysic of Hope* TB/397

Religion: Oriental Religions

TOR ANDRAE: Mohammed: *The Man and His Faith* § TB/62
EDWARD CONZE: Buddhism: *Its Essence and Development.* ° *Foreword by Arthur Waley* TB/58
EDWARD CONZE: Buddhist Meditation TB/1442
EDWARD CONZE et al, Editors: Buddhist Texts through the Ages TB/113
ANANDA COOMARASWAMY: Buddha and the Gospel of Buddhism TB/119
H. G. CREEL: Confucius and the Chinese Way TB/63
FRANKLIN EDGERTON, Trans. & Ed.: The Bhagavad Gita TB/115
SWAMI NIKHILANANDA, Trans. & Ed.: The Upanishads TB/114

Religion: Philosophy, Culture, and Society

NICOLAS BERDYAEV: The Destiny of Man TB/61
RUDOLF BULTMANN: History and Eschatology: *The Presence of Eternity* ° TB/91
RUDOLF BULTMANN AND FIVE CRITICS: Kerygma and Myth: *A Theological Debate* TB/80
RUDOLF BULTMANN and KARL KUNDSIN: Form search. *Trans. by F. C. Grant* TB/96
LUDWIG FEUERBACH: The Essence of Christianity. § *Introduction by Karl Barth. Foreword by H. Richard Niebuhr* TB/11
KYLE HASELDEN: The Racial Problem in Christian Perspective TB/116

MARTIN HEIDEGGER: Discourse on Thinking. *Translated with a Preface by John M. Anderson and E. Hans Freund. Introduction by John M. Anderson* TB/1459
IMMANUEL KANT: Religion Within the Limits of Reason Alone. § *Introduction by Theodore M. Greene and John Silber* TB/FG
H. RICHARD NIERUHR: Christ and Culture TB/3
H. RICHARD NIEBUHR: The Kingdom of God in America TB/49
JOHN H. RANDALL, JR.: The Meaning of Religion for Man. *Revised with New Intro. by the Author* TB/1379

Science and Mathematics

W. E. LE GROS CLARK: The Antecedents of Man: *An Introduction to the Evolution of the Primates.* ° *Illus.* TB/559
ROBERT E. COKER: Streams, Lakes, Ponds. *Illus.* TB/586
ROBERT E. COKER: This Great and Wide Sea: *An Introduction to Oceanography and Marine Biology. Illus.* TB/551
F. K. HARE: The Restless Atmosphere TB/560
WILLARD VAN ORMAN QUINE: Mathematical Logic TB/558

Science: Philosophy

J. M. BOCHENSKI: The Methods of Contemporary Thought. *Tr. by Peter Caws* TB/1377
J. BRONOWSKI: Science and Human Values. *Revised and Enlarged. Illus.* TB/505
WERNER HEISENBERG: Physics and Philosophy: *The Revolution in Modern Science. Introduction by F. S. C. Northrop* TB/549
KARL R. POPPER: Conjectures and Refutations: *The Growth of Scientific Knowledge* TB/1376
KARL R. POPPER: The Logic of Scientific Discovery TB/576

Sociology and Anthropology

REINHARD BENDIX: Work and Authority in Industry: *Ideologies of Management in the Course of Industrialization* TB/3035
BERNARD BERELSON, Ed., The Behavioral Sciences Today TB/1127
KENNETH B. CLARK: Dark Ghetto: *Dilemmas of Social Power. Foreword by Gunnar Myrdal* TB/1317
KENNETH CLARK & JEANNETTE HOPKINS: A Relevant War Against Poverty: *A Study of Community Action Programs and Observable Social Change* TB/1480
LEWIS COSER, Ed.: Political Sociology TB/1293
ROSE L. COSER, Ed.: Life Cycle and Achievement in America ** TB/1434
ALLISON DAVIS & JOHN DOLLARD: Children of Bondage: *The Personality Development of Negro Youth in the Urban South* || TB/3049
ST. CLAIR DRAKE & HORACE R. CAYTON: Black Metropolis: *A Study of Negro Life in a Northern City. Introduction by Everett C. Hughes. Tables, maps, charts, and graphs* Vol. I TB/1086; Vol. II TB/1087

PETER F. DRUCKER: The New Society: *The Anatomy of Industrial Order* TB/1082
LEON FESTINGER, HENRY W. RIECKEN, STANLEY SCHACHTER: When Prophecy Fails: *A Social and Psychological Study of a Modern Group that Predicted the Destruction of the World* || TB/1132
CHARLES Y. GLOCK & RODNEY STARK: Christian Beliefs and Anti-Semitism. *Introduction by the Authors* TB/1454
L. S. B. LEAKEY: Adam's Ancestors: *The Evolution of Man and His Culture. Illus.* TB/1019
KURT LEWIN: Field Theory in Social Science: *Selected Theoretical Papers.* || *Edited by Dorwin Cartwright* TB/1135
RITCHIE P. LOWRY: Who's Running This Town? *Community Leadership and Social Change* TB/1383
R. M. MACIVER: Social Causation TB/1153
GARY T. MARX: Protest and Prejudice: *A Study of Belief in the Black Community* TB/1435
ROBERT K. MERTON, LEONARD BROOM, LEONARD S. COTTRELL, JR., Editors: Sociology Today: *Problems and Prospects* || Vol. I TB/1173; Vol. II TB/1174
GILBERT OSOFSKY, Ed.: The Burden of Race: *A Documentary History of Negro-White Relations in America* TB/1405
GILBERT OSOFSKY: Harlem: The Making of a Ghetto: *Negro New York 1890-1930* TB/1381
TALCOTT PARSONS & EDWARD A. SHILS, Editors: Toward a General Theory of Action: *Theoretical Foundations for the Social Sciences* TB/1083
PHILIP RIEFF: The Triumph of the Therapeutic: *Uses of Faith After Freud* TB/1360
JOHN H. ROHRER & MUNRO S. EDMONSON, Eds.: The Eighth Generation Grows Up: *Cultures and Personalities of New Orleans Negroes* || TB/3050
ARNOLD ROSE: The Negro in America: *The Condensed Version of Gunnar Myrdal's* An American Dilemma. *Second Edition* TB/3048
GEORGE ROSEN: Madness in Society: *Chapters in the Historical Sociology of Mental Illness.* || *Preface by Benjamin Nelson* TB/1337
PHILIP SELZNICK: TVA and the Grass Roots: *A Study in the Sociology of Formal Organization* TB/1230
PITIRIM A. SOROKIN: Contemporary Sociological Theories: *Through the First Quarter of the Twentieth Century* TB/3046
MAURICE R. STEIN: The Eclipse of Community: *An Interpretation of American Studies* TB/1128
FERDINAND TONNIES: Community and Society: *Gemeinschaft und Gesellschaft. Translated and Edited by Charles P. Loomis* TB/1116
SAMUEL E. WALLACE: Skid Row as a Way of Life TB/1367
W. LLOYD WARNER and Associates: Democracy in Jonesville: *A Study in Quality and Inequality* || TB/1129
W. LLOYD WARNER: Social Class in America: *The Evaluation of Status* TB/1013
FLORIAN ZNANIECKI: The Social Role of the Man of Knowledge. *Introduction by Lewis A. Coser* TB/1372

8